When Should America Fight?

Donald M. Snow

ROWMAN & LITTLEFIELD
Lanham • Boulder • New York • London

Executive Acquisitions Editor: Michael Kerns
Assistant Editor: Elizabeth Von Buhr
Sales and Marketing Inquiries: textbooks@rowman.com

Credits and acknowledgments for material borrowed from other sources, and reproduced with permission, appear on the appropriate pages within the text.

Published by Rowman & Littlefield
An imprint of The Rowman & Littlefield Publishing Group, Inc.
4501 Forbes Boulevard, Suite 200, Lanham, Maryland 20706
www.rowman.com

86-90 Paul Street, London EC2A 4NE

Copyright © 2023 by The Rowman & Littlefield Publishing Group, Inc.

All rights reserved. No part of this book may be reproduced in any form or by any electronic or mechanical means, including information storage and retrieval systems, without written permission from the publisher, except by a reviewer who may quote passages in a review.

British Library Cataloguing in Publication Information Available
Library of Congress Cataloging-in-Publication Data

Names: Snow, Donald M., 1943– author.
Title: When should America fight? / Donald M. Snow.
Description: Lanham : Rowman & Littlefield, 2023. | Includes bibliographical references and index.
Identifiers: LCCN 2022042248 (print) | LCCN 2022042249 (ebook) | ISBN 9781538169438 (cloth) | ISBN 9781538169445 (paperback) | ISBN 9781538169452 (epub)
Subjects: LCSH: United States—Military policy. | United States—History, Military—21st century—Case studies. | United States—Strategic aspects. | Strategy.
Classification: LCC UA23 .S526244 2023 (print) | LCC UA23 (ebook) | DDC 355/.033573—dc23/eng/20221205
LC record available at https://lccn.loc.gov/2022042248
LC ebook record available at https://lccn.loc.gov/2022042249

Contents

	Preface	vii
Introduction	The Withdrawal from Afghanistan and the Continuing Use of American Force	1
	Introducing the IF Factor	4
	Vietnam, Afghanistan, and Beyond	7
	The New Way of Fighting: Asymmetrical Warfare	11
	The IF Contribution	12
	Conclusion: The Legacy of Vietnam, Afghanistan, and Ukraine	13
	Bibliography	15
Chapter 1	The United States in Vietnam and Beyond	17
	The Context: Why Students Need to Know about War	17
	The Post–World War II Evolution of Warfare	18
	The Post–WWII Transition	18
	The Effects on Thinking about Warfare	21
	The Impact of Vietnam	24
	The Longer-Term Effects of Vietnam	28
	Vietnam and the Future of War	30
	The End of the Draft and Americans' Connection to Military Activity	31
	Conclusion	34
	Bibliography	35

Chapter 2	The Twentieth-Century Legacy: The European Model of Warfare, the Impact of Nuclear Weapons, and the Transformation of the Uses of Force	39
	The European Style of War	43
	The Impact of Nuclear Weapons	46
	Evolution of the Nuclear Impact on War	47
	The Nuclear Weapons Age: China and America	49
	The Nuclear Age and Traditional War	52
	Conclusion	55
	Bibliography	58
Chapter 3	The Systemic Shock of 9/11: Afghanistan, Iraq, and Beyond	61
	America in Iraq	65
	The Gulf War and Beyond	67
	Invasion and Conquest	69
	Justification of the IF Criteria	71
	The War in Afghanistan	73
	The Original Motive: Avenging 9/11	74
	Conclusion: The Past in the Future?	77
	Bibliography	80
Chapter 4	Russia and Ukraine in 2022: The Face of Modern Mayhem?	83
	Defining Parameters in 2022: The Ukrainian Case	87
	The Incendiary Potential of the 2022 Crisis: A Presage to a Larger War?	89
	And Then There is Putin	92
	The War Worthiness of the Ukrainian Crisis: Before and After the Impact of Nuclear Weapons	95
	Resolving the Ukrainian Crisis	97
	Conclusion: The Nuclear Prophylactic?	102
	Bibliography	103
Chapter 5	Contemporary Warfare and American Force: Conventional and Asymmetrical Warfare in the World	105
	Fighting in the Developing World: The IF Factor in Application	108
	Contemplating Involvements: The Challenges of Asymmetrical Warfare	110

	Assessing the Prospects: The Middle East Quagmire as Rejoinder	112
	The United States and Potential Deployments beyond the Traditional Middle East Conflict	116
	Asymmetrical Warfare 101	117
	Asymmetry and the IF Factor	119
	Asymmetrical Warfare Is Not Easy	122
	The Dynamics of Defeating Intervention	124
	Conclusions	127
	Bibliography	129
Chapter 6	The Briar Patch of Intervention in a Complex Environment: The Developed World	131
	Dealing with the Modal Threats	133
	The Russian Invasion of Ukraine	135
	The Return of Major Power Conflict: Why Did Putin Do It?	135
	The American Response: Aggression and Nuclear Weapons	140
	Is Ukraine Russia's Vietnam—Or a Reprise of Afghanistan and Iraq?	144
	Ukraine and the IF Factor	147
	Conclusion: The Legacy of Ukraine?	150
	Bibliography	154
Chapter 7	Coping with Asymmetrical and Conventional Forms of War: The Challenge for American Expeditionary Forces	157
	"Traditional" War: Russia and Ukraine	160
	Asymmetrical Pasts and Futures?	164
	Asymmetrical Warfare in Europe?	166
	The Ukraine War in Perspective	169
	The Ukraine War, the American Response, and When America Should Fight	172
	The IF Factor and the Ukrainian War	175
	The Ukrainian Precedent	179
	Bibliography	180
Chapter 8	Conclusion: Where Will and Should the United States Fight: The Road Ahead	183
	The Recent Past as Prologue?	183

The Past as the Model of the Future?	187
The Ukrainian War	188
Asymmetrical War in the Developing World	192
Back to the Future: Where Should America Fight?	194
Peering into the Future	196
Projecting Forward	199
Bibliography	200
Index	203

Preface

In 2000, I published a book titled *When America Fights*. It sought to describe the circumstances and ways the United States has employed military force throughout its history and tentatively tried to extrapolate that experience into a future unsettled by the end of the Cold War and the resulting effect that change might have on the future. The interim period since has seen change continue, and in some cases literally explode. Both the pattern of force and the reasons for employing it have evolved in the process, and the questions of how the United States uses force and for what reasons it has and *should* use it in the future have changed along the way. Revisiting that subject factually and as a matter of US strategic preference has changed as well.

The early 2020s provide a prominent example of that evolution. The violence in much of the world during this epoch has been concentrated in the developing world and especially the Middle East, and this setting represents both a unique venue and a set of problems for policy makers. Its sources include the interconfessional conflict between Judaism and Islam that is currently undergoing some change largely due to Israeli initiatives, the rise and persistence of terrorism as a signature part of Middle Eastern relations, and, of course, Middle Eastern oil. The form such violence often takes is in so-called asymmetrical warfare, an approach that the United States has encountered problematically in the past (notably in Vietnam). The Russian invasion of Ukraine has reintroduced conventional war into Europe and reminded us that the disintegration of the Soviet Union was not the same thing as the end of conflict between Russia and the West. Each of these sources of conflict will continue to highlight the landscape of international conflict and violence and thus continue to be necessary elements in understanding the landscape of violence that can and may continue to concern the student of world peace and war.

The early 2020s present a pregnant period in the places and for the reasons the United States employs force to achieve and defend its interests. Conflict in the developing world presents both a unique venue and set of problems making so-called asymmetrical warfare a high priority for management. The Russian invasion of Ukraine has made parts of Europe a war zone. The result has been, in some ways, a return to a system of conventional and unconventional uses and reasons for employing force. The danger of escalation to major, systemic (including, in the most extreme case, nuclear) war was always a limiting force in relations during the Cold War but which receded during the 1990s and into the new century.

The possibility of the Cold War going hot was always present, although that concern has faded as have memories of the post-1945 competition. Until the end of the Vietnam conflict, interest in war was particularly acute among those who might be involuntarily required to fight it. But that interest has cooled. War has become a more impersonal and seemingly remote possibility for most Americans, although it remains a possibility for which the country must prepare itself.

This book attempts to provide an overview of these problems and prospects, and thus to serve as a reminder to Americans that the world is still a dangerous place in which policy must be navigated. More to the point, the cohort of formerly draft-vulnerable young Americans who have not been concerned about involuntary service since the draft was suspended (but not revoked) in 1974 are well advised to be cognizant about what could go wrong and thus change their privileged, aloof status.

The drafting of this text got caught in the middle of this process of change. When it was first undertaken, asymmetrical warfare was by far the dominant form of international violence; Ukraine has forced a broadening of that perspective. Russia's invasion has reintroduced a whole set of traditional European-based dynamics that include the continuing role and prospects of nuclear weapons and their continuing role in moderating international outbreaks of war added to the unconventional war problem. The question of whether and how to operate a conflictual international system remains a concern for those who think about and plan for possibilities of employing force. The pages that follow attempt to survey the possibilities. This entreaty applies especially to young males (and in the future, potentially females) who have been potentially vulnerable to being drafted since the suspension in 1974 but often were unaware of their vulnerability.

What has simultaneously (and counterintuitively) changed has been the implicit but significant impact of nuclear weapons and the possibility of nuclear war—no matter how improbable such a prospect may be. The Ukrainian war is the first violent conflict in Europe since these weapons became widespread and possessed by both sides in a conflict, and their possession has enlivened the potential battle space. The issues and fighting in Ukraine have both directly raised the nuclear specter, and Putin has referred to them ominously upon occasion. A bad outcome for Russia in Ukraine is certainly possible, in which case escalation could become an option that is preferable to a loss in the minds of Putin and his supporters. He has not specified circumstances that might make the threat or use of such weapons attractive, but who knows what a desperate Putin faced with humiliating defeat and challenge to his leadership might create?

Among developing world conflicts, the only region directly affected by major power competition is the Middle East. Russian influence is largely confined to Syria, and a nuclear-armed Israel has become a geopolitical power throughout the region. In a world gone geopolitically mad, some have hinted at the possibility of Sino-American confrontation that might devolve into conflict, particularly over Taiwan, but the two countries are too economically and financially bound together to make such a possibility likely.

War involving the United States in a major way seems remote at this point, but things change as circumstances change. The pages that follow look at the dynamics of the dominant forms of international conflict that exist and how they could affect the United States and potentially others in the world. It focuses on two major scenarios—unconventional wars, almost entirely in the Middle East and, thanks to the Ukrainian-Russian conflict, the prospects of more conventional European war.

Many thanks to the reviewers who offered feedback on the project, including Joseph P. Bassi, University of Texas at El Paso; Peter Davies, California State University, Sacramento; Patrick Haney, Miami University; and Wesley B. O'Dell, Virginia Military Institute.

Introduction

The Withdrawal from Afghanistan and the Continuing Use of American Force

On July 31, 2021, the last American C-17 transport plane departed from Kabul airport in the early evening local time. It carried the last remaining US forces symbolizing American military participation in the seemingly endless civil conflict in Afghanistan. It was an essentially open-ended conflict in which the United States had been a major combatant since American forces originally entered Afghanistan in late 2001 to capture the Al Qaeda terrorists responsible for the September 11, 2001, attacks on American soil and where they had been given sanctuary. The action was justified because the Taliban government refused to remand the terrorists to the Americans. The United States invaded Afghanistan to capture them; the operation failed, however, as Al Qaeda escaped to Pakistan. Even though that American mission failed, the United States stayed for nearly twenty years until the summer of 2021, when the Taliban returned to power as the Afghan government and military collapsed.

On July 16, 2021, Taliban had entered and subdued the Afghan capital of Kabul without opposition from either Afghan government's forces or NATO forces. The takeover was accompanied by the utter collapse of the 300,000-man Afghan army recruited, paid for, and equipped by the Americans. This nearly twenty-year US military presence represented the longest war in American history, far exceeding the length of the US intervention in Southeast Asia. Afghanistan has thus been the longest war in American history to this point. In terms of American combat deaths—2,352 killed, according to the Department of Defense—it was the tenth deadliest American war, sandwiched between the Spanish-American War and the War of 1812.

It ended, like Vietnam, messily. In Southeast Asia, the South Vietnamese allies of the United States ultimately collapsed in the face of an offensive by the National Liberation Force (NLF, or Viet Cong) that most famously overran the US Embassy grounds. The most vivid visual image beamed to the world was clearly desperate American diplomatic personnel scrambling onto helicopters hovering above the embassy.

The scene in Kabul was evocatively similar. The Taliban entered and subdued the city without opposition, and President Ashraf Ghani Ahmadzai fled the capital before they arrived. Most Americans and many Afghan nationals (especially those with connections to the Americans) panicked as people fled to the Kabul airport hoping to board planes and flee the country. In scenes eerily reminiscent of Saigon in 1975, some Afghans clung to the undersides of airplane wings of departing aircraft and some lost their grips and plunged to the earth to their deaths. Apparently seeking to moderate their images as fanatics, the Taliban did not oppose the exodus, and in some cases even acted to make it less chaotic.

The Afghan withdrawal marked major change in the answer to the question raised in the title of this book: When should America fight? The rationale has changed significantly across time from periods of expansive willingness to use force to geopolitical and internal political influences limiting that willingness. This vacillation has in turn been affected by changing assessments of what exactly are the national interests and what would be needed through American military capabilities to achieve those interests. The answers change periodically. The end of the Afghan involvement will almost certainly usher some retrenchment and reluctance to enter what could become the next generation of "endless wars," but experience suggests that change could be transitory. "No More Vietnams," was the mantra of a generation after 1975, but it was largely deemed inapplicable to the challenges of the twenty-first century. The simple fact is that the United States has never developed an enduring, consistent answer to the question of when America should fight.

Answering this question is neither simple nor easy. If it was, there might be a consensus that most Americans agreed on across the range of possibilities. There is not. Such a consensus does not exist and has become increasingly difficult to attain in the hyper-partisanship that has become a signature feature of American politics in the twenty-first century, and the results are unfortunate. The response to the disorder on the ground in Kabul was an American military attempt to whisk Americans and sympathetic Afghan refugees out of Afghanistan through airlift and evacuation from the Kabul airport. It was a chaotic, seemingly disorderly process, and it was captured in exquisite detail by global media. President Biden was widely blamed for the chaos, though the messiness and brutality of the process was probably an unavoidable artifact of its nature and timing; that it all appeared in essentially real time on global television was its distinction from earlier examples. The difference from similar events in the past was largely in the ubiquity of electronic media in 2021.

If there was a "cause" of the chaotic conditions in Afghanistan as the Taliban asserted their victory and began to impose their domain, it was the truly desperate nature of the situation on the ground that was at the core of the response. This was, after all, the crescendo of a civil war that had been going on for a quarter century or more and which may continue. It was a bitter, long-standing contest over what group of Afghans would rule the rest of the Afghan population, and the feelings that it created ran very deep. In such conflicts, the losers often have good reasons to fear the victor's law that ensues. That they panicked and ran for the exits was not the fault of the American decision to depart a situation into which it probably should never exposed itself in the first place. The cause of the chaos was the quite genuine fear of the losers at their postwar situation. In this case of the use (misuse?) of American military force was not how it was withdrawn, but whether it should have been applied in the first place.

Not all situations surrounding the applications of American force end up being as tragic as Afghanistan. There are situations where there is agreement that force is necessary. Almost everyone agrees about those extreme cases. There is little dissent that the United States must respond appropriately if its most important interests are directly attacked by a hostile military force, although there is some disagreement about appropriate responses in a world of nuclear weapons. At the same time, some interactions and international outcomes are clearly not important enough to commit US force to solving. The boundaries and range of possibly appropriate responses is more difficult at this end of the spectrum. It can, for instance, be argued that there was nothing important enough in anything that happened in Vietnam or Afghanistan to justify the level of American commitment in either place. Situations where the worth (interests involved) and the propriety of force to achieve desired outcomes at acceptable costs form the parameters of answering the title question of this book. The answer is neither easy to determine nor will it be universally embraced.

On February 24, 2022, Russia invaded Ukraine in what it assumed would be a quick and easy campaign motivated presumably by sentiments among some Ukrainians to join NATO. Vladimir Putin's rationale was not so clear. Was it an attempt to demonstrate Russian status as a superpower, to provide a crown jewel for Putin's legacy, or was there some other motive? The answer is not clear, but the Russians clearly underestimated Ukrainian and international reactions to their actions.

Ukraine offers a very different problem for the United States than the long war in Afghanistan. American forces are not participating directly in the fighting; it is not directly an American war. It is a war started by the Russian invasion of the sovereign state of Ukraine, and the forces of those two countries have done the fighting and dying. The United States could have become actively involved with fighting troops but did not, even though the Russian action was a provocative breach of the general European peace that has held since the end of World War II. The United States, instead, limited itself to massive material support for the Ukrainians and helping to rally international force behind the overmatched Ukrainian armed forces.

Why did the United States exercise restraint in Ukraine? The answer, quite simply, is to avoid the possibility of a nuclear war. The result is an anomaly of sorts, which will be explored through the text—the contrast between plausible intervention in the developing world where US interest may be less vital, and avoiding intervention in European wars where the United States may have more at stake. This effectively means the United States can fight where our most important interests are not involved but not where they are.

The purpose of what follows is not to try to convince the reader of a "proper" solution to the root question. Rather, it is to try to build a framework of questions and considerations that can be reference points both for decision makers and for citizens evaluating those choices. One vehicle for doing this is what I will call the *IF Factor*. There are two underlying operational concepts in this formulation, which proposes to help order whether possible interventions are advisable. The first concept is the assessments of *American interests (I)* in contemplating involvements in particular situations and whether proposed outcomes achieved are worth the costs. The second is *feasibility (F)*, which asks whether the application of force can be effective in achieving those outcomes. They are, in essence, asking two questions: what is the interest involved and is it worth pursuing with American force? And can American force achieve those goals?

Introducing the IF Factor

In an earlier book (*When America Fights*), I argued Vietnam provided the strongest and most poignant examples of how not to assess the wisdom of engaging in military interventions and the outcomes of those engagements. Vietnam was ultimately an adventure where the assessment of each of the major criteria proved wrong in retrospect.

The US war in Southeast Asia was the first example of the relevance of this distinction as a theater of the Cold War, where a nationalist movement was led by a communist, Ho Chi Minh, who was opposed by an anti-communist government in South Vietnam that happened to be less worthy of support than it might have been. The Vietnam War was framed in terms of the Cold War competition and in the fear that if the South Vietnamese government fell, it would be a major advancement in the effort to turn the world map decisively "red," that is, communist. There were elements of truth in this formulation: the North Vietnamese insurgency was led by communists, and it did succeed in recoloring a small part of the world political map. The more dire consequences proved mostly to be false. Nearly a half-century after the final American withdrawal, the country remains nominally one of the four communist states in the world (the others being China, North Korea, and Cuba), but they are hardly a menace to the United States. Vietnam is now a peaceful trading partner, not a geopolitical opponent. For most of the former American soldiers who visit there, it is a vacation site.

Had something like the IF Factor been considered at the time, concerns captured in it might have been helpful in framing the early 1960s decision to intervene in this internal conflict. Instead, the situation was viewed as an East-West, communist-anti-communist conflict in the global struggle for domain, a not atypical assessment of the situation at the time. It was almost certainly not a conflict that warranted the expenditure of more than 58,000 young American lives in a failed geopolitical enterprise.

The IF Factor is intended to channel concerns that may affect the contemplation of American military involvement in conflict situations. Its effects—and to some extent its intent—is cautionary for the United States, because careful consideration and analysis of its criteria raises the bar for involvement to higher levels than have always been applied. In essence, the post-Vietnam entreaty of "no More Vietnams" is an application of its principles, learned and unlearned in Southeast Asia and now to be relearned again after the Afghanistan experience. The two experiences were not perfectly analogous, but they can illustrate the factors in application.

The IF Factor is largely compatible with the realist paradigm, a formulation of the principles of classic realism to national foreign and security policy goals and applications that still heavily influences many decision makers. I have discussed the paradigm in various other places—most fully in my book, *National Security*, currently in its seventh edition. The construct has roots in the classic balance of power political systems of the eighteenth and nineteenth centuries but fell into some disrepute in the twentieth century because it was associated with most of the leaders who fought the two world wars. Nonetheless, it is a useful construct for thinking about when to use—and not to use—military force to achieve national goals in international relations. Its premises and applications are found prominently in both basic concepts of the IF Factor.

The first IF Factor is *interests*. To meet this factor's standard of applicability, participation in a potential conflict must first be in the country's vital interests to achieve or maintain. It begins with the question of what the national interest is in any situation, how the actions of a potential opponent may preclude the achievement of that condition, and whether a negative outcome is sufficiently damaging to justify taking strong measures, including the threat or use of armed violence. In classic realist usage, the bar between situations worthy or unworthy of contemplating the application is the *vitality* of achieving a successful resolution of the conflict of interests with another party. In classic realism, the use of force is reserved for situations where that achievement is *vital*, meaning the national interest must be unacceptably compromised if the situation is not resolved successfully before force is contemplated.

The IF Factor examination begins with the question of the vitality of interests that the state has in creating or preserving a particular situation or relationship. According to the paradigm, the standard of *vital interests* is the dividing line between those interests that are so important that force may be justified to achieve them and those that are not. All other interests are considered *less than vital (LTV)* and presumably fall below the standard for considering or threatening to use force to secure them. It sounds like a straightforward division, but as in so many actual national security concerns, it is not so easy to determine in practice.

The simple fact is that people have sometimes broadly divergent concepts of what is and is not vital to the national interests. The problem arises from the philosophy of science concept known as *intersubjectivity*. This term refers to the idea that to meet scientific standards, all phenomena must appear the same to all observers. Questions whether vital interests apply often do not achieve that status. A condition that seems necessary (vital) to one observer, in other words, may appear less important to someone else. If the achievement of vitality is the necessary criterion for proposing the application of force in a specific circumstance, the parties presumably must be in accord on whether the situation warrants that exertion: is a favorable outcome truly necessary to national well-being? The answer is often contentious, as some of the decisions to engage in Vietnam and Afghanistan during the Cold War demonstrate, and they contrast with the reasons for American nonintervention in Ukraine.

Vietnam, Afghanistan, and Beyond

If the public record is a fair indication, decisions to engage in both Vietnam and Afghanistan were reached based on limited knowledge of the situation, with less-than-perfect understanding of the military and political situations in the two countries and an assessment of American interests that was imperfectly rigorous. In both of the earlier cases, for instance, American interests were decidedly limited and did not capture the nature of the situation. The Southeast Asian adventure, for instance, was conceptualized primarily as an effort to stop the spread of communism in the region. That emphasis had a potent political appeal in the 1950s when it was articulated: Vietnam was seen as a vital element in arresting the spread of the global communist menace. The position had some salience: the leader of the insurgency, Ho Chi Minh, was a communist who wanted to establish a communist regime in all the country. It was not, however, the total story: for many South Vietnamese, it was also a revolution to end oligarchic rule in the country by largely Chinese absentee landowners; if the incumbents remained in power, most *Vietnamese* residents were politically and economically repressed. The United States was, in effect, aligning itself with a political outcome opposed by a larger part of the population than it realized at the time.

In Afghanistan, the battle over political control has always been at heart tribal: it is about whether Pashtuns or non-Pashtuns will control the country. This is a dominating theme of Afghan history. The excesses of the Taliban suppression of women is factual and reprehensible from a Western vantage point, but it was never the heart of the conflict. The United States entered the country in 2001 to capture the leadership of Al Qaeda. That failed, and we stayed for twenty years to keep them from coming back. As Afghan history demonstrates, that put us at odds with fundamental Afghan history.

American interests are different in the Ukrainian case. The United States has minimal direct interests in Ukraine, but significant interests in the broader European balance. And Russia's desire for expansionism collides with American interests in a free and peaceful European environment. In addition, the brutality and war criminal nature of aspects of the Russian invasion is incompatible with American global interests and a peaceful, humane world order.

The question of levels of interest takes on a different meaning when framed in these terms. There is a direct, if partial, justification of the Vietnam decision based in Cold War terms: the National Liberation Front was indeed communist and imposed a Marxist regime after achieving power. A focus on this outcome provided an American interest in the war, but it ignored the other dynamic: the United States fought in support of one side in a civil war, and that side was not the popular choice of many Vietnamese, nor was it a political outcome the success of which (other than preventing communists from achieving success) was particularly in the United States' interest. The South Vietnamese whom we supported and tried to keep in power lost, and we lost with them.

There was an analogous combination of motivations in Afghanistan. When the United States failed to capture Al Qaeda following our post-2001 intervention, the question was what interest remained to justify a continued American effort. If there was an internal debate about this (which presumably there was), it has never been widely shared publicly. Instead, the Americans stayed, entered an effective alliance with the so-called Northern Coalition of Pashtuns and others seeking to dislodge the Taliban from power, and remained after that effort succeeded in sending the Taliban into exile in Pakistan in 2002. It was not clear at the time what purpose was served by staying beyond that goal, but it evolved to a post hoc goal of ensuring the Taliban did not come back to power and invite the terrorists to return from exile—the official rationale when the occupation ended in 2021. The remaining question has always been whether the United States could have ensured Afghan unwillingness to allow Al Qaeda to use the country as a sanctuary short of a twenty-year occupation. It is a question raised in chapter 3.

The point of this discussion is to suggest that a careful delineation and critique of the interests served by a proposed military action is necessary before committing force for at least two reasons. First, it can (and should) determine whether the interest is indeed important enough to warrant achieving or maintaining it through an American military commitment. Was keeping the Taliban out of control in Afghanistan important enough to justify the ultimately failed effort to achieve it? How important is a free Ukraine to the United States? Second, it facilitates a careful examination of whether there were alternative ways short of inserting American forces into the situation that could have been employed to secure American objectives. In other words, were there alternatives to fighting America's longest war in Afghanistan but avoiding a direct clash in Ukraine?

The second part of the IF Factor is *feasibility*. This criterion basically asks whether American military force can effectively be employed to achieve the interests for which it is proposed. Can the United States "win"? The determination of interest leads to the question of whether US force secures that interest.

The logically prior question to the achievement of objectives is whether whatever objectives that may underlie a proposed application of force can be secured with force: is force the appropriate and effective means to the end? This has always been a beguiling question for the US military. The tradition is unrelentingly positive and is captured in the slogan "Can do." It reflects a self-image of the American military as being consistently up to any task and suggests that the question of reliability is essentially universally positive. If given a military chore, the American armed forces "can do," are capable of and willing to overcome any obstacle, and can achieve any objective that they are asked to carry out.

This "myth of invincibility," as it is sometimes called, has been a durable part of the American military self-image, and it is an important element in that institution's self-image and sense of worth. Like all myths, of course, it is exaggerated to some degree, amplifying the successes of the country at arms and downplaying instances where that application was not as successful or glorious. This is not so much a criticism as part of the military's elan and myth of all countries to some extent. The most often-cited evidence of can-do prowess is the role the United States played in the world wars. It carried over to the post–WWII environment, when the country was the world's preeminent power and a large part of that status was attributed to its military capabilities.

In the post–WWII world, the military situation has changed in ways at odds with that self-traditional image. A dominant form of politico-military activity since the 1950s has been dealing with the emergence of the so-called developing world as a force in world politics. That movement has had two major characteristics. The first is self-determination and independence of the Afro-Asian world from colonial rule by Westerners. The second is internal turmoil within and between those countries to establish their boundaries and leadership. Both factors are related to one another and are far enough removed from the American democratic experience to be alien to American policy makers. The United States had a limited role and interest in much of the early phase of this process, except when it included Cold War concerns: the competition between communism versus market-based systems. This confrontation created considerable interest for the United States and enticed it into the contest for ideological control as the Cold War spread to the developing world. It also meant the United States ended up taking sides in many of the internal struggles that dominated the emerging countries and tempted the United States to assert interests that had not previously existed. Vietnam was the prototype.

Ukraine offers a different profile: from the vantage point of feasibility, the United States was placed in a different operational environment that featured military return to the European traditions. The war in Ukraine is a form of fighting that has some roots in the historical American military experience. Its difference, of course, is in the potential destruction it could create should the Americans and Russians somehow meet on the battlefield and nuclear weapons be employed. That process of escalation is to be avoided at all costs, so the thinking in Washington has gone. Operationally, that means the Russians and Americans will not meet on the battlefield at all.

This nontraditional style of warfare has its roots in Eastern practice that goes back literally thousands of years. Its best-known expression was in Sun Tzu's *The Art of War*, an exposition on the style of warfare that stands in stark contrast to the Western tradition of fighting. The Western style of warfare favors the larger and stronger competitors (both physically and in terms of deadly equipment) and disadvantages the party that cannot field the same size and quality of resistance. The emphasis of the Eastern style is on deception, maneuver, and the erosion of enemy morale, whereas Western-style warfare is exemplified by the large armies of the eighteenth century where the two sides lined up in long lines of soldiers who marched directly at one another and crashed together in deadly combat. The linear battle is the epitome of the Western approach; the ambush is the heart of the Eastern, indirect approach. The Eastern approach is also more psychological: it seeks to demoralize the opponent by showing that it cannot succeed; the Western approach succeeds by bringing the enemy to its knees. It is sometimes said, in this analogy, that conventional Western-style forces must "win by winning," while unconventional Eastern forces "win by not losing."

The indirect approach (another description of the Eastern style) is not entirely unknown in the American tradition; it is just not a part of the experience Americans equate with victory and success. These techniques have been borrowed and adopted by American forces at different times. A prime example is the Battle of Saratoga in the American Revolution. British General Burgoyne marched an army south out of Canada with which to attack New York. As they proceeded southward, American revolutionaries harassed and killed many of his troops through techniques such as hiding in the mountains and hills along the way and ambushing and killing British troops (who considered the attacks cowardly). By the time the British reached the outpost at Saratoga overlooking the Hudson River, they were so depleted and exhausted that Continental troops easily defeated them. Because this style was unconventional and disparaged by the Europeans, it was not incorporated into basic American military doctrine and practice. This may have been just as well, because had the Confederates adopted some of these techniques in the waning year or so of the Civil War in the Appalachians, the outcome of the war might have been different than it was (this possible scenario helps introduce chapter 4).

This style of warfare became popular in the late nineteenth and early twentieth centuries, especially among adherents of the Chinese revolution orchestrated by Mao Dzedung, and is thus associated with the communist movement of the Cold War. The term *guerrilla mobile warfare* is one of the terms used to describe it, but it has had the unfortunate effect of allowing the equation of mobile-guerrilla warfare and communism. The more proper term is unconventional or asymmetrical warfare.

The New Way of Fighting: Asymmetrical Warfare

As is discussed in some detail in chapter 5, the problems created by asymmetrical warfare are very different from those arising from the European-style fighting with which the United States is most experienced and most adroit. Asymmetrical warfare is not a method so much as an approach to fighting. Its conduct evolves and changes. This is done purposely, because the forces available to asymmetrical warriors are normally inferior to those of conventional forces in terms like firepower, and the asymmetrical warrior must find a way to negate the advantage the traditional warrior has in order to stand a chance of surviving and prevailing.

The United States has tried to adapt to this style of warfare but has met resistance from internal opponents, some in the American military hierarchy. The first large-scale American exposure to an enemy using the techniques associated with asymmetrical warfare was in Vietnam, and the United States was not particularly successful in negating it. Part of the meaning of the charge that Vietnam was the first war the United States lost is that the United States was never able to crush the Vietnamese resistance to the South Vietnamese government we supported. Another way of saying this is that the United States failed to defeat the enemy, which was able to outlast American patience and willingness to continue fighting a seemingly unwinnable war. Eventually the American people turned against the effort, and the United States was forced to leave. Other groups in other countries watched this phenomenon, and the outcome was that many adopted their own variant of the asymmetrical model, especially if there was the danger or actuality of American intervention in their affairs. The problem for the United States is that these adaptations have worked, and future developing world opponents will almost certainly replicate them. The Taliban in Afghanistan have been among contemporary successful practitioners. Fighting in Ukraine has been overwhelmingly conventional.

The problem of asymmetrical warfare is at the heart of the feasibility factor in developing world conflict. It is virtually a given that any developing world opponent the United States may contemplate facing in the future will employ some variant of asymmetrical warfare strategy against the Americans. The reason is simple: it is the only way they have a chance against arguably the world's premier conventional armed force. Confronting the Americans on their own military grounds and "playing" by their rules virtually guarantees that such adversaries will lose. The last country to try fighting the Americans in European-style warfare was Iraq during the 1990–1991 Persian Gulf War, and they were crushed in the process—a lesson for all potential opponents of the Americans. Among others, the Iraqis themselves learned this lesson well, and in 2003 when the Americans marched into their country, they offered essentially no armed resistance, simply allowing the conquest and occupation they could not prevent, and they mounted a limited asymmetrical campaign of resistance. And it worked. The Americans remained for eight years and then they left, whatever mission they were pursuing unattained or only partially attained.

As the recently concluded American occupation of Afghanistan demonstrated, the strategy of unconventional warfare against the Americans works in other developing world settings as well. At the risk of getting ahead of the major train of analysis, the reason is largely a matter of impatience: the goal of American military engagement is quick and decisive victory on the battlefield, followed by capitulation of the opponent, the imposition of peace terms, and a return to peace. It is the peace-war-peace model that is at the heart of European-style warfare, but it is a model that developing countries cannot adopt, because they lack the resources to prevail in this kind of struggle. Instead, they must fight a war of attrition, where they can simply outlast the enemy, deny its ability to achieve its goals, and eventually frustrate it to the point that the more powerful state simply concludes its goals are unattainable within acceptable bounds of the conflict and leaves. The strategy worked against the Americans in Vietnam, in Iraq, and now Afghanistan. Why?

The IF Contribution

The principles of the IF Factor help to unravel the dynamics of the American use of power both in the developing world and in places like Ukraine. The heart of the limits imposed by the IF criteria is that a military action must meet two conditions. It must have an important enough rationale to sustain support for the actions it demands, and the United States must have a force designed to realistically prevail in this kind of contest. The Afghan example illustrates both the importance of each criterion and their interconnection. Summarily put, pursuing an objective that is not vital enough to the country runs the risk of public opposition developing before the mission can be concluded successfully (if it can be under *any* circumstances). An objective that cannot be successfully secured on the battlefield will likely prove unpopular enough that public opposition will grow to the point that continuation will become a political and economic liability that is impossible to sustain.

Feasibility takes on a different and more complex meaning in a place like Ukraine. In that conflict, the United States faced two conflicting imperatives. One, of course, was to help the Ukrainians defeat and repel the Russian invasion. The second was to avoid escalation to nuclear war. The solution was a compromise: first, aiding the Ukrainians by providing material assistance so they could more effectively defend themselves, but not committing American forces into direct conflict with the Russians, which could have escalated into direct war between the two superpowers. The other was helping to mobilize the coalition of NATO countries providing aid and support for the victims of the war, as well as publicizing and excoriating Russian brutality.

The problem of extraction from these kinds of adventures must be addressed within this framework given the notoriety and controversy that surrounded the American withdrawal from Afghanistan. It was a messy, humiliating process for the United States and a terrifying, life-threatening experience for the thousands of Afghans who had collaborated with the American effort and who feared deadly revenge if they were left behind. The lasting symbol of the final takeover centered on the Kabul airport, from which Americans and their Afghan allies sought escape through a massive, hastily assembled American airlift. Ending the Ukrainian involvement remains a work in progress.

Why dwell particularly on the sad results of the unfulfilled purpose of the twenty-year involvement of the United States in Afghanistan? Unfortunately, something like what happened in Kabul has been a recurring feature of American military intervention in developing world politics since World War II. The final flight from Kabul was conceptually akin to the abandonment of Saigon forty-five years earlier. The main difference was that Afghanistan was covered in much greater media detail, the result of the greater ubiquity of electronic media coverage today. The United States largely avoided the cameras when it slunk out of Iraq in less than triumph in 2011, but there was nothing resembling a triumphal departure either.

Conclusion: The Legacy of Vietnam, Afghanistan, and Ukraine

The lasting lesson of the harried American departure from Afghanistan will probably be that it is likely to be a recurrent nightmare if the United States involves itself in future situations that do not clearly meet the criteria of the IF Factor. Unless the Americans are totally successful in helping a chosen side to triumph, it is almost bound to be a messy, unpleasant process. The heart of asymmetrical warfare strategies is to avoid losing, and that is accomplished by dragging out combat and avoiding defeat until the opponent tires of the effort and leaves. This is essentially what happened in both Vietnam and Afghanistan. It is hard to portray the US departure in positive terms.

Citizen outrage with Vietnam has not been repeated in Ukraine. The situations have, of course, been different. Vietnam was a long, protracted affair that involved the involuntary participation of many young Americans, and President Nixon ran for reelection on a promise to extract the United States from Southeast Asia. He reinforced this promise by suspending the unpopular selective service system to assure an angry population that more young Americans would not face involuntary combat duty in a future war they opposed. In contrast, Americans were not committed to the fighting and dying in Ukraine, because there was no draft and the shadow of potential escalation loomed over the conflict. The United States learned a lesson in the Vietnam war effort that it did not forget in Ukraine.

The end of the draft also relaxed considerably public opposition to military intervention in wars that arguably violate both principles of the IF Factor. The reason is self-evident: the only Americans with a personal interest in how and where the United States uses its armed forces are the actual volunteers who constitute the All-Volunteer Force (AVF) and their families and loved ones. No American who was not at least eighteen years old in 1972 when the draft was suspended has had to confront the possibility of being conscripted and forced to fight and possibly die in an American military effort. Putting your own life in jeopardy in the line of fire will inevitably change the calculation of what is in the nation's vital interest and worth sending forces to advance. Military service has become an abstract concept the possibility of which does not directly affect many voters and their elected officials. Does this not change how citizens and political figures think about military actions? How can it not?

These introductory observations help form some broad parameters within which determinations about the use of military power in the post-Vietnam, post-Afghanistan era can be made. If the Vietnam experience is any indicator, the immediate scenario will be a reduction in support for submitting American forces into harm's way for a time, but exactly for how long is speculative. The immediate post-Vietnam period was dominated by public support for restraint ("No More Vietnams") in using those forces. The military itself welcomed the change both because it created a respite for the force and because the volunteers were more professional and committed, because they had freely chosen the military as a career. The drawback was reducing public reluctance to use and reuse those forces. No one publicly raised the possibility of committing US forces in Ukraine.

The thirteen American troops slaughtered at the Kabul Airport were the first American casualties in Afghanistan since 2020. With the American withdrawal complete and only a few troops remaining there to guard American assets like the embassy grounds and staff, the United States has entered a period where there is not a major deployment of its forces overseas in direct harm's way, and this trend will be reinforced if the Biden administration or a successor continues to deemphasize the military presence of this country in the Middle East generally (a possibility the dynamics and appeal of which I have examined recently in *The Middle East and American National Security*). But will that restraint endure? The purpose of the rest of this volume is to explore how and in what circumstances the United States should choose to use its armed forces in the contemporary environment. It will do so by looking first at the Afghan commitment, the more physically restrained approach in Ukraine, and then by comparing those experiences with an eye toward their cumulative impact in the future.

Bibliography

Allison, Graham T., and Dimitri K. Simes. "Trump and Russia." *The National Interest* 147 (2017): 25–34.

Art, Robert A., and Kenneth M. Waltz, eds. *The Use of Force: Military Power and International Relations*. 7th ed. Lanham, MD: Rowman & Littlefield, 2009.

Bacevich, Andrew J. *America's War for the Greater Middle East: A Military History*. New York: Random House, 2016.

Brodie, Bernard, and Fawn M. Brodie. *From Crossbow to H-Bomb: The Evolution of Weapons and Tactics of Warfare*. Revised and Enlarged Edition. Bloomington: Indiana University Press, 1973.

Caputo, Phil. "The Temperature in Saigon is 105 and Rising: What I Learned About American Power Watching the U.S. Leave Vietnam—and Then Afghanistan Decades Later." *Politico* (online), August 21, 2021.

Fontaine, Richard. "The Nonintervention Delusion: What War Is Good For." *Foreign Affairs* 98, no. 6 (November/December 2019): 84–98.

Fromkin, David. *The Independence of Nations*. New York: Praeger Special Studies, 1981.

Lawrence, Mark Atwood. "The Real Saigon Analogy: Vietnam Wasn't the End of American Credibility, and Neither Is Afghanistan." *Foreign Affairs* (online), August 21, 2021.

Liddell-Hart, B. H. *Strategy*. New York: Meridian Press, 1991.

Malley, Robert. "The Unwanted Wars: Why the Middle East Is More Combustible than Ever." *Foreign Affairs* 98, no. 6 (November/December 2019): 38–47.

McKinley, P. Michael. "We All Lost Afghanistan: Two Decades of Mistakes, Misjudgment, and Collective Failure." *Foreign Affairs* (online), August 16, 2021.

Nasr, Vali, and Maria Fantappie. "The Promise of Diplomacy as the United States Withdraws." *Foreign Affairs* (online), August 2, 2021.

Nuechterlein, Donald. *America Recommitted: United States National Interests in a Reconstructed World*. Lexington: University of Kentucky Press, 1991.

Packer, George. "The Longest Wars: Richard Holbrook and the Decline of American Power." *Foreign Affairs* 98, no. 3 (May/June 2019).

Schelling, Thomas C. *Arms and Influence*. New Haven, CT: Yale University Press, 1966.

Shifrinson, Joshua, and Stephen Wertheim. "Biden the Realist: The President's Doctrine Has Been Hiding in Plain Sight." *Foreign Affairs* (online), September 9, 2021.

Snow, Donald M. *Distant Thunder: Patterns of Conflict in the Developing World*. 2nd ed. Armonk, NY: M. E. Sharpe, 1997.

———. *The Middle East and American National Security: Forever Wars and Conflicts?* Lanham, MD: Rowman & Littlefield, 2021.

———. *National Security*. 7th ed. New York and London: Routledge, 2020.

———. *Uncivil Wars: International Security and the New Internal Wars*. Boulder, CO: Lynne Rienner, 1996.

———. *When America Fights: The Uses of American Military Force*. Washington, DC: CQ Press, 2000.

———, and Dennis M. Drew. *From Lexington to Desert Storm and Beyond*. 3rd ed. Armonk, NY: M. E. Sharpe, 2010.

Stares, Paul B. *Preventive Engagement: How America Can Avoid War and Keep the Peace*. New York: Columbia University Press, 2018.

Summers, Harry G. Jr. *On Strategy: A Critical Analysis of the Vietnam War*. Novato, CA: Presidio Press, 1982.

Sun Tzu. *The Art of War*. Translated by Samuel B. Griffith. Oxford, UK: Oxford University Press, 1963.

Waltz, Kenneth. *Theory of International Relations*. Rev ed. Long Grove, IL: Waveland Press, 2010.

CHAPTER ONE

The United States in Vietnam and Beyond

The Context: Why Students Need to Know about War

Although a war like the one that recently concluded American involvement in Afghanistan may today seem the "normal" way the United States uses force in the modern world, it in fact represents a historically radical departure from how the United States has employed political and military force and how and why to use force before the latter part of the twentieth century. The American experience up to the middle of the twentieth century was quite different. The country has gone through a major evolution in how and for what purposes it uses force to protect and promote its national interests. It now will have to adapt to the outcome of the Afghanistan War as it thinks about future geopolitical scenarios employing its armed might.

The period from the American Revolution through World War II was dominated by thought and actions within the conventional, European framework, and this intellectual construct dominated how both political and military thought was directed and focused. Before the twentieth century, the United States was a marginal international actor, a distant outsider that did not add much to the power balance in the European system and was not unlike the way developing world countries are thought of today. American military action was mostly confined to internal obstructions to its westward movement across the North American continent from Indian tribes who occupied the lands and in dealings with Western Hemispheric neighbors. The only major American military event was the Civil War, which might have been a harbinger of the future, but was not conceived in those terms (see chapter 5). That war was conducted on both sides by leaders trained in European-style warfare, ultimately to the benefit of the Union and the detriment of the Confederacy.

The world wars of the first half of the twentieth century changed American status dramatically. During the last decades of the nineteenth century, the United States emerged as a robust and potentially consequential economic power. It was not a major global player, due largely to its disdain toward European power politics. Its primary geopolitical emphasis was on securing its control over the territory that became the lower forty-eight states of the union. The military tradition it developed closely mirrored European-style warfare.

The world wars effectively destroyed the viability of its status as an aloof, marginal member of the international system. At the end of the second world conflagration, the United States emerged as the world's most powerful country and the only state with the resources to finance and lead the restructuring of the international system. The only other country that could be said meaningfully to have won WWII was the Soviet Union, although Soviet losses dwarfed American sacrifices by most measures. The consequences of these new realities included a changed international order led by opposing neophyte major powers, and global international geopolitics were greatly changed.

The Post–World War II Evolution of Warfare

Korea was the first harbinger of change. That war to restore the political order on the Korean Peninsula also featured warfare in transition physically. It was a conventional war in terms of the organization of the forces of the countries that dominated its conduct, but the participation of the Chinese "volunteers" also introduced elements of the Eastern military tradition into the fighting. The war was a victory of sorts for the United States and the traditional Western style, but it also included Chinese-inspired elements of nontraditional, Eastern-style warfare. The influence of Sun Tzu and other Eastern thinkers (e.g., Mao Dzedung) introduced elements of what became asymmetrical warfare into the conflict. The door was opened a crack for the style of warfare so often fought today.

The Post–WWII Transition

The process of change has gone through several basic stages since. The first was the Cold War itself. With Europe largely exhausted and dependent on the Americans to help rebuild and replenish themselves, the conflict was dominated by the two most geopolitically inexperienced major states from the wartime coalition that had defeated fascism. It was also a period of maximum pessimism and subsequent geopolitical change to respond to the new realities that defined the postwar world.

The period was marked by both political and military change. Politically, it featured two ideologically diametrically opposed powers who had managed to cooperate to repulse the Axis, but whose values and aspirations were so different and opposed that many could not see how they could be reconciled. As a result, the prevailing pessimism was that a violent clash—something like World War III—between them was inevitable to see which ideology would prevail. Since the confrontation began so close to the end of the second world war, it was presumed that the clash would be an extension of the recently concluded conflict. That projection included an unprecedented amount of death and destruction that would, among other things, have largely destroyed Europe physically and transformed the world in unpredictable ways.

The military unknown in the emerging scenario was the existence of nuclear weapons. These deadly explosives had become operational in 1945, and the war in the Pacific was essentially ended by their use against Japan in nuclear attacks by the Americans on Hiroshima and Nagasaki. These attacks caused a Japanese surrender that they had stubbornly resisted until the mushroom-shaped clouds arose over those largely incinerated civilian population centers. The American nuclear monopoly existed from 1945 to 1949, when the Soviets exploded their own nuclear device and, in the process, transformed traditional military geopolitics.

It took several years for the major powers to adapt to this innovation in the ability to make war. At first, thinking about the military components of the emerging Cold War remained essentially conventional, based on the application of European-style armed forces in a much deadlier version of the recently concluded hostilities but led by the two World War II collaborators (the United States and Union of Soviet Socialist Republics) in a much bloodier reprise of the second global conflict. Such a war would have been incredibly more destructive than its predecessor, but it would have been a conceptual extension of the other global conflicts of the twentieth century. The implicit assumption was that one side or other would have emerged incredibly bloodied but victorious from this paroxysm of violence. It was, however, the only kind of war that military planners could envision.

Nuclear weapons were the wild card in these calculations. During the Korean conflict, basic military thinking remained essentially conventional until the impact of the employment of nuclear weapons on modern warfare. Between the end of WWII and the North Korean invasion of the South in 1950, a whole new generation of nuclear weapons analysts had emerged, led by figures like Bernard Brodie and Thomas C. Schelling. The consensus that was emerging by the time of the Korean War was that the principal, and even total, utility of nuclear weapons was to avoid a nuclear weapons possessor from using those weapons in war—deterrence. This emerging consensus regarding nuclear deterrence grew as the number of states possessing them increased (horizontal proliferation) and the size of arsenals grew (vertical proliferation). Thinking about the use of military force was being transformed in the process, although this adaptation was less publicized within military planning circles than it was among the civilian nuclear deterrence writers who studied and hypothesized on the impact of these unique instruments of war.

The morbid fascination with nuclear weapons grew and matured in the period including and following Korea. Their employment on the Korean peninsula between 1950 and 1953 seemed at least a physical possibility: the United States possessed the only truly developed arsenal of nuclear weapons, although in far smaller numbers than they eventually achieved, and Russia, which had tested its fission bomb in 1949, presumably could have fielded and detonated a few nuclear weapons to influence the outcome, but all possible users declined to do so and Korea never became the world's first nuclear conflict.

After that war, much military and civilian thinking about future war centered, directly or indirectly, on the military and geopolitical impact of these awesome explosives on warfare. Within the civilian community, the tenor was obsessive and fatalistic, dominated by the possibility of a nuclear Armageddon that would destroy human civilization. Students (including this author) learned how to evacuate their schools as part of nuclear "fire" drills and to "duck and cover" their heads beneath their school desks to protect themselves from the effects of a nuclear detonation (exactly how this would protect us was never entirely clear). The obsession extended to popular culture, as exemplified by motion pictures such as *Doctor Strangelove Or: How I Learned to Stop Worrying and Love the Bomb* and *On the Beach*. The fatalism about whether there would be a surviving culture in the 1960s or beyond was debated in great, if hypothetical, detail. Paranoia and pessimism were widely held emotions.

The military was attempting to determine how to adapt as well. In the 1950s, nuclear weapons possession and possible use were widely debated and "tactical nuclear weapons" were deployed as part of nuclear defenses in Western Europe. Many Europeans concluded that although it was theoretically possible for the Americans to employ a nuclear defense of NATO of Western Europe that stopped short of a homeland exchange between the United States and the Soviet Union, the idea that a nuclear defense was possible fell from favor in Europe, and thus the primary, and possibly sole, utility of these weapons was the deterrence of their use.

General Lesley Groves, the military commander of the American Manhattan Project (the code name of the weapons project) that reached fruition at the Trinity Site in rural New Mexico in early 1945 with the first nuclear detonation, captured the change that day with the simple but profound observation that "this is the end of traditional warfare." His observation was largely ignored at the time but was both prophetic and profound as the nuclear age progressed.

We might elaborate and qualify Grove's remark somewhat today. The traditional warfare to which he referred was the European-style warfare that had reached its zenith in the world wars and a reprise of which was presumed to be the future of warfare between the major powers—in the 1950s and 1960s with the United States and the Soviet Union as the lead warriors. Because both sides had gradually made their nonnuclear arsenals more lethally efficient, it was projected—almost certainly accurately—that an ensuing nonnuclear war between them would be a reprise on an even bloodier scale that would dwarf the carnage of the last war. In 1946, that prospect was what most feared but accepted as likely. By the middle 1950s, a superpower clash would have added nuclear weapons usage as a distinct possibility, and this entered a crucial variable that ironically made such a cataclysm less likely and eventually all but unthinkable. In the late 1940s, humankind viewed World War III with trepidation but not as a threat to human civilization. Nuclear weapons made the prospect of destroying the world something truly to be feared—a potential literal apocalypse. The world of traditional geopolitics to which General Groves had referred was a casualty of that change. More specifically, traditional geopolitics was a victim of the weaponization of nuclear power.

The Effects on Thinking about Warfare

The impact of this change was a topic of considerable concern among thinkers about military employment during the latter half of the 1940s. Led by analysts like Brodie, whose evocatively titled book *The Absolute Weapon* captured the emotional impact, the effect was to alter the acceptable uses of military power in the future in two basic ways. On one hand, analysts feared the possibility that military leaders would treat atomic weapons as mere extensions of more traditional explosives, a sort of "more bang for the buck" impact that did not change the calculus of war fundamentally. Atomic bombs had, in this view, a salutary impact on World War II, causing the Japanese to surrender but otherwise not greatly affecting the conduct of hostilities.

The analysts, of course, disagreed, especially when the Soviets perfected their atomic device and the two antagonists prepared for what they believed was an inevitable slide to World War III, which could feature nuclear weapons should war begin. As they projected a future of more nuclearization, the fear that these civilization-threatening devices would be treated as just another addition to military affairs came to dominate their thoughts, and they virtually unanimously concluded that nuclear weapons could not be used in war without civilization-threatening effects. This led to the belief that their sole utility was in preventing their use by another nuclear possessor against you: deterrence.

This recognition had another effect that is more pertinent to the central thrust of this work. Nuclear weapons, in this view, not only made war employing those weapons unacceptable; it meant that *any* war between nuclear weapons states became very difficult to contemplate, rationally plan for, and conduct, and any disagreement between nuclear powers had to be handled with extreme caution. The reason was simple: any war between nuclear possessors had to be avoided at all costs because such a conflict was a *potential* nuclear war that could escalate to nuclear "combat" by processes and dynamics that were literally unpredictable: there were no precedents for an escalation process from European-style war to nuclear holocaust. This conviction, in turn, led to a conviction that the purpose of nuclear arsenals not only made nuclear war unacceptable; it made nonnuclear war unacceptable as well. Any war between nuclear powers was, after all, a potential nuclear war, and the only sure way to avoid that possibility was not to fight at all.

This message was initially more apparent publicly to civilians, including political leaders and academic and other analysts, than it was to military leaders. From Eisenhower and Khrushchev in the 1950s forward, American and Soviet political leaders all warned of the consequences and thus the unacceptability of nuclear weapons use, and their arguments reflected the growing consensus of scholars and analysts in the field of nuclear deterrence.

The event that sealed the ascendancy of nuclear deterrence was the Cuban missile crisis of 1962. That crisis was precipitated by the attempted implementation of Soviet plans to transfer satellite state Cuba into an offensive launch site for Soviet nuclear weapons aimed primarily at the American eastern coast. If completed successfully, it would have provided the Soviets with a valuable lever to bring pressure on the United States in a crisis, and Soviet leader Nikita Khrushchev apparently believed he could get away with the bold action because he had concluded a comparatively youthful US President John F. Kennedy was too weak and inexperienced to stop the Soviets from installing these offensive missiles on the island. He guessed wrong, and Kennedy dispatched American naval vessels to intercept incoming Soviet ships bearing missiles headed for Cuba. For thirteen suspenseful, nerve-wracking days, the world watched to see what would happen when the Soviet ships encountered the blockade.

Ultimately, Khrushchev blinked, and the Soviet ships broke off their delivery of the missiles and returned home. The thirteen days during which this crisis unfolded were, in the estimation of virtually everyone involved, the closest humankind ever came to nuclear war, and it frightened them all. After the Cuban crisis, the United States and the USSR relaxed their confrontation, arms control measures regulating nuclear weapons were negotiated with regularity, and the military aspect of the Cold War began to relax. The two superpowers did not become friends, but they did implicitly agree that their rivalry did not warrant a nuclear holocaust. This dynamic underlay much of their interaction over Ukraine.

Somewhere buried and publicly unnoticed in these remarkable changes was the impact of nuclear weapons on great-power traditional warfare. As nuclear arsenals proliferated to the gargantuan proportions they eventually achieved (over ten thousand warheads apiece for the United States and the USSR), it became increasingly obvious to some that they could not fight one another at all, because any war between them was a potential nuclear war, and neither side could predict based on previous experience how such a war might begin or, more importantly, end. Given the dire potential consequences of nuclear hostilities, neither side wanted to find out the answers to these questions. Not only was nuclear war between them unacceptable, so too was *any* shooting conflict between them.

These dynamics were well publicized as they were occurring, but one prominent and profound effect was not: the impact of the unacceptability of direct superpower conflict on the structure of warfare with which the superpowers, and especially the United States, would have to compete in the future. At the time of the Cuban crisis, the American armed forces were essentially a materially adapted replica of the forces they fielded in World War II. They were developed to use against the forces of the Soviet Union and its allies in Europe, but the specter that such a war would likely escalate to nuclear exchange made Europeans understandably skeptical of such plans. It took the danger of direct superpower engagement raised by Cuba to bring this prospect soberly obvious to the superpowers themselves. After the Cuban crisis, they moved to defuse their direct confrontation to continued rhetoric. This meant there was no place left in the world where the European model of war was obviously applicable. A reminder of this has been evident in the Ukraine war.

The model has died hard in the United States, whose military was firmly wedded to the twentieth-century model of the world wars. But in the process, direct war between nuclear-armed states had essentially disappeared as an acceptable phenomenon. In an odd sense, nuclear weapons have contributed to greater peace and stability in major power disputes than their absence may have produced.

The breakout event that exposed the inadequacy of the old model for the evolving international system was growing American involvement in Southeast Asia. Vietnam was a hybrid international phenomenon in at least two ways. First, it was fought unconventionally, with the insurgents who faced the United States and its South Vietnamese allies employing an adaptation of Maoist-derived asymmetrical war style fighting. It was the first time the United States had personally encountered Mao's war of national liberation strategy on a large scale, and the adaptation was not a total success. Second, the conflict was a harbinger of warfare to come. From a Cold War standpoint, it was an indirect form of conflict fought primarily by surrogates of the major powers, and it would be repeated in future internal conflicts that have attracted American attention even since the Cold War ended. The Vietnam War was essentially the prototype of warfare to come for the United States.

The Impact of Vietnam

Vietnam has frequently been described as the first war the United States ever lost, thus earning it a special place of ignominy in American military history. This simply stated judgment is, however, incomplete, because there are two different meanings to the terms "won" and "lost" in the typification of wartime outcomes. The first and most common designation is military defeat: did the United States decisively defeat and subdue the enemy and cause that enemy to accept American peace terms? Or was it defeated? In that sense, Vietnam was neither victory nor defeat: the Americans did not vanquish the North Vietnamese and their southern allies so that those enemies were forced to accept the American peace terms. That did not occur. It also was not forced to leave because it was beaten militarily. The criterion of military victory or defeat on the battlefield does not apply.

The second, political definition of war outcomes is measured by the postwar peace, and by this criterion, Vietnam was a victory for our opponents. The American political definition of victory was the retention of an independent South Vietnam, while our opponent sought to unify the Vietnams by force. By that measure, the enemy clearly prevailed and the United States failed: we lost the war in the sense of failing to attain any of the political objectives for which we entered it. Ultimately, that definition is more important than the battlefield outcome, but in the popular sense of battlefield outcome, it is not as satisfying. Vietnam was not a defeat on the battlefield; it was a failure to achieve any of our political objectives. This sense of victory and defeat has continued to haunt many American military applications ever since, making Vietnam an important precedent for understanding when the United States should continue to use force in the future. Militarily, the United States was not defeated on the battlefield in Vietnam, but it neither crushed the opposition nor achieved its political goals. The political outcome was probably about the same as it would have been had we not intervened—only a great deal of American blood was shed in the process.

An overview of the American experience can thus be phrased in terms of the IF Factor. Regarding American interests, Vietnam represented the first Cold War situation where US interests and the interests of those we intervened to keep in power were distinctively divergent from one another. The American purpose was Cold War geopolitical: to halt the spread of communism into Southeast Asia. This interest was extrapolated to other parts of Asia as part of the opposition to the process of communist global expansion (preventing the so-called domino effect). If Vietnam fell, other countries in the region would also fall like a row of dominos was a popular way to describe this purpose. That interest, in other words, was about the global consequences of communism should the North Vietnamese and their southern sympathizers succeed rather than it was about the welfare of the South Vietnamese people we sought to protect. For large portions of the indigenous population, the struggle was over land tenure and centered on wresting South Vietnamese territory from largely absentee Chinese landowners and giving it back to Vietnamese. American opponents saw the war as a civil conflict over control of government and ownership of land; the Americans tended to justify the war as a part of the global Cold War.

Had the domino effect been the real underlying dynamic of the Vietnam War, it might have met the criterion of being of vital interest to the United States to prevent. This assumption, however, was arguable. For one thing, it was not what most Vietnamese were fighting about. Ho Chi Minh, the leader of the North Vietnamese government seeking to unite the country, was indeed a communist who intended to create a united communist system for Vietnam, but there is no clear evidence that he was a willing agent of the International Communist Conspiracy seeking world dominion as part of a Soviet-led communist conspiracy. The best evidence of this assertion was that although the outcome of the war was indeed the victory of the communist North and the unification of the Vietnams, there was no visible domino effect of neighboring countries falling under the dominion of the Vietnamese communists. Most of those countries (e.g., Cambodia and Laos) instead saw the Vietnamese as their natural enemy, a fact of which the United States was apparently unaware or sought to ignore. The American interest in stopping the spread of global communism may have represented a vital American interest; unfortunately, it was not what the war in Southeast Asia was about to most who lived there. The dynamic of intervening in situations where our interests differed from the interests of those we aided would be repeated in subsequent military actions.

This misapprehension about what level of American importance of interests were served by intervention was the first clear developing world instance of the United States marching into an armed conflict the dynamics of which it did not understand politically. It also illustrated a violation of the criterion of feasibility of an achievable military outcome. Although it had gotten a small exposure to asymmetrical warfare in parts of the World War II campaigns in Asia and in Korea, the United States was a clear neophyte in this form of warfare on a large-scale basis, and it required a significant learning curve adapting to that problem.

The United States intervened with a thoroughly conventional, firepower-dominant European-style force that it assumed, based on limited historical comparison, would brush aside the presumably inferior insurgents it faced. In the initial clashes between the two sides in places like the Ia Drang Valley, American firepower was applied with great effect, but the enemy quickly determined the folly of confronting the Americans on their own terms and quickly reverted to nonconventional strategies and tactics that effectively stifled the Americans in the mountainous jungles of the Southeast Asian Peninsula. The combination of enemy strategy and the hostile physical and political environment effectively made the war unwinnable for the Americans.

Vietnam thus violated both criteria of the IF Principle. It was a situation where the levels and content of interest involved for the two sides were different. For those the United States opposed, the outcome was a matter of survival and the fate of their country, and they fought with remarkable tenacity and self-sacrifice in the face of enormous odds and staggering losses. Literally millions of Vietnamese were killed fighting the Americans, and they absorbed those losses because the outcome was vital to them. The United States lost 58,000 killed, a high number given active American opposition to the war, and that casualty total helped drive the Americans from Vietnam. The interests for which the Vietnamese opposition fought were simply more important to them than American interests were to the Americans. In the end, American unwillingness to absorb losses exceeded American cost-tolerance and we simply left. It is a pattern that has recurred, because the balance of interests and feasibility of success are similar in other developing world state situations. Both IF principles were violated, and the United States failed to "win" the war.

Opposition to the war grew gradually as it progressed. Particularly before the influx of newly drafted eighteen- to twenty-five-year-old males into the military services and onto the Vietnamese battlefield began to swell, it was mostly confined to college campuses where anti-war sentiment was predictably highest among those who would be called to serve involuntarily and for whom justifications for being there rang most hollow. Success or failure was difficult to measure, report, and thus to claim progress about. There were no fronts in the conflict. Recoloring the map to depict progress toward victory was difficult and often impossible. In order to report what was occurring, the American high command resorted to the daily body count as the grisly depiction of what was occurring on the battlefield. Democratic Republic of Vietnam-Viet Cong fatalities always greatly exceeded those of the Americans and the Army of the Republic of Vietnam (ARVN) and portrayed a situation where success appeared to be occurring, but this proved to be a hollow, almost ghoulish measure of success to those who opposed the war anyway.

To the extent there was a truly decisive event in the war, it was the Tet offensive of 1968. Launched during the Tet Buddhist holidays, it was an all-out offensive attack by Viet Cong rebels across the country. It came on the heels of optimistic pronouncements by the American high command at the end of 1967 that great progress toward victory in the war was occurring or about to occur. As Viet Cong insurgents surged through the country's major cities, those pronouncements were shown to be false. With television cameras rolling, VC cadres attacked everywhere in the country, most visibly including penetration of the American embassy grounds in Saigon. After that, it was impossible effectively to sustain the assertions of progress. American cost-tolerance was effectively overcome in the process, although it would take several more years after that realization for the war to end.

Both sides were affected. The mostly South Vietnamese Viet Cong provided the shock troops for the attacks, and they were decimated by the effort to the point they were never again a factor in the war or its settlement. It has long been suspected that this effect was intended by the North Vietnamese government to eliminate a postwar rival for power. The more decisive effect was on the United States. Before Tet, the anti–Vietnam War movement was mostly isolated to the country's college campuses. Tet undercut the arguments of success among those who supported the war. Much of the US government's official argument for perseverance was based in the assertion that progress was being made toward a victory that would keep the

American-supported South Vietnamese government in power and thus contain communism in that part of Asia. That argument was impossible to sustain effectively after Tet.

American public opinion about the war changed in the wake of Tet. Although not proclaimed at the time, the American political objective was scaled back from defeating the insurgents to an orderly withdrawal that did not admit failure. The catchphrase was "peace with honor." In Tet's wake, President Lyndon B. Johnson, who had presided over the American buildup, announced on March 31, 1968, that he would not seek reelection for a second term, and the Republican Party nominated Richard M. Nixon, a Cold War hawk turned Vietnam dove, whose platform prominently featured a promise to end American participation in the war. After his election, formal peace negotiations began, and they dragged on. American military had not lost the war on the ground, but neither had they been able to defeat the insurgents and thus avoid the communization of a unified Vietnam.

The Longer-Term Effects of Vietnam

American interposition in the struggle for control of Southeast Asia and the reasons for doing so can be critiqued using the categories of the IF Principle. First, the United States arguably lacked sufficiently important interests in that struggle to make war there, and so American support was never strong and wavered as success proved elusive. At heart, the United States did not really understand the nature of the situation into which it was getting itself. To the indigenous contestants, the issue was not primarily the expansion of communism in the Cold War competition, although it may have been crucial to countries like the Soviet Union and China that supported the insurgents. For most Vietnamese, the struggle was about land reform for the peasant-dominated Vietnamese majority. Ho Chi Minh was a communist, but he was also the George Washington figure to the Vietnamese. The United States aligned itself with a South Vietnamese government that did not represent the kind of reforms the Vietnamese desired; it was, instead, viewed as the protector of a hated status quo. By supporting the South Vietnamese government, the United States was the ally of the side they opposed. There is little indication in the public record at the time that those in power in Washington realized this distinction. The Americans were fighting a war against communist expansion, while the Vietnamese were fighting a war of national and personal self-determination. Had the United States fully appreciated the situation on the ground, it might not have decided to intervene and let the Vietnamese civil war run its course. This is what happened in the long run anyway. To the Americans, Vietnam was a theater of the Cold

War. To the Vietnamese, it was a struggle over national identity. The latter purpose was more important to them than the former was to us.

What has always struck this writer is that no long-term American interests were irreparably damaged by the outcome. Vietnam indeed has been a communist state since the Americans withdrew, but the United States and Vietnam are at peace, have evolved essentially congenial economic and political relations, and Vietnam is even a tourist destination for American tourists (mostly veterans of the war) and a trading partner in areas like textiles. American interests, such as they were, have basically been achieved despite, rather than because of, the American military effort there. Had the vitality of those interests been recognized and assessed at the time, this country would probably have declined the urge to intervene: the war was simply not important enough to the United States to shed the blood of the dead American veterans remembered on the Vietnam Wall memorial in the nation's capital.

The war also violated the IF standard of feasibility of success, although it did set in motion dynamics that would allow for a better chance in similar situations in the future—a debatable virtue. The professional American military was dominated by a leadership best prepared to fight a conventional war in Europe, and that leadership resisted the development of forces primarily trained for unconventional warfare. The Kennedy administration had created a brouhaha within professional military ranks when it created an emphasis on the Special Forces and gave them the distinctive green berets. Although the army had long employed some troops fighting unconventionally in situations like the World War II island-hopping campaign in the Pacific, the designation of the Green Berets was first systematically applied in Vietnam. The distinction between asymmetrical warfare and more conventional approaches, among other things, was at odds with basic American doctrine and practice, and it was resisted by the army's hierarchy. The Special Forces were the only American forces trained specifically in the approaches necessary for asymmetrical warfare. The Vietnamese experience caused an expansion and elevation of the status of Special Forces after the war and was one of its few military successes. Some resistance to the unconventional nature of special forces lingered within the armed forces, but especially the US Army.

The post-Vietnam impact on America's use of force flows from this experience in two directions. One is the nature of the kind of opponents the United States would face in the future. This was largely the result of a combination of where future wars would occur and the observation by future opponents of what worked against the Americans. The other effect was on the nature of the relationship between the US military and citizenry. Actions taken as the war became more unpopular had a profound effect on separating military actions from American public opinion and control. The chief culprit in this change was the weakening of citizen connection with its military and how it is employed, an artifact of relieving the citizenry of any fear of being forced physically to participate in military affairs.

Vietnam and the Future of War

The style of warfare the United States faced in Vietnam was what is now called asymmetrical. This designation describes warfare in which both sides fight in different manners and do not accept the conventions or rules of the other side. In Vietnam, this meant that the opponent fought using variants of the tradition chronicled by Sun Tzu and refined during the campaign by Mao Dzedung and his communist insurgents in China. This style of warfare is difficult to describe in precision, because it is more an approach to fighting than it is a doctrine governing military conduct of war. It is intended, rather, as a methodology the purpose of which is to negate the advantages of a more conventional, heavily armed opponent.

In direct clashes with European-style warfare, the side adopting this kind of approach generally does so out of necessity since it lacks the "mass" to compete with that kind of force on its own terms. It is a style designed to negate the enormous advantage of a conventional opponent in firepower and heavy equipment. It does so largely by denying that opponent the advantages that opponent possesses by refusing to stand and fight using conventional methods that heighten the advantages in lethal efficiency the conventional warrior possesses. The basic preference of the conventional fighter is pitched battle, the legacy of the linear formations that crashed against one another in eighteenth- and nineteenth-century European-style battles. The asymmetrical approach, by contrast, rejects such confrontations and prefers to fight more indirectly. If conventional forces prefer pitched linear battles, the unconventional warrior prefers the ambush.

Unconventional, asymmetrical approaches to warfare have become the chief form of fighting that the United States has faced since Vietnam. The reasons are obvious and straightforward. First, almost all violent conflict in the world occurs in the developing world. Ukraine is the exception. The process of national political development is least developed and the political order less established in many of the countries and regions that have emerged from colonial rule since World War II, and some of the time the result of such development is political violence. During the Cold War, Western, including American, interest was concentrated on arresting or reversing the spread of communism in those emerging countries and regions. Vietnam was one of the most dramatic examples. Since 1991, terrorism has replaced communism as a prime American motivation. Afghanistan and Iraq are primary examples.

Second, the asymmetrical style fits the physical and political circumstances of the regions. European-style warfare was largely crafted for fighting on the relatively developed, topographically flat northern European plain, and very little of the developing world replicates that geography. Moreover, the firepower-intense style of the European model is best suited to developed countries with the resources to develop and field "heavy" forces that can rely on weapons systems' superiority to support their efforts. Developing countries almost uniformly lack the necessary kinds of resources for such forces, and thus an approach that deemphasizes material superiority (or mass) fits them better. Third, guerrilla-style fighting, a prime characteristic of most asymmetrical warfare, is better suited to the terrain and human resources available to developing countries. There are generally few areas in these countries that feature the kind of relatively flat, open plains favored by conventional warriors. Rather, the terrain tends to be some combination of hilly/mountainous, heavily forested or with significant barriers to movement of armed forces (e.g., the barren, rocky mountains of Afghanistan), with underdeveloped transportation systems. The terrain tends to be more compatible with small units acting independently rather than large armies, the logistics of which are often very complex. Non-European-style warfare is most compatible with these conditions and circumstances.

Fourth and arguably most importantly, the most developed countries, and particularly the United States, have not proven particularly adept at or successful against forces employing asymmetrical warfare strategies and purposes. This is not a coincidence: most asymmetrical approaches have been developed specifically and consciously as means to counter the European style of warfare.

The End of the Draft and Americans' Connection to Military Activity
The Vietnam experience had other, and arguably more profound but less acknowledged, effects on the American way of war. Throughout most of American history, American forces had been small enough that their ranks could be adequately filled by volunteers most of the time. When military crises confronted the United States that were too large to be successfully dispatched by these volunteer forces, the United States imposed a military draft on the citizenry to raise adequate forces to do the job. The Civil War and the world wars, all of which were too extensive to be prosecuted without some form of conscription, are prime examples of successful applications of this model of military manpower procurement. What is importantly common

about those examples is that conscription was not widely resisted in situations where almost everyone agreed that war was necessary for American interests. The Civil War, which was opposed widely in parts of the Union, was a partial exception.

This tradition was challenged and breached in the post–World War II period. The United States had a large pool of World War II veterans it could call upon in the Korean War, so that adequate manpower procurement there was not a major problem. Many veterans were still in the reserves and could be called back to duty, meaning less of those who fought in Korea were there involuntarily than was the case in Vietnam. Conscription was in force during the 1950s (Elvis Presley and Muhammed Ali—née Cassius Clay—were among the most famous draftees), but since those drafted were not thrown into combat in a foreign war, resistance and refusal to serve were not overwhelming problems. That all changed as the American buildup grew in the early 1960s for Vietnam. The American military involvement in Southeast Asia grew to the point that volunteers for military duty could not meet the manpower needs of that burgeoning commitment. The only alternative to arresting or reversing the level of American manpower was conscription.

Even when the commitment was well below the half-million American personnel consigned to Vietnam at its highest point, there was substantial, very vocal opposition to it. That opposition was loudest among young Americans, and particularly students enrolled in higher education, who were part of the pool of people most vulnerable to being drafted when they left college (deferments of service were routinely issued to undergraduate and most graduate students while they remained in school). Anti-Vietnam demonstrations broke out on college campuses across the country, notable in the form of "teach-ins" explaining why the United States should not be involved in the conflict, but they were ignored by the Johnson administration, which had inherited growing involvement after John Kennedy's assassination.

In 1965, large numbers of American military conscripts were deployed in Vietnam, and this was a turning point in the war. Earlier in the 1960s, before massive American troop influxes occurred, most of the American presence was carried out by voluntary, mainly career, service members, but the size of force that was committed eventually could not be sustained by these soldiers. The shortage was largely filled by conscripts, many of whom opposed the war and resented having their lives placed in jeopardy in a cause in which they did not believe they should be involved. The Johnson administration's justifications of the war were most famously captured in the "domino effect" asserting if South Vietnam was not maintained as a noncommunist bastion, its neighbors would face insurgencies that would cause them to fall, and the effect would be the fall of more states like a row of dominos, which could eventually imperil the United States itself. Supportive arguments like this were not sufficiently convincing to prevent the rapid growth of a burgeoning anti-war effort led by potential draftees and their loved ones who did want their progeny killed in what they viewed as a conflict that did not justify that level of sacrifice.

The war thus became a partisan political battleground. In early 1968, President Lyndon Johnson announced his decision not to stand for reelection in that year's general election. Richard M. Nixon, President Eisenhower's vice president and a fervent anti-communist, defeated sitting Vice President Hubert H. Humphrey. Nixon ran on an anti-war platform, promising to extract the country from the war, a position with some irony, since Nixon had risen to political fame largely due to his fervent anti-communism.

The year 1968 also featured an intensification of the fighting—and dying—by American forces. The most notable event was the 1968 Tet Offensive already introduced. More than 80,000 communist forces, mostly South Vietnamese Vietcong, attacked major southern cities, including the South Vietnamese capital of Saigon. Covered in detail by the electronic media, the rampage gave the apparent lie to administration claims of progress in the war and helped solidify Nixon's ascension.

The war continued throughout Nixon's first term, with the president extolling efforts to bring it to an end that were not matched by actions at the peace table. As the 1972 election campaign began, Senator George McGovern, a fervent opponent of the war, received the Democratic nomination for president opposite incumbent Nixon, who continued to portray himself as a dedicated anti-war advocate, despite the continued carnage on the ground. Nixon countered McGovern's charges that he would continue the war indefinitely by announcing the end of the draft as evidence of his commitment to peace. The last American fighting forces left the country on March 29, 1973, and the final evacuation accompanied the fall of Saigon on April 30, 1975, amid a level of disorder that was a visual precursor to the fall of Kabul, Afghanistan, forty-six years later.

The longest and most profoundly important effect of the Vietnam conflict was arguably its impact on the level of scrutiny of the American people on the country's employment of military force. Suspension of the Selective Service system and its replacement with the All-Volunteer Force was popular with the draft-age cohort that had provided the loudest opposition to the war, and it occurred at a time when American force levels in Vietnam were drawing down. It was also welcomed by many in the armed forces because it reduced disciplinary problems caused by unhappy, unruly conscripts and created a more effective and well-disciplined force of willing volunteers. Moreover, it relieved the anxieties of the parents and other relatives of many draft-vulnerable young men.

It also had a pernicious effect that became most apparent after 9/11. The mantra of "No More Vietnams" effectively dampened any militancy favoring the major employment of American forces for the balance of the century, which was consistent with American public sentiment, but it also decreased the interest and thus level of critical scrutiny of the public regarding military employment in other situations. The draft had, as it turned out, been a critical component in motivating citizen and Congressional oversight and restraint of when and how the military was employed to achieve national interests, and by suspending it, that scrutiny was reduced. This effect was not immediately obvious, because the "Vietnam hangover," as it was sometimes called, provided a restraint on the casual use of American forces, and citizen interest was also diminished by the fact that under the AVF, American youth were no longer involuntarily required to fight for their country; only those who had volunteered for that status did. For the balance of the century, the oversight and restraint of using force was moderated by events. The most notable of these, of course, was the collapse of the Cold War, which had both dictated a large force that required involuntary recruitment and had created the framework for American security policy.

Both disappeared when the Soviet flag was lowered for the last time. The 1990s were exemplary: As the international system adjusted itself to the disappearance of the Cold War structure, American military operations were reduced to small, limited deployments in places like Bosnia, Somalia, and Haiti that are footnotes in the history of America at war and that could be covered by voluntary forces. The only action that resembled a full-time operation was the eviction of the Iraqis from Kuwait in the Gulf War in 1990–1991, and in military terms, it was a minor, very brief event. There seemed little need to show vigilance in citizen oversight of the ways in which the military was employed. Citizen interest waned as a result. All that, of course, was about to change with the turn of the century.

Conclusion

The period between the end of World War II and the end of the twentieth century was one of the most important half centuries in thinking about and executing American military power in the world. The changes it witnessed have been momentous. When the twentieth century began, the United States was a large and rapidly developing member of the international system, but partly as a result of choice and partly of chance, it was not a globally regarded great power. That status was largely reserved for the militarily active countries of the European balance of power. Those countries had held sway at least since the Thirty Years' War of the seventeenth century, had placed much of the world under their colonial tutelage, and were the undisputed countries of international consequence.

The world wars erased the dominant status of Europe. In two extraordinary orgasms of bloodletting in the first half of the twentieth century, Europe literally bled itself virtually dry, and its status in terms of sway over the international system was permanently weakened in the process. As the second half of the 1940s unfolded, the two boisterous but muscular junior members of the World War II winning alliance emerged as the two musclebound pillars of the balance of power. They were probably destined to be rivals, even antagonists, because of their size and opposing, incompatible views of themselves and of the world: American political democracy versus Soviet politico-economic communism. They quickly recognized that their wartime alliance would not hold and that they could not cooperate in shaping a common successor world order.

The result, of course, was the slide into confrontation in the form of the Cold War. Its symbolic formalization came in 1950 when North Korea attacked and nearly conquered South Korea. Acting under the formal auspices of the new United Nations, the United States responded and drove the invaders back northward, and the Cold War as a competition with a distinct military emphasis was born. In the end, that conflict began with the restoration of the status quo on the eve of the invasion: a Korean peninsula that had historically been a single political entity was divided into two states, one communist and one anti-communist. The event both symbolized and was the precedent for the geopolitical standoff that would dominate the Cold War period. It also left in its wake a structure of conflict that included adjustment to the operational reality of the awesome power of nuclear weapons and their dampening effect on global change by force.

Bibliography

Ambrose, Stephen E. *Americans at War*. Jackson: University of Mississippi Press, 1997.

Blair, Clay Jr. *The Forgotten War: America in Korea, 1950–1953*. New York: Random House, 1987.

Brodie, Bernard. *The Absolute Weapon: Nuclear Power and World Order*. New York: Harcourt Brace, 1946.

———. *War and Politics*. New York: Macmillan, 1973.

———, and Fawn M. Brodie. *From Crossbow to H-Bomb: The Evolution of Weapons and Tactics of Warfare*. Revised and Updated Edition. Bloomington: Indiana University Press, 1973.

Brown, Harold. *Thinking About National Security: Defense and Foreign Policy in a Dangerous World*. Boulder, CO: Westview Press, 1983.

Clausewitz, Carl von. *On War*: Translated and edited by Michael Howard and Peter Paret. Princeton, NJ: Princeton University Press, 1984.

Davis, Burke. *Gray Fox: Robert E. Lee and the Civil War*. New York: Fairfax Press, 1981.

Dupuy, R. Ernest, and Trevor N. Dupuy. *The Encyclopedia of Military History*. New York: Harper and Row, 1977.

Giap, Vo Nguyen. *People's War, People's Army*. New York: Praeger, 1962.

Gurr, Ted Robert. *Why Men Rebel*. Princeton, NJ: Princeton University Press, 1970.

Haass, Richard N. *Intervention: The Uses of American Military Force in the Post-Cold War Period*. Washington, DC: Carnegie Endowment for International Peace, 1994.

Herring, George. *America's Longest War: The United States and Vietnam, 1950–1975*. New York: McGraw-Hill, 1995.

Kattenburg, Paul. *The Vietnam Trauma in American Foreign Policy, 1945–1975*. New Brunswick, NJ: Transaction Books, 1980.

Kennedy, Robert F., and Arthur Schlesinger Jr. *The Thirteen Days: A Memoir of the Cuban Missile Crisis*. New York: Norton, 1969.

Mao Tse-tung. *Mao Tse-Tung on Guerrilla Warfare*. Translated by Samuel B. Griffith. New York: Praeger, 1961.

———. *The Collected Works of Mao Zedung*. Vols. 1–4. Beijing: Foreign Languages Press, 1967.

Miller, David. *The Cold War: A Military History*. New York: St. Martin's Press, 1969.

Schelling, Thomas C. *Arms and Influence*. New Haven, CT: Yale University Press, 1966.

———. *The Strategy of Conflict*. Cambridge, MA: Harvard University Press, 1960.

Snow, Donald M. *Cases in International Relations: Principles and Applications*. 9th ed. Lanham, MD: Rowman & Littlefield, 2022.

———. *Distant Thunder: Patterns of Conflict in the Developing World*. 2nd ed. Armonk, NY: M. E. Sharpe, 1997.

———. *National Security*. 7th ed. New York and London: Routledge, 2020.

———. *Thinking about National Security: Strategy, Policy, and Issues*. New York and London: Routledge, 2016.

———, and Dennis M. Drew. *From Lexington to Baghdad and Beyond: War and Politics in the American Experience*. 3rd ed. Armonk, NY: M. E. Sharpe, 2009.

Summers, Harry G. Jr. *On Strategy: A Critical Analysis of the Vietnam War*. Novato, CA: Presidio Press, 1982.

Tecott, Rachel. "Why America Can't Build Allied Armies: Afghanistan Is Just Another Failure." *Foreign Affairs* (online), August 26, 2021.
Weigley, Russell F. *The American Way of War.* New York: Macmillan, 1973.
Williams, T. Harry. *A History of American Wars: From Colonial Times to World War II.* New York: Alfred A. Knopf, 1981.

CHAPTER TWO

The Twentieth-Century Legacy
The European Model of Warfare, the Impact of Nuclear Weapons, and the Transformation of the Uses of Force

If there is one overarching force that provides the essential parameter around which the calculation and use of force by modern states—and especially those countries that possess them—it is the existence of nuclear weapons and the fear that some possessor will use them in an act of "war." Weapons based in nuclear physics have now been a part of the dynamics of warfare for over three-quarters of a century, and so far no state has exploded one in anger since the United States, the first country successfully to weaponize the fruits of nuclear physics, incinerated the Japanese cities of Hiroshima and Nagasaki and their inhabitants to convince the Japanese government to surrender, thereby effectively ending World War II, on August 6 and 9, 1945. Since those events, no nuclear possessor has attacked an opponent with these weapons, and virtually all countries and their leaders remain verbally committed to the maintenance of this condition universally known as nuclear deterrence.

This record is exemplary, and given the reality that an armed conflict in which nuclear weapons states were participants could destroy human civilization, maintaining nuclear deterrence is the highest of human imperatives. The simple fact, however, is that nuclear deterrence *could* fail and that the result could be the end of life on the planet as we know it. Avoiding that catastrophe has been a primary fixation of military thinkers and planners since 1949, when the Soviet Union joined the nuclear "club." Developing intellectual constructs to guide possessors of the necessity of avoiding nuclear usage has been what some would argue to be the most important priority of the world since, and it has succeeded to this point. The simple, stark fact, however, is that nuclear deterrence *could* fail. Avoiding that consequence lies not far below the surface of all military and potential military actions. The "shadow of the mushroom-shaped cloud" (as I called the problem in a 1978 monograph) looms over us, even if we sometimes appear intent on ignoring it.

This enormous change in the role of force in international relations is no better illustrated than by an incident that became public in typically partisan fashion in September 2021 in the United States. It centered on General Mark Milley, the chairman of the Joint Chiefs of Staff. According to a new bombshell book written by Bob Woodward and Robert Costa, Milley called his Chinese counterpart in October 2020 and again in January 2021 to assure the Chinese that the United States was not planning to nor would it attack the Chinese with a nuclear strike, something the Chinese were concerned about given the apparent instability of President Trump triggered by his defeat in the 2020 presidential election. Their concern apparently was based on fears that an attack might be a pretext by Trump to void the 2020 election and hold power, and Milley sought to assuage such fears. Part of Milley's message was that even if Trump ordered such an attack, such an order would not have been carried out. Trump did not know of the calls at the time and called Milley a traitor after he left office and learned what the chairman had done.

This extraordinary event showed how the dynamics of violence have changed in two fundamental ways. First, it was recent evidence of how nuclear weapons have transformed the calculation of war. Direct war between major powers has simply disappeared from the international stage because it is a possibility truly feared by nuclear-armed countries whose continued existence depends on the avoidance of nuclear war. Second, if the major powers can no longer fight, it raises serious questions about the sensibility of maintaining large, conventional war-fighting configurations aimed at one another as the backbone of force structure.

Recognizing the inadmissibility of warfare between nuclear-armed China and the United States reflects how institutionalized the taboo of war between nuclear powers has become since the Cuban crisis. In the case of the United States and China, anything beyond very limited air-based attacks (e.g., American strikes on Chinese targets in the South China Sea, measured attacks or harassment of US military installations in the region by China) is probably impossible in any practical sense. The countries are simply too far apart for launching a conventional attack against one another by a force that would almost certainly be intercepted and destroyed well before it got to the other's soil. The only way they can fight is by attacking one another with intercontinental missiles, which would almost certainly be nuclear if fighting became serious. No one knows or wants to know what might trigger the escalation process, and the clearest way to avoid that situation is to avoid war between them altogether. War between America and China either becomes nuclear or it fizzles out. European forces simply do not play much of a role in thinking about or conducting such a war. Chinese testing of a missile system that apparently can evade detection after launch threatens this equation at the margins but not fundamentally: it may increase the amount of devastation that would occur in the United States, but not the fundamental calculation of mutual devastation.

Milley apparently contacting his Chinese counterpart to say that the United States had no intentions of attacking China arose from fears regarding the increasing mental unpredictability of Trump. He was talking about a nuclear attack, not a twentieth-century war fought with conventional forces. That realization is both frightening and reassuring at the same time. It is terrifying because of the likely outcome of such a conflict: the nuclear incineration of both countries and probably most of the rest of the world. It is reassuring because the way the crisis was handled also shows how well the understanding of possible nuclear dynamics has permeated the structure of military thinking at all levels of military consideration. It also, one must add, suggested the need somehow to create a more institutionalized, less idiosyncratic way to deal with the instability of amateurs in positions of political leadership with neither the experience nor appreciation of the potential consequences of such calculations. Hosting a reality show on television, in other words, may not provide an adequate preparation to master nuclear war dynamics. Milley's action demonstrated this dynamic is understood and appreciated in professional military circles.

The realistic need to place a primary priority on a conventional military force designed at least implicitly for another large European-style war is a commitment that is rarely discussed publicly in the general debate on when and where to use military force. Historically, much of the resistance to starting this discussion has come from inside the professional military itself, and their reluctance to do so is understandable. The US military has historically been structurally based on the European model, and that traditional preference is reflected in this configuration. Its rationale is the preparation for and prosecution of warfare against a similarly configured opponent, with the outcome largely the result of which side has the most muscle, skill, and resources to prevail. It is a style and configuration that the United States evolved successfully in the first part of the twentieth century. The United States prevailed in both world wars, and that legacy has been cemented into the country's military consciousness and force composition. It is the style of warfare that Americans have excelled at and thus are comfortable thinking about and conducting. It is "the American Way of War," to borrow from a book title used by numerous authors, notably Weigley, and many in the military are very devoted to it and have made career choices congruent with its endurance. That preference and tradition are largely the base for much of the organization and roles of the various American services, although there has been some erosion and adaptation of how traditional roles are interpreted as time and the absence of another European-style war have evolved. The question is conceptually a matter of adaptability of the model to contemporary challenges.

The problem, of course, is that warfare is essentially no longer fought the way it was during the first half of the twentieth century. Major powers no longer confront one another directly. The last time a conventional war was fought between major powers was in 1998, and the combatants were India and Pakistan. Both had recently joined the nuclear weapons "club," and the world watched nervously to see if one side or the other might escalate the fighting to nuclear exchange and thus possibly trigger an unpredictable escalation process that spread to other countries. As usual, the incendiary issue was Kashmir in this case, about which emotions run high on both sides, but apparently both were cognizant of what they might cause inadvertently if they let the nuclear genie out of the bottle, and they quickly stopped the fighting. No two countries with nuclear weapons have gone to war since in a dynamic that has affected the character and nature of US participation in the Ukraine war.

European-style forces and accompanying strategies and tactics for their use have been the luxury of large, powerful, and rich countries that can afford them, and these are the same countries that possess nuclear weapons that could be the logical end of the escalation trail if similarly configured armed forces clashed on the battlefield. Traced backward, one can argue that nuclear weapons have made war between such states too potentially destructive to contemplate, and this means the European-style forces possessed by these states cannot be employed against the kinds of foes for which they are designed.

Robbed of the intended missions for which they have been designed, traditional European-style forces must instead be employed against different kinds of foes in different political and military environments. These newer foes employ ways of fighting that differ significantly from the European tradition. The European model has not proven overwhelmingly effective in these settings, at least partially because the new foes fight in different ways and in different kinds of settings that are partly designed to neutralize these heavy forces and to maximize advantages such as terrain that enhance that neutralization. At the extreme, it leaves heavy forces as dominant in the kinds of warfare that are hardly ever fought anymore but as less effective in the kinds that are fought.

This anomaly does not mean there are not good reasons to maintain the traditional forces. Were those forces reduced as anachronistic or as too expensive to maintain when their utility is reduced, other states might use those changes to their advantage. Ironically, these forces could then become relevant again against opponents that exploited their absence. Thus, traditional forces gain some relevance as a deterrent against a return to the brutality of traditional European-style warfare. This rationale is not dissimilar to the conventional dynamic of nuclear deterrence at a lower level. Conventional and nuclear forces both help deter great-power conflict, and that is worth something. They remain expensive, however, and limit the exploration or emphasis on alternate forms of forces. There are no obviously easy solutions to this conundrum.

The European Style of War

The European style of war evolved over time, culminating in the world wars of the twentieth century. It is the quintessence of what is also called heavy warfare, and its salient characteristics include large, heavily armed forces whose preference for engagement features the direct, frontal clash of forces in direct battle. It is firepower intensive and bloody, and the basic purpose of engagement is either to destroy or break the fighting will and ability of the opponent. The classic conclusion of warfare fought in this manner is the functional destruction of one side's armed forces by those of the other side. Wars fought using this model have historically been concluded when one side or the other quits the contest because of the depletion of its resources or because of the loss of will or cohesion of those forces. It is warfare at its most brutal and often bloody.

The distinctive style that emerged in the twentieth century and that continues to provide the model for recruiting, organizing, and employing those forces was largely the product of two forces after the Thirty Years' War. The first was the rise of nationalism in newly forming European states that emerged during that period. In terms of military organization and usage, nationalism created a bond and attachment to the political unit of which one was a member that had traditionally not existed. This attachment, in turn, created a willingness to become part of and participate in the state's military affairs. Before this occurred, the average citizen had little interest or attachment to the international politics of his or her country and was certainly unwilling to join or be forced into military service in the name of the state, and this limited the size of forces and the purposes they could undertake.

Nationalism created that attachment and willingness. Its first momentous impact came in France in the revolutionary period and Napoleonic era. France was able to raise heretofore unseen numbers of armed forces from an activated population base, and this mass ran roughshod over Europe until the other countries managed to agree to cooperate to counter this citizen mass with numbers of their own.

The other factor was technological. Growing political nationalism occurred alongside the fruits of the growth of the Industrial Revolution in Europe. Particularly during the nineteenth century, major fruits of that economic process were devoted to the innovation of new and more lethal forms of weaponry that could be produced in adequate quantities to support the burgeoning citizen armed forces of the emerging states of the European balance. Nationalism and industrialization became the dual sparks that continued to produce the lethal character of the European warfare.

This process occurred gradually. In the eighteenth century, the standard battlefield tactic between countries adhering to the European style was to place two armies in linear formations several ranks deep on an open field facing one another. One side or the other would then begin marching across the field as the other side waited for direct contact. As the attacking force approached, the defenders would fire volleys into the approaching ranks, thinning it as some attackers were hit. The defenders would then reload, with those who had fired retiring to the rear of the formation to reload before firing again. The fusillade of fire could be withering and deplete both the attacker's and the defender's ranks, but since it took a minute or more for this to occur, attackers would face a limited number of fusillades before making physical contact with the defenders, at which point the muskets effectively became clubs that doubled as spears, since the weapons often had bayonets. The process was enormously bloody with high casualties, but it was the kind of warfare that technology permitted.

Technological developments leading to the twentieth-century orgies of blood made these tactics obsolete. Breach-loading guns could accommodate and fire multiple bullets before having to be reloaded, meaning the defenders, particularly if they secured themselves from attacking fire, could decimate the attacking formations before they made direct contact, and advancements in artillery and later the development and weaponization of aircraft enhanced the change. In addition, the linear method required that battles take place on reasonably flat fields with few obstacles (rocks, trees, etc.) that could break up the lines. Technology effectively freed military actions from these topographical bounds, and they allowed, even demanded, a change from classical European warfare. That effectively meant converting styles of war to greater compatibility with the Eastern tradition of war.

The European style of warfare reached its epitome in the conduct of World War II. Over eighty million direct combatants and civilians are estimated to have been killed in that clash of coalitions fighting mostly by European standards and methods. The Eastern way of war, based on principles that would emerge and be imitated later, was part of the fray in Asia and introduced methods and philosophies in that theater effective enough that they were emulated in the developing world afterward. The war was, however, the pinnacle of violence based on European fighting methods and premises.

As the Cold War began to take shape, both the United States and the Soviet Union as the leaders of the opposing sides in that competition prepared themselves for the exigency of war between them, and the model for that conflict's conduct was what had preceded and which they had experienced and had success fighting. It was augmented by developments in the preparation for war after WWII. The prospect was for a "conventional" conflict conducted by the model of the second global war that would dwarf that war in bloodletting by orders of magnitude of carnage. European-style warfare had developed to the point that it was not clear what could be accomplished by its repetition. During the early part of the postwar period, military action in the developing world (mostly in the form of wars of independence against colonial rule) was in its infancy, and it was simply assumed that the overwhelming superiority of practitioners of the European model would be adequate and appropriate for whatever needs arose in very different parts of the world.

The new geographic and geopolitical realities did not, however, prove the death knell of planning and preparations based on the same assumptions that had dominated European-based military thinking. The underlying logic of the European model was total war: the clash of large, heavily armed forces until one side was physically defeated or weakened to the point that it sued for peace. Nuclear weapons turned those dynamics on their heads. The principal way it did so was the feared impact of these weapons if employed. When warfare was based on the total defeat of the enemy, the focus of war planning was the subjugation of the enemy: its final acceptance of its defeat. Threatened or actual physical invasion were the tools for accomplishing that defeat, but nuclear weapons replaced that means with the threat of actual physical annihilation to produce an enemy's surrender. Although unrealized (or unadmitted publicly) at the time, that was the true lesson of the atomic attacks against Hiroshima and Nagasaki. Given the destructive capacity of nuclear weapons, their gradual sophistication, and the spread of their possession to multiple, antagonistic powers, the victim was the relevance of the European warfare in a nuclear-armed world.

Nuclearization gave a whole new meaning to total warfare and effectively rendered it obsolete. Military thinking has been reacting to that reality ever since. Another way to think of the conceptual basis of change was that conventional war was bloodletting on a major scale that was to be dreaded but that could be rationally contemplated and its likely results survived. Most prominently, it produced winners and losers and a postwar peace. War with nuclear weapons threatened, even eliminated, most of those calculations. It was not clear whether anyone could "win" a war in which both sides possessed and used these weapons. The consensus gradually grew that nobody could win and everybody would lose.

The Impact of Nuclear Weapons

Research on understanding what became nuclear science was one of the less well known but most important underlying dynamics of the period leading to and during World War II. The weaponizing of that science was a priority of the effort. Teams of scientists in several countries had discovered the possibility of the vast potential of nuclear energy before the war, but the war sent many of the nuclear scientists scattering for political asylum. Ironically, the core of prewar nuclear science was in Germany and was conducted by researchers many of whom were German Jews. These scientists fled to the West to avoid the Nazi conquest and suffering the consequences of the Holocaust. Had this migration not occurred, it is entirely possible that German weaponization would have resulted in a Nazi victory in the war. Nazi racism was a critical reason for a brain flight to the West, and notably the United States and Britain, and that migration helped lead to the fascist defeat.

The impact of nuclear science outcome was thus indirectly responsible for Allied victory in Europe by denying Nazi Germany a weapon the use or threat of use against Allied targets could have brought the Western coalition to its knees. At the same time, that same research led to the success of the American Manhattan Project and the dropping of the only two nuclear weapons to date to be used against human targets, causing Japan to surrender rather than forcing the Americans to conquer the Japanese home islands at enormous human costs on both sides. Like so much of the nuclear age, the impact was decidedly double-edged.

Evolution of the Nuclear Impact on War

The nuclear weapons age coincided with enormous geopolitical change generally in the world that magnified the role, but also the limitations, of these weapons in war. By 1949, the American nuclear monopoly had vanished, as the Soviet Union exploded a nuclear device (with technology it had largely purloined) that year. Nuclear weapons were not employed in the first Cold War confrontation on the Korean peninsula, but by 1952, the fission-based processes that produced the Hiroshima-class bombs had been eclipsed by thermonuclear "hydrogen bombs" that increased the explosive yield of early bombs produced from the equivalent of thousands of tons of TNT to megatons (the equivalent of *millions* of tons of TNT).

Simultaneously, enormous progress was occurring in designing and operationalizing more sophisticated ways to deliver these weapons to their targets. The principal thrust of these efforts was in rocketry, an area of emerging technology that had applications in both the civilian space program and in military development. At the same time, new ways to store and launch these weapons were emerging in forms like hardened land-based missile silos and submarines that served as both secure places to store the weapons and from which to launch them at an adversary that had no way to defend itself.

By the end of the 1950s, the nuclear landscape had changed fundamentally from 1945. The attacks against Japan had been carried out by conventional bomber aircraft that were able to penetrate to target because Japanese air defenses had largely been depleted, allowing bomber aircraft like the *Enola Gay* to penetrate them and reach their targets. The munition these bombers carried was novel and far deadlier than anything previously fielded, but the logistics of the attack remained within the framework of traditional military thought. The thermonuclear explosive and delivery of that munition by an indefensible offensive weapon changed the entire parameter of traditional warfare.

The chief effect was on the inability to calculate victory, even societal survival, from a military clash in which nuclear weapons were used. The development of the thermonuclear warhead combined with delivery platforms that could not be intercepted took away any illusion that nuclear war could be contained below catastrophic levels. A potential war between nuclear-armed opponents presented a prospect truly to be avoided. Since any war between such opponents could escalate to nuclear exchange by dynamics so unique as to be unpredictable, the implication was clear: the only sure way to avoid nuclear war was to avoid war between nuclear weapons possessors altogether.

The distribution of nuclear weapons in the early days was significant. The initial possessors were the adversarial Cold War superpowers. Although the United States and Soviet Union had been leading partners in World War II, there was virtually universal belief that this fellowship would not continue into the postwar order.

The two countries were the two postwar standing giants, even though the United States was arguably strengthened by the war (one of whose effects was, after all, to end the Great Depression of the 1930s), whereas the Soviet Union suffered enormous damage and carnage in the conflict, in which they were a much more direct object of Hitlerian ire than the Americans. That said, they were the only states with great residual capability after the war, they held diametrically and irresolvable worldviews about political organization and power, and both, especially the Soviets, were particularly evangelical in seeking to spread their worldviews. The Soviets demonstrated this proclivity most distinctly by extending their sway over virtually all central and eastern Europe and installing communist puppet governments in those countries. By the end of the 1940s, it was clear that the leitmotif of world power politics would be the contest between communism and democracy, and that this contest might well be decided by recourse to arms, a continuation of the geopolitics of the first half of the twentieth century.

That belief and fear have not been actualized, and it is arguable (and is argued here) that nuclear weapons have probably been the main reason they have not. During the 1950s, the nuclear arms race was at its most feverish levels, and arsenals on both sides grew quantitatively and qualitatively. The destructive capacities of both sides grew to proportions that made it a virtual certainty that an all-out nuclear war between them would destroy both, and that belief was reinforced as new nuclear powers (Britain and France) joined the "club." China joined them in 1964. India, Pakistan, and North Korea have since publicly acknowledged they have acquired nuclear capability, bringing the world total of official possessors to eight in 2021. Although they neither publicly admit nor deny membership, Israel has possessed them since 1968. Iran is considered the leading candidate to become the next member after that.

Nuclearization created an intellectual pall in world politics. The reason, based on the experience of the first half of the century, was that World War III would likely follow if things did not change fundamentally, and that this contest would feature the ultimate use of nuclear bombs, the consequences of which would be to reduce the planet to irradiated rubble beneath which lay the remains of the world population. The result was a thoroughly depressing vision of the end of human civilization.

None of the apocalyptical prophecies and fears have been realized, of course. The atmosphere and dynamics surrounding the Cuban crisis of 1962 provided a sober reassessment of the situation. More importantly in the long run, it produced a determination to avoid self-annihilation that has endured ever since. Humankind proved itself to be more intelligent and resilient than the 1950s doomsayers believed it to be. In essence, nuclear weapons both led humans to the edge of the abyss of nuclear war prospect *and* inspired them to back away from it. Before Cuba, nuclear war between East and West was thought to be virtually inevitable. After coming so close to the brink, that prospect receded to the point that the subject is rarely raised today, except surrounding proliferation of the weaponry to new, and presumably less mature, countries. Nuclear weapons are still possessed in very large numbers by the major powers in the world, but one rarely hears about nuclear war breaking out between them. Such conversations were commonplace among people within and on the fringes of the national security community before Cuba started the process of controlling those weapons and reducing the likelihood of their use. World politics are fundamentally different as a result of this epiphany.

The Nuclear Weapons Age: China and America

Nuclear conflict is still a physical possibility, and this affects both international politics and the recourse to other physical violence, principally involving the major powers. Although it is controversial and somewhat unfashionable to state that effect, I believe fear of the consequences of nuclear weapons has contributed to a more peaceful world than many thought possible in 1950, and certainly it has essentially eliminated the prospect of war between major nuclear weapons possessing states. Ukraine may challenge that assumption.

Ironically, the very real prospect that a nuclear war would destroy the world has made that destruction by willful possessors much less likely than feared. In the 1950s, when those weapons were becoming the critical elements in the war and peace system, they seemed to be the instrument of inevitable (or at least highly likely) human extinction. Except for a small coterie of experts who concentrate on the possible dynamics of nuclear interchange, that potentially macabre dynamic has largely disappeared. It is still possible that a nuclear war could somehow occur, and if it did, the results would likely destroy us all. What is different is that we no longer believe this is an imminent or inevitable prospect and have endeavored to reduce the prospects that world politics ever devolves to the point that it might occur.

If one accepts this premise (and not everyone does), its implications are enormous. Take a contemporary scenario that concerns many analysts: the possibility of confrontation that could lead to war between the United States and China. The two countries have many geopolitical issues between them. They are the dominant major political actors in eastern Asia. China is a traditional Asian power, and American interests largely are holdovers from the outcome of World War II and later the Korean War. China, at heart, wants to be regarded and treated as *the* major player in the area, whereas the United States wishes to maintain its influence in places like South Korea, Japan, and the Philippines, and believes that Chinese influence and expansion in the region threatens those countries and the American relationship with them. Specific sources of irritation include the status of the South China Sea and relationships with North Korea. Friction has also entered the enormous economic relationship between the two countries. Countries in the past have gone to war over issues no more momentous than those that divide the two twenty-first-century powers, but how realistic are those dangers in a nuclear-armed world?

The short answer is that the prospects are probably not great. Why? There are physical barriers, such as the distance (over 7,000 miles) between the two, which means neither could mount a successful conventional invasion of the other without having its forces intercepted and probably destroyed during their trans-Pacific voyage. At the same time, the economies of the two countries are so intertwined that the disruption of that relationship in major war would be economically ruinous to both countries. As has been argued for some time, China and the United States may not be friends, but both recognize the color of money and its fundamental importance to their relationship and prosperity. They are, to borrow a term, "frenemies."

The most ultimately real prohibitive factor, of course, is the impact of nuclear weapons. Because of other barriers like physical distance between them, a Sino-American conflict of any size would almost inevitably become a nuclear war if either or both sides decided to pursue it to some conclusive outcome. There are certainly contentious issues between the two countries, but are any of them important enough to pursue to what could be an escalatory process that eventuates in Armageddon?

The major schisms are economic and geopolitical. The Chinese economic miracle is at or close to peaking for reasons such as a rapidly aging population. A resultantly shrinking working population and thus a growing retired cohort place increased pressure on Chinese assets. As global warming becomes a more prominent item on the world agenda, China's status as the world's largest polluter will increasingly multiply demands on them to scale back their emissions (which they realize), with economic consequences. Trump-era economic sanctions notwithstanding, the United States can only marginally be blamed for these problems, and certainly not enough for them to start a war with the Americans that could escalate to the nuclear level.

Geopolitically, the two do face off over primary geopolitical status in East Asia, a position the United States has informally occupied but that history and geography tells the Chinese is rightfully theirs. The primary American geopolitical interest is protecting the independence and status of Asian Rim countries with whom they have important economic and security ties like South Korea, the Republic of China (Taiwan), and Japan, and the containment of a nuclear North Korea. China has placed some pressure on Taiwan; the two countries are at odds over developments in the South China Sea and North Korea, but it is hard to imagine that the balance would cause the serious contemplation of war unless fundamental (and largely unanticipated) deterioration in relations occurs from some exogenous source. Both sides are aware of these possibilities and work hard to keep any resulting tensions between them well below the boiling point. Would the two sides display the same restraint if the "shadow of the mushroom-shaped cloud" did not hang over them to remind both countries of the consequences of letting things get out of hand?

Although the analogy is seldom raised, the Chinese-American relationship in security terms may be more analogous to the dynamics of relations between the superpowers in Europe in the building years of the Cold War. As already mentioned, there was the widespread fear that Soviet-American confrontation might lead to World War III, where the European continent would become the irradiated battleground of this titanic conflict. The United States, for instance, might well not have been able to mount a successful defense to a massive Soviet ground invasion westward, and the only hope at defense would probably have been by using so-called "tactical" nuclear weapons to defeat the invading force. Europeans (led by the French) quickly determined that this "admirable" American action would leave Europe an irradiated wasteland where most of those defended would be dead but where the United States and the USSR stopped short of their own destruction. This debate went on especially furtively in the fatalistic 1950s, and bellicose posturing by both sides dissipated along the way. Who talks about a nuclear defense of Europe anymore? Did the existence of the very weapons that could destroy mankind make the contemplation of such a war less likely?

This is not to suggest that the possibility of nuclear war has disappeared. It has not, and it might well be destabilizing if the military prudence it has created did fade away. Lurking in the background—the great subtext—of geopolitical interactions between the major (i.e., nuclear-armed) powers is the realization that nuclear war could happen if they were to allow the worst of their conflicts to devolve to something like all-out military proportions. The nuclear threat does condition their interactions with the recognition that a violent conflict between them could destroy not only them both. That possibility stands at the heart of the dynamic of assured destruction, the nuclear dynamic that provided the conceptual boundary line for the Cold War and that has effectively been extended to all violent interactions that possessors of large arsenals may contemplate.

The implications are clear. All violent conflicts between nuclear possessors can become nuclear wars. Given the consequences of such escalation, *all* violent conflicts between nuclear powers must be avoided. The bottom line is clear: nuclear weapons not only deter the use of nuclear war between their possessors; they deter *all* war between the major powers. That is a considerable positive dynamic. It also, however, has considerable implications for the development, purposes, and use of military forces designed for those traditional roles.

The Nuclear Age and Traditional War

Before Ukraine, it had been nearly three-quarters of a century since traditional European-style armed forces have been used in the ways and situations for which they evolved into the twentieth century. The reasons for this are complex, but they begin from the first premise that those forces are not well suited for the kinds of contemporary violent situations for which they may be required. These forces evolved, after all, to fight on the relatively confined northern European plain and to confront and defeat similarly configured opponents. It was a form of warfare appropriate through World War II, but it is no longer politically or militarily effective or appropriate in parts of the world where there is instability and violence that might attract the attention of outsiders.

Nuclear weapons have contributed significantly to this major change in the character of warfare. They have altered military thinking about the utility of force by their possessors and the pattern of using force effectively. The main impact is that it is a major, if not *the* major, reason that traditional European-style warfare between major powers has become among the most remote force likelihoods. States simply do not use force in situations and against opponents where there is any likelihood things could get out of hand and escalate to potential nuclear war.

The reason for this is obvious enough. Any major war between traditional powers, and especially nuclear possessors, is now considered unacceptable, because it is potentially a nuclear conflict, because no one knows the dynamics of escalation in which opposing nuclear powers are engaged, and thus when such conflict might escalate from conventional means to nuclear exchange. The legacy of the early nuclear arms race in the 1950s was the gradual realization that nuclear war was unacceptable and that as a result, the primary purpose of those weapons was to persuade an adversary not to use their nuclear weapons against you. The idea of assured destruction became a virtue, because the impossibility of knowing where the nuclear threshold was translated into the principle that all war between nuclear possessors must be avoided to keep from finding out.

This dynamic transformed the military dynamics of the Cold War. That competition originally was based on the implicit assumption that war between the major contestants was likely, and that it would be fought in Europe as a more intense version of the world wars. The Soviets had the geographic advantage of being closer to the scene than the Americans, and it was admitted privately that they might well win a strictly conventional war fought in and over Europe by virtue of sheer numbers and proximity to the battle. The Western alliance, and more particularly the United States, had the unpalatable options of defending Europe conventionally and possibly losing, or of adding nuclear weapons to defense plans (which they did). The use of nuclear weapons could escalate the conflict to homeland nuclear exchange that would destroy both the United States and the Soviet Union. Neither option was attractive, especially to the Europeans, who would lose in either case.

Happily, there was a third option, which was to recognize that the deterrent value and imperative of nuclear weapons had to be extended to conventional war as well, specifically war in the European context: any clash there had to be made impermissible as a practical matter. The forces continued to confront one another across the Iron Curtain after this "blinding insight of the obvious," but a major thrust of continental diplomatic relations became reduction of the tensions and provocations between the sides that might lead to WWIII.

That determination took hold, and the realistic likelihood of active military clashes between the major powers is no longer the urgent concern it was a half century ago. The major Cold War rivalry with the Soviet Union obviously disappeared with the implosion of the Soviet state. Although Russia under Putin has attempted to reassert its former status as a world force and returned warfare to the continent in Ukraine, that effort has not translated into major conflicts between East and West. Also, the power trajectory for Russia over time is not promising for them. Like China, Russia faces demographic challenges in the forms of an aging and shrinking population that will gradually reduce its relative position in the world, and Putin's "petrolist" strategy of using its petroleum wealth to promote national power and support has also proven to be a long-range geopolitical losing plan. Russia will remain a military power of consequence for some time, but its long-range dreams of returning to something like superpower status are not bright, especially given its military performance in Ukraine.

China is obviously the other international rival of consequence, as already suggested. It is not clear what the current Chinese regime's global power aspirations are: does it seek the more geographically limited goal of something like a hegemonic position in eastern Asia and the Pacific, in which case the Americans must be considered a rival for influence rather than a direct military threat, or does it aspire to more? Demographic trends are also not particularly favorable for China, and rivals like Japan, South Korea, and even Taiwan pose a significant barrier to any hegemonic dreams the Chinese may entertain. A massive land war in eastern Asia between the United States and China is a difficult prospect to envision. If there is a threat of violent clash, it would likely be air and even space based and involve weapons of mass destruction (including nuclear weapons). The dynamics and protocols of assured destruction provide a framework for managing that kind of potential eventuality. European-war-style military forces do not fit well into any scenarios one might devise, except in a few places like Ukraine. Predictions of war between the two powers, while representing a scenario that must be considered, are probably remote.

The American conventional force structure and ways to employ it have not, however, experienced a major epiphany toward these threats, although the institution has modified its missions and structures to accommodate newer, primarily developing world, priorities. That force has clearly evolved and changed across time. The army somewhat grudgingly has elevated the role and centrality of Special Forces, because their skills are needed for the kinds of ground challenges the United States faces in most developing world situations, but the army philosophically remains quintessentially a "heavy" force built to operate on the principle of mass and emphasizing the kinds of capabilities it inherited from the European tradition. The navy has not been engaged in significant naval battles since World War II, and its role now emphasizes naval air support where the United States does not have significant basing access for conventional operations. The marine corps, organized as a form of light, highly mobile infantry, has seen its role expand, because developing world crises more closely resemble the kinds of operations at which it excels. The air force has modified its roles to include the embrace of using assets (including drones) that can attack targets in countries where topography and politics make using traditional ground force impractical or impossible.

Conclusion

The landscape of violence has obviously changed since the last time the major powers fought one another. In the first half of the twentieth century, that landscape seemed clear and forthright. If one starts from the premise that a country should (and often must) fight when its truly vital interests are threatened, then the case for American participation in the two world wars seems obvious and compelling, especially in retrospect. It is useful to remember that they were not as clear-cut then as they are now. It took three years of fighting in the trenches of Europe in World I before President Wilson was able to convince the American public to join in the effort to defeat the German-led Central Powers, and there was substantial resistance to entering World War II until the Japanese attack at Pearl Harbor.

Both wars, of course, were classic European-style clashes, with some of the fighting in East Asia and the Pacific sprinkled with elements that were more like conditions and situations in the developing world today. Both wars created massive carnage and physical destruction, especially in Europe. The European way of war reached a crescendo on the European continent in 1944–1945 and in the irradiated ruins of Hiroshima and Nagasaki.

The postwar situation was both very similar to and different from the conditions it supplanted. The situation in the latter 1940s seemed analogous to 1939: two increasingly hostile military coalitions facing one another. The United States led one coalition; the Soviet Union dominated and commanded the other. These conditions seemed similar enough to the past that military planning and policy prepared for another round that would have been a more violent and destructive reprise of what had preceded it.

There were, course, two differences. One was nuclear weapons. Until 1949, nuclear employment, thinking, and planning was basically the United States deciding when or whether it would use them and under what circumstances. When the Soviets began to field an arsenal and supplies of the weapons expanded greatly, humans became truly capable of eradicating themselves, and nuclear deterrence was born to prevent that from happening. The victim of this development was the military assumption that a next war under the rules of the European style was inevitable. Nuclear deterrence was born of this recognition, and it gradually spread to the realization of the need to avoid all war based on the model of European warfare. There has not been anything vaguely resembling the world wars since, and the notion that great powers could gradually confront one another directly without risking destroying the world has gradually come to dominate thinking and planning. Imagine, for instance, how the US–Russian interface might have been different if neither side had to calculate and fear a war between them that could become nuclear and potentially destroy both.

The other difference was the emergence of the developing world as the focal point of military activity. This factor is related to the second world war in that the conduct of that war had exhausted and bankrupted the colonial powers of Europe enough that they no longer had the energy or resources to maintain their control over their colonies. This change was recognized in colonies, where independence movements felt emboldened to throw off the colonial yoke. The developing world became the epicenter of international violence.

The potential of nuclear weapons provides a basic, defining reason that direct big-power conflict has not occurred since 1945. The reasons for such conflicts in the past had not disappeared, primarily because of the Cold War. Historically, this kind of politico-military division was fundamental and potentially explosive enough to form the basis for a World War III fought between heavily, lethally armed European-style armies. As the realization of the implications of nuclear weapons use spread during the pessimistic 1950s, so too did the calculus of such a war change. Such warfare is still theoretically possible, because the weapons still exist and could be used as a result of inadvertent escalatory processes, but that prospect seems far less inevitable than it did then.

The result is that the age of war based in the European style has, at least for a time, largely passed from the scene. There have been no direct military conflicts between major powers since World War II, and saber rattling by major powers against one another has essentially disappeared from international interaction, for the simple reason that the prospect of Armageddon has made such conflict unthinkable. Ukraine has revived some of that dynamic.

The interchange between American Chairman of the Joint Chiefs Mark Milley and his Chinese counterparts illustrates how the dynamics of military affairs have changed. The two countries are the opposing superpowers of the early twenty-first century, with China replacing the former Soviet Union as America's primary protagonist, with their conflict grounded regionally in East Asia and substantively in economics. During the turbulent transition from Trump to Biden, there were international fears that Trump might start a war to prevent the transition, and Milley called his Chinese counterpart to assure the Chinese government that the United States had no intention of starting a shooting conflict with them and to assure them that despite volatility in American politics, the international posture of the United States had not changed and that China did not need to worry about the possibility. At the time of the calls, their occurrence remained secret, including not telling Trump, who was apparently furious when he learned they had occurred.

The exchange, which did not elicit a public Chinese response, was extraordinary. Talk about the possibility of Sino-American conflict pops up occasionally, but those in the national security establishment were shown clearly to believe that the devolution of the situation to active war is simply an unacceptable possibility. The two countries may spar occasionally over control of the South China Sea, China may occasionally make threatening gestures over Taiwan, and the two countries have clearly different views on North Korea. In the past, any of those could have activated the slide toward violence, but no longer. Nuclear weapons have made such wars between possible nuclear powers simply unacceptable. A nuclear exchange could physically occur, and that realization helps form the greatest military deterrent to that occurrence. The potential deadliness of what could happen has made international politics less dangerous, if much more potentially deadly. There has, to repeat, not been a direct major military conflict between the most powerful states in nearly three-quarters of a century, and speculation about Sino-American relations deteriorating to war seems increasingly fanciful. Ukraine is a possible test of that dynamic, and the lingering fear of that possibility will affect how punitive the peace may be. That is something in an international environment that often seems unstable, even volatile.

The retention of European-style forces as the backbone of this long peace has been a continuing practice, but the appropriateness of such a high level of emphasis is increasingly questionable in an international environment for which they are not entirely suited and in which their employment could lead to catastrophic consequences. Some elements of the armed forces have been more adaptable than others to this changed reality. Among the armed forces, the army is probably still the most conspicuously "heavy" in its orientation.

If an unconventional opponent, for instance, recognizes that it is going to be attacked by a large and heavy army, it simply gets out of the way—leaves and avoids that contact. Heavy artillery requires a massed target to get the "most bang for the buck," and battle tanks must have adequate physical infrastructure to be deployed effectively to the battle area. As an example, in Kosovo during the 1990s the army wanted to move physically heavy American tanks from nearby countries to the theater, but Kosovo did not have adequate roads and bridges strong enough to allow the tanks to use them. As a result, the only means of available transport was large American transport aircraft that could only carry one tank at a time to the combat area.

European-style armed forces require developed environments that can accommodate them and allow them to have maximum effect, and this is often not the case in places where contemporary fighting rages.

Conflict and the places it has drawn American force have changed physically and in the kind of conflict situations and problems it encounters. This has implications for the structures of forces and the way they are used. Armies no longer mutually search for large open fields in which to advance against one another as they once did; Pickett's charge at Gettysburg during the Civil War is a description of history, not contemporary reality, and today's soldiers do not view it as part of their operational universe. The nature of warfare has indeed changed.

Those changes reflect the quantum leap in destructive capability associated ultimately with nuclear weapons and the venues in which war now occurs. The two factors are, of course, related. The advent of nuclear weapons made direct clash between nuclear powers unthinkable and caused those powers to erect platforms in which they could compete without undue fear of direct confrontation and escalation. The decolonization movement in the Afro-Asian world provided the surrogate platform where conflict could occur "safely," as the two sides took and supported opposing sides in developing world internal conflicts. This form of surrogacy started while the Cold War was still being hotly contested, and it continued after that global competition was replaced by the war on terrorism. Heavy forces were designed for and are most effective in military engagement with similarly configured opponents in physical environments compatible with their preferred usage. Such circumstances hardly exist today in terms of how and for what ends force is intended. The possible implications are profound. How the war in Ukraine ends will be an indicator of how much change there has been.

Bibliography

Allison, Graham T. *Destined for War: Can America and China Escape Thucydides Trap?* Boston: Houghton-Mifflin Harcourt, 2017.

———. *The Essence of Decision: Explaining the Cuban Missile Crisis.* New York: HarperCollins, 1972.

Bacevich, Andrew. *Washington Rules: America's Path to Permanent War.* New York: Henry Holt and Company, 2010.

Benjamin, Daniel, and Steven Simon. "America's Great Satan: The 40-Year Obsession with Iran." *Foreign Affairs* 89, no. 6 (November/December 2019): 55–66.

Betts, Richard K. "Pick Your Battles: Ending America's Permanent State of War." *Foreign Affairs* 83, no. 6 (November/December 2014): 15–24.

Brzezinski, Zbigniew. "The Cold War and Its Aftermath." *Foreign Affairs* 71, no. 4 (Fall 1992): 31–49.

Clark, Ronald W. *The Greatest Power on Earth: The International Race for Nuclear Supremacy, From Earliest Theory to Three-Mile Island*. New York: Harper and Row, 1980.

Economy, Elizabeth. *The Third Revolution: Xi Jinping and the New Chinese State*. Oxford, UK: Oxford University Press, 2018.

Farrow, Ronan. *War on Peace: The End of Diplomacy and the Decline of American Influence*. New York: W. W. Norton, 2018.

Fontaine, Richard. "The Nonintervention Delusion: What War Is Good For." *Foreign Affairs* 89, no. 6 (November/December 2019): 84–98.

Fukuyama, Francis. *The End of History and the Last Man*. New York: Free Press, 1992.

Gaddis, John Lewis. *The United States and the End of the Cold War: Implications, Reconsideration, Provocations*. New York and Oxford: Oxford University Press, 1992.

Gates, Robert M. *Exercise of Power: American Failures, Successes, and a New Path Forward in the Post–Cold War World*. New York: Alfred A. Knopf, 2020.

George, Roger, Harvey Rishikopf, and Brent Scowcroft, eds. *The National Security Enterprise: Navigating the Labyrinth*. 2nd ed. Washington, DC: Georgetown University Press, 2017.

Jarmon, Jack. *The New Era in U.S. National Security: An Introduction to Emerging Threats and Challenges*. Lanham, MD: Rowman & Littlefield, 2014.

Meacham, Jon. *The Soul of America: The Battle for Our Better Angels*. New York: Random House, 2018.

Mearsheimer, John J. "Why We Shall Soon Miss the Cold War." *Atlantic Monthly* 262, no. 2 (August 1990): 35–50.

Reveron, Derek S., Nikolas K. Gvosdev, and John A. Cloud. *The Oxford Handbook of U.S. National Security*. New York: Oxford University Press, 2018.

Snow, Donald M. *The Case Against Military Intervention: Why We Do It and Why It Fails*. New York: Routledge, 2016.

———. *National Security*. 7th ed. New York and London: Routledge, 2020.

———. *The Necessary Peace: Nuclear Weapons and Superpower Relations*. Lexington, MA: Lexington Books, 1987.

———. *The Shadow of the Mushroom-Shaped Cloud*. Columbus, OH: Consortium for International Studies Education, 1978.

———. *The Shape of the Future: The Post-Cold War World*. Armonk, NY: M. E. Sharpe, 1999.

Stoessinger, John G. *Why Nations Go to War*. 11th ed. Belmont, CA: Wadsworth, 2010.

Sun Tzu. *The Art of War*. Translated by Ralph A. Sawyer. New York: Basic Books, 1991.

Vine, David. *The United States of War: A Global History of America's Endless Conflicts, from Columbus to the Islamic State*. Berkeley: University of California Press, 2020.

Weigley, Russell F. *The American Way of War: A History of United States Military Strategy and Policy*. Bloomington: Indiana University Press, 1977.

Woodward, Bob, and Robert Costa. *Peril*. New York: Simon and Schuster, 2021.

CHAPTER THREE

The Systemic Shock of 9/11
Afghanistan, Iraq, and Beyond

The period leading to and including the change of centuries has been difficult for the United States in terms of its military involvements and transitions. Because of the outcome of the Vietnam conflict, the United States had retreated from an aggressive defense posture while it absorbed the lessons of its failure and adjusted its personnel to the all-volunteer force concept. The period between 1975 and 1990 was marked by a period of introspection, even tranquility, compared with what was to follow.

The 1990s were a period of great change stimulated by bookend traumas at either end of the decade. The first major trauma was the collapse of the Soviet Union and the ripple effects that momentous event created after 1991. The Soviet fall cascaded through the communist world generally, and country after country shed themselves of Marxist Leninism. The twenty-first century has seen the communist "empire" effectively shrink to four countries: the People's Republic of China (PRC), the Democratic People's Republic of Korea (DPRK), Vietnam, and Cuba. The "threat," such as it was, thus moved from Eastern Europe to Asia, and it was far different, less threatening to national security for the United States than during the Cold War. China replaced the Soviet Union as the major US competitor, and China and the United States have become major rivals with some military overtone. North Korea's nuclear emergence is a concern, but the military confrontation in the Far East is not yet as great as the twentieth-century central conflict with the Soviets. Vietnam has become a tourist destination for some Americans (especially Vietnam veterans), and many American wardrobes now include apparel marked "made in Vietnam." Cuba remains, well, Cuba. It counts in American security terms mainly because the American naval base at Guantanamo Bay helps protect access to and military control of the Panama Canal.

The other seminal event, of course, was 9/11 in the first year of the twenty-first century. It was, in a sense, the first full-blown national security crisis that the United States had faced in over a half century, rivalling the attack on Pearl Harbor in 1941 both as a direct assault on American soil and in the treachery of its commission and the psychological effect it had on the American public. The "war on terror," declared by President Bush in its wake as he stood on the New York World Trade Center towers, galvanized the American public and created a singularity of purpose not seen since the end of the Vietnam War.

It was also, of course, a very different event in significant ways. Pearl Harbor was an act of war committed by the armed forces of a hostile power as the signal that convinced Americans who had wanted to stay on the sidelines of World War II that the United States could not continue its neutrality. The Al Qaeda terrorists who carried out 9/11 represented no government or country, and their action was directed almost exclusively at the civilian population of the United States. The Japanese attacked an American military installation in a clear act of war. The goal of the Japanese was to sink enough of the American Pacific Fleet for them to consolidate the empire they were establishing in East Asia. It is not clear what the political goal of Al Qaeda was, as is often the case with terrorist acts.

The responses by the American people were similar in both cases, however, galvanizing public opinion against the perpetrators and creating a unity that did not preexist the attacks. On the day after Pearl Harbor, the United States declared war on Japan and joined the coalition that successfully won WWII. When George Bush exhorted Americans after 9/11, American support for retributive action was widespread, and the United States was joined in the campaign against terror by its NATO allies. Symbolically, they invoked Article 5 of the NATO Charter (which declared that an "attack against one" was an attack against all of them) in support of the United States. It was the only time since NATO was formed in 1949 that the "collective self-defense" provision of the alliance had been invoked.

The major difference in the two events was in the nature of the response. In 1941, the United States joined an ongoing defense coalition with the clear political objective of defeating the opposing coalition led by Germany and Japan. It was a specific and clear objective, it was clearly identified, and it did not change. The attacks of 9/11 were different. They were acts of terror by a nongovernmental entity, not clearly military acts by a sovereign actor.

Al Qaeda was not the government of a state, and its actions did not conform to the rules of war that govern interstate conflicts, its goals in the attack were not clearly evident, and it was an elusive foe with no accepted territorial base. Its acts were, however, atrocious and frightening (which is the purpose or reason for many terrorist actions). Americans were united in their resolve to punish the perpetrators and to prevent them from reprising the atrocity. How and against whom to do so was more difficult than identifying the nationality of those who had attacked Pearl Harbor.

The "war on terror," as it was quickly identified, thus did not have the same kind of enemy against which to concentrate retributive responses as did the Japanese perpetrators of Pearl Harbor, and this lack of clarity has been responsible for much of the difficulty of combating a terrorist foe that still exists in various guises worldwide. Because it was such an unanticipated and unique event in the American experience, it also created an outrage the fury of which was difficult to articulate and confront. Someone had to pay, but whom, how, and where? The response to Pearl Harbor was more concrete and identifiable: the Japanese government had authorized the attack on American soil as a deliberate provocation and act of war for which there were well established, if difficult, prescribed means of recourse: war. The 9/11 attacks were clearly of the same qualitative intent and effect, but they were not associated with an international entity of the legal stature of a state. Although Al Qaeda was quickly identified as the perpetrator and thus the object of vengeance, it was not a physical state with an identifiable political status and territorial base. The analogy with the act of infamy it represented was quickly compared with the Pearl Harbor experience by declaring the response as the "war on terror."

The analogies are not, of course, identical. The attack on Pearl Harbor was a sneak attack, as was 9/11, and both created a public outrage and demand for retribution partially fueled by the covert nature of the operations. Specifying what that response should be was much easier after Pearl Harbor because the attack was by another state with whom relations had deteriorated and that was aligned with the more obvious fascist alliance against whom war was deemed inevitable by most public officials. The action taken by Congress the next day demanding a formal declaration of war was a traditional international response for which there was established precedent, and the response included a mobilization to form the unified force that would prosecute the war. It did serve to cancel any remaining sentiment for neutrality in the world conflict and to fill the American public with what Japanese Admiral Isoroku Yamamoto described as a "terrible resolve" that translated into solid support for war.

The attacks of 9/11 produced a similar outrage, but it was also different in content and direction. The attacks were clearly acts of war, even though they violated the laws of war, notably by being directed at civilian targets, which are prohibited under the laws of war. They were also not conducted by the identifiable armed forces of any country or organized political group.

The prime commonality was that each galvanized American opinion behind military action. The implicit anti-military sentiment that was an effect of the post-Vietnam period evaporated immediately as Americans demanded retribution for the unprovoked (at least in American minds) nature of the terrorist attacks. This sentiment was magnified since the attacks were directed at significant landmarks of the country's largest city and killed more than three thousand civilians. Committing the attacks directly on American soil was both offensive and frightening, and millions of American citizens around the country wondered aloud if they were not personally vulnerable to injury, or even death.

The result was a metamorphosis in thinking about and using American force that survived for two decades. That change has been interrupted and presumably altered by the American withdrawal from Afghanistan in possible ways that will be explored in these pages. Since the Vietnam excursion, American military activity had gradually been moving toward engagements in the Middle East, stimulated by interests in protecting Israel, in access to Persian Gulf oil, and in influencing the results of the Iranian Revolution of 1979. Those goals have always been partially incompatible in practice, because the Persian Gulf oil producers have historically opposed Israel (at least rhetorically), and because Shiite Iran (almost all the producers except Iran and Bahrain were overwhelmingly Sunni) is a former American stalwart ally in that part of the world.

This foray into the byzantine intricacies of Middle Eastern geopolitics has placed the United States on unfamiliar ground where there was resultantly little consensual agreement about American security interests beyond the familiar Cold War–era troika of protecting Israel, guaranteed uninterrupted access to Middle East oil, and minimizing Soviet penetration of the region. These priorities are no longer so dominant. A nuclear-armed Israel is quite capable of taking care of its own security, an effort heavily subsidized by the United States (see my *The Middle East and American National Security* for a discussion). American dependence on Middle Eastern oil is declining in the face of growing climate change effort, and although Russia continues to push for greater regional influence, its only real success has been a pro-government presence in the Syrian Civil War. America's traditional policy priorities have been largely overcome by events.

The year 1979 was when these changes began to surface due to events in the region. America's principal ally in the region, Iran, was converted from its staunchest pillar to an enemy with the overthrow of the Shah and his replacement by an antagonistic, fundamentalist, and expansionist Shiite regime in Teheran that continues to this day. An already unstable Iranian regime and perceived role further exacerbated conflict in the Muslim Middle East and led the United States to make decisions positioning itself as a major barrier to Iranian ambitions and thus into the intricacies of regional power politics, an area that was not an American historic forte based on experience and expertise. Middle Eastern international politics became more unstable than usual, and the United States found itself dragged into violent conflicts about which its knowledge and expertise base was debatable. In many ways, it was unfamiliar ground for the United States, for which its experience had not prepared it very well. Its previous lenses for viewing the region had been filtered through the vantage points of Israel versus the "Arabs" and its warm personal relationship with the Shah of Shahs, and both perspectives changed. Its expertise in other parts and problems of the region were not deep nor great and did not provide an adequate frame for how to react in other places like Iraq and Afghanistan. This lack of perspective was clear when the country came into conflict with these countries and in the quality of its responses to their conflicts. This difficulty was particularly evident on whether and how to use force when conflict arose generally, and this controversy that continued into the 2020s. However one assesses the validity of the shifts that have occurred, it is hard to maintain that the experience has been an overwhelming success. The forays into Iraq and Afghanistan have been the most public examples of the morasses into which the United States has placed itself and from which it has long struggled to extricate itself. For this reason, the discussion turns to American military actions in both countries and how they color thinking about force in the region and elsewhere.

America in Iraq

The United States and Iraq have historically had a basically marginal, cool relationship, most of which has been adversarial and has been an offshoot of American interest in Israel. This basic tension also has formed the base of rivalry with the Iraqis, and it has included Iraqi participation in the various wars between Israel and its neighboring Muslim states from 1948 to 1973. Interest increased after the Iranian Revolution of 1979 drove a wedge between the United States and Iran, and it was particularly stimulated by the Iran-Iraq War that broke out in 1980 and continued for nearly a decade thereafter. The outcome was to create an ambivalent American perception toward the Iraqis and the beginning of the slippery slope toward the American invasion, conquest, and occupation of Iraq from 2003 until 2011.

The initial point to be made is that American interest in Iraq was derivative, not basic, and that is still true. Prior to 1980, the relationship was casual at most. The only thing that rose to anything resembling vital interests between them was the possibility (remote by 1980 given Israeli nuclear weapons) that the coalition of Islamic states that opposed Israel—and of which Iraq was a member—might somehow imperil Israel. The United States received some oil from Iraq, but it was not much and was replaceable from other sources. There was, in other words, nothing to suggest the probability of a war between them or an eight-year American occupation of Iraq. The Iran-Iraq War raised Iraq to a higher level of US awareness and concern.

Iran and Iraq share a 1,600-kilometer (1,000 mile) border from Turkmenistan to the head of the Persian Gulf. Both are Muslim states, but their similarity ends there. The Iraqis consider themselves to be Arab, and the Sunni minority has been dominant politically, although there are many more adherents to Shiism in the country. The Iranians, by contrast, are almost all Shiites and non-Arab, speak a different language, and have a shared history as one of the oldest countries and civilizations in the region. By contrast, Iraq is a largely artificial state that gained independence in 1932. Iraq was ruled by a series of strongman dictators, including Saddam Hussein, who gained power in 1973 and maintained it until the American overthrow of the government in 2003.

Saddam had large ambitions within the region, hoping to succeed Egypt's Gamal Abdul Nasser as the titular leader of Arab "nationalism." The quotation marks are appropriate, since there is essentially no sense of unity among the various "Arab" states (most of which are artificial with little shared national identity), but Nasser minimally sought to identify himself as the leading figure of the Arabs. The Iran-Iraq War was the platform for making his leadership case. Taking on the Iranians and hopefully protecting the Arab Sunni states from the Shiite Iranian infidels was his way to do so. Because the US government opposed the new Shiite regime in Teheran, they provided some military aid to the regime in Baghdad, the first visible manifestation of anything more than the most casual relationship between the two countries. The aftermath of the war between Iraq and Iran began the interaction between them that eventually devolved into probably the most senseless military adventure in US history in 2003.

Among other things, the Iran-Iraq war effort had virtually bankrupted Iraq, and after it was over, Saddam Hussein went to the principal wealthy

Arab neighbors he had protected from the Iranians and asked for financial assistance in the forgiveness of loans he had received to fight the war and that were needed to pay for his country's recovery. At the top of the list of the countries he solicited were Kuwait and Saudi Arabia, both of which dismissed his requests. Enraged by this lack of gratitude, Saddam ordered the Iraqi invasion of Kuwait in August 1990 to get the funds he felt he needed and his "reward" for protecting the other Sunni Arab states from the radical Shiite Iranians. This act of aggression engaged the United States in a process of interaction that devolved into the American conquest of Iraq and its occupation until 2011.

The Gulf War and Beyond
The Iraqi invasion and conquest of Kuwait was a walkover. A seasoned, battle-trained Iraqi force entered Kuwait and many of the Kuwaitis fled to Saudi Arabia. As a result, the Iraqis were in control of the small country, and they were standing on its border with the Saudi state and peering toward the main Saudi oil refining complex less than a hundred miles away. In typical Saudi fashion, the Saudi royal family addressed the crisis by looking for someone else to defend them from the potential Iraqi onslaught (which they were incapable of turning back themselves despite bloated expenditures on military preparedness based on foreign mercenary forces). Among those who volunteered to come to their aid was the United States (at that time, still thoroughly addicted to Saudi oil) and a Saudi national with experience in the Afghan resistance to Soviet occupation named Osama bin Laden, who had a force of veterans of the recently concluded expulsion of the Soviets from Afghanistan, and who volunteered the services of that force to protect the Saudis from the Iraqis. The Saudis chose the Americans as their protector, a decision that infuriated bin Laden, and his reaction was partly responsible for his growing obsession with excluding the apostate Americans from the region that crystallized in the 9/11 attacks.

The result was the 1990–1991 Persian Gulf War, in which the Americans and the Iraqis faced off against one another for the first time. Militarily, of course, it was no real contest for the United States, which brought a well-trained, thoroughly superior force to bear against an Iraqi opponent that had just completed its decade-long fight with Iran and the invasion of Iraq itself. The fighting was brief: the United States assembled a coalition of thirty-five countries to participate in the removal of the Iraqis from Kuwait, and fighting began on January 17, 1991. The physical war ended in late February, when the Iraqis retreated back across the Kuwaiti border to Iraq. The Americans lost 143 soldiers in combat and a slightly larger number to other causes. No one knows exactly what Iraqi losses were, although the estimates begin at about twenty thousand.

If the war itself was hardly noteworthy, its effects on American policy in the area and specifically regarding Iraq were significant. During Iraq's war with Iran, relations had warmed between the two countries to the point that the United States sent some military equipment to support the Iraqis. The war in Kuwait caused a sharp reversal of that amicable condition. To justify the use of force, the US government was forced to demonize the Hussein regime, its motives, and particularly its political leadership. The Iraqi president, Saddam Hussein, was a picture-book villain and made the latter effort easy to do, and as the Americans prepared to withdraw, there were political calls for American forces to follow the Iraqis back into their homeland and overthrow Hussein. President Bush resisted these calls as likely to precipitate the United States being dragged into a prolonged occupation (a prophetic prediction given events in 2003), and the case was closed.

Unfortunately, the closure in US attention to Iraq was short-lived. The Persian Gulf War experience had transformed warm (or at least proper) American feelings toward Hussein to opposition, and both opposing and deposing him became the goal for a group of conservatives in the United States known as the neoconservatives (neocons for short), among whom the desire to overthrow him was greatest and went back to 1990. Saddam fulfilled many of their direst descriptions in his postwar treatment of elements in Iraq who had been opposed to or were indifferent toward the attack on Kuwait. Hussein attacked his internal opponents (mostly Kurds from the north and Shiites in the south), including air attacks with poison gas that sent many Iraqi Kurds fleeing across the border into Turkey, where they were not welcome. After the refugees' plight was publicized on global cable TV (a novelty at the time), the United States declared the affected areas as no-fly zones for the Iraqi air forces and, along with NATO allies, kept the Iraqi air force out of its own airspace until the invasion of 2003.

What is particularly interesting about the process leading to the American invasion and occupation was the strategic unimportance of Iraq to the United States. The murder of Iraqis after the Persian Gulf War and the institution of Operation Northern Watch (the no-fly zone implementation) to preclude further aerial bombardment of his own people by Saddam Hussein had created tension between the two regimes, and it was not clear how the United States could relieve itself of the open-ended obligation it had incurred toward the Kurds and the Shiites in the process. None of the options were attractive. Abandoning the Kurds and others to Saddam's revenge was unacceptable to the American government on humanitarian grounds; managing to exact a commitment from Saddam to cease his oppression would not satisfy those Iraqis whom he had suppressed, and they did not trust his word not to resume that activity if not constrained by outside force. The other option, rarely discussed in public during the remainder of the 1990s, was to get rid of Saddam. This was the preference of the neocons, but they did not hold sway before the end of the century. The 2000 election of George W. Bush and the 9/11 attacks unlocked the conceptual door for that remedy.

Invasion and Conquest
The case for invading Iraq was born of the same frenzy that pervaded so much of national security politics and decision making surrounding the terrorist attacks and ensuing turmoil in the country. This fervent feeling of the need to act—and to punish—anyone in the Middle East who might be suspicious in one way or another was felt especially strongly by the neocons, who had argued for an invasion of Iraq in 1991 to overthrow Saddam. As noted, they had been turned down by the senior President Bush, and they reasserted their case to his son, a much less experienced President George W. Bush, who lacked his father's background in the national security field and was more open to their entreaties. They built their case around accusations that the Iraqi regime was building prohibited weapons of mass destruction (WMD) and that they might be negotiating to share these with the Al Qaeda terrorists. In a harbinger of executive branch politics that would be reprised in 2021, most of these claims were false (or at least unproven), but they were accepted by anti-Iraqi advocates in the administration and formed the basis of US Iraqi policy. The saddest example of the conceptual malaise was the speech by Secretary of State Colin Powell, who accused the Iraqis of these transgressions and which accusation he later admitted was false and a stain on his otherwise most distinguished career.

War fever came to grip the Bush administration, and in May 2003 the United States invaded and quickly brushed aside Iraqi armed forces, which put up a perfunctory resistance and then moved underground. American Secretary of Defense Donald Rumsfeld exultantly predicted as the invasion was underway that not only would the Americans prevail, but that all American troops would be withdrawn by Labor Day. He was, of course, half right: American forces prevailed on the battlefield as they had in 1991, but the effort to equate that physical triumph with achieving whatever political objectives were being pursued was elusive. Although it was not recognized at the time, the Iraqi response was a classic example of asymmetrical warfare: with no chance they could successfully compete with the American military in standup confrontations (a lesson they had learned the hard way in 1991), they chose to revert to the shadows and wait for opportunities to harass the occupiers to the point that the invaders tired of the conflict, decided its continuation was not worth the continuing sacrifice, and left. It took eight years rather than the predicted several months to accomplish, but in 2011 the Americans did substantially leave. Whether US goals were achieved in the process was debatable.

The conquest of Iraq has earned the designation by many analysts (including this author) as the dumbest, most misguided military adventure in American history. Although a handful of remaining apologists argue that all the motivation has not become public (which is a debatable assertion, to say the least), but if clear and defensible motives were to surface, the reasons for the war might be rehabilitated.

The entire enterprise arguably violated fundamentally both tenets of the Interest-Feasibility (IF) formula: the United States did not have adequate interests at stake in what was going on in Iraq to justify military action, and American ignorance of Iraq circumstances almost assured that the effort, while apparently successful in the short run, had little prospect of succeeding in whatever the long-term goals were.

At this point, participants seem to be more intent on erasing the memory than in justifying it. We had inadequate understanding of a country in which we had minimal stake, and the invasion thus made essentially no sense in any geopolitical way, a judgment that has gained analytical ascendancy as a means of avoiding a conceptual repetition.

The Bush administration tried to make the case that the Saddam Hussein regime indeed posed a threat to the United States. It maintained that it had evidence that Iraq had an active program seeking to perfect and field weapons of mass destruction, that the regime had ties to regional terrorist groups with whom it might well share those weapons, that the terrorist groups would use these weapons against the United States, and that as a result, the government of Iraq, by virtue of these activities and intentions, posed a national security threat to the United States. If the combination of these allegations was true, Iraq posed a strong, even compelling, case for American military action against it and its political leadership. The dual problems with this assertion is that it has never been proven and that its defenders have largely quit trying to do so.

There was, in other words, one major problem with these assertions and the conclusions drawn from them: the administration offered no convincing evidence that they were true. They were serious charges that, if proven true, made a strong case that the Saddam Hussein regime posed a threat to American vital, including survival, interests and that as a result, the United

States was justified in taking military action to remove that regime and to destroy those capabilities. The hysteria caused by the 9/11 attacks was still strong enough that such accusations tended to be accepted uncritically (or at least not strongly contested) by many Americans, including their elected leaders, many of whom have recanted or reinterpreted their absence of objection since. Well after the fact, many of those American elected officials voiced reservations about the veracity of the charges, but their voices were, to put it mildly, muted while the decisions to invade Iraq were being hatched and developed.

These accusations have still not been proven, at least in public. The invasion did occur in March 2003, and American forces searched fervently but vainly to find any evidence of an Iraqi WMD active program or any stockpile of WMD to be shared with the terrorists. The Saddam Hussein government had no documented history of anything but animosity with the terrorists and despite having shown a willingness to attack their own citizens with chemical weapons, they had little history otherwise with weapons of mass destruction. Nearly two decades since the accusations were made, there is still no public record substantiating the accusations that formed the basis for the invasion. Why not?

Justification of the IF Criteria
This truth of the accusations is absolutely crucial to whether the invasion was justifiable as an act of vital national defense or not. At heart, they are necessary to establish that the United States had *any* national security interests in Iraq that could possibly rise to the level that American force was an appropriate and justifiable tool to secure them. Aside from noting that Iraq was a member of the coalition of Islamic states dedicated to destroying Israel (although not a prominent part of that forlorn movement), the two countries had largely ignored one another prior to 1980 because they had so little in common (or at odds). Taking on an Iran that had become an enemy in 1979 cast what relationship there was in a favorable light.

When they invaded Kuwait and threatened American "ally" Saudi Arabia, it recast them as an enemy among some American policy makers, as did Saddam's postwar actions in retaliation against his own people. On their own, however, these hardly created such a high level of animosity and clash of interests as to justify the physical invasion and overthrow of the regime and the eight-year occupation of the country. There should have been a more threatening set of circumstances to justify the use of American force, and the neocons failed to provide them. The problem then and now is thus that those apologists have never demonstrated the charges were true. If anything, time has suggested those assertions to be lies (or to be charitable, highly inflated). Such a revelation may seem unexceptional in 2022; it was not something one assumed to be likely when the invasion and occupation were being justified.

The second IF criterion, plausibility of success, was achievable at the physical level of brushing aside the Iraqi armed forces and overthrowing the regime, but poor planning and occupation policy undercut the success of the overall effort. Once again, the American lack of understanding of the situation into which it placed itself was largely to blame for the resulting catastrophe that marked the occupation. A major reason for the mistakes that were made, however, was the absence of important American interests in Iraq over time that meant the Americans lacked an adequate contextual interest and understanding of the country to know if its policies would succeed or fail. Ironically, the most important mitigating factor was that the actions simply reinforced the instability of the country without making things terribly worse than they were, and they did result in the overthrow of a notorious leader in Saddam Hussein. These were justifiable goals at some level, but were they adequate to justify the extent of the American effort that was mounted?

It is not clear what specific goals the United States had in making war on Iraq beyond removing Saddam Hussein and finding and destroying the places he was supposedly building WMD and capturing any stores of these weapons he had in his possession. Neither were inherently bad ideas, if true, but were they important enough to justify an all-out invasion and eight-year occupation of a country seven thousand miles from American soil? Saddam Hussein was certainly an arguably reprehensible dictator who had ruthlessly suppressed the Shiite majority in the country and the minority Kurds of northern Iraq. His removal was certainly not an undesirable outcome, but if removing all the people we dislike through war was standard American policy, there are lots of candidates in addition to Saddam who could keep the US military active in lots of countries. Saddam's guilt, while real, arose because he allegedly went farther, building and using WMD against his own people and supposedly being prepared to share it with terrorists who would use it against the United States. If that were true and could have been proven, the war effort would have been justifiable and depictions of it as an utterly needless war would not have arisen. If such evidence was available and made public, the effort might rehabilitate what was decided and done. What does it say that it has not been?

The problem was that the WMD accusations were never confirmed by the public capture of any WMDs or records documenting the weapons' existence, although not for a lack of effort on the part of the occupying Americans. Defanging such an Iraqi capability before it could be used against Americans would have provided a clear reason for war. The problem was that such a discovery was never made, or at least made public. The vitality of removing a WMD threat (which at times included accusations of nuclear weapons development) would have been clearly a violation of vital American interests and would have justified war. Removing a Saddam Hussein who was not doing these things was arguably not.

There is a residual irony that reinforces the point. After the war was concluded, some foreign leaders suggested that had Iraq developed the kinds of capabilities of which they were accused—especially nuclear weapons—the United States would likely not have invaded in the first place for fear of a nuclear retaliation by the Hussein regime. Whether this would have occurred or not is speculative and may or may not have influenced the American decision, of course, but it is an assertion believed in some developing world countries. It is certainly compatible with the discussion of nuclear dynamics in the last chapter. In the same vein, had the Iraqis been engaged in a serious WMD/nuclear weapons effort, the United States probably would not have had to carry out an invasion, because the Israelis would probably have acted preemptively to destroy their programs, something they have done in the past.

The conclusion that emerges from analyzing the Iraq War was that it was a justifiable response to a threat that did not in fact exist and an overreaction to a danger that did exist. If the threat that was alleged had been real, in other words, the use of military force would have been entirely justified. Against the threat that did exist, the effort was clearly an overreach. In the end, the only "strategic" goal served by removing Saddam was to cancel the need for Operation Northern Watch overflights of parts of the country formerly menaced by the Iraqi dictator. The assertion that the Iraq War was the most unjustifiable assertion of American military power arises from these concerns. If the question of when the United States should use force in the future is evaluated partially in terms of how and when it has been used in the past, the conclusion seems to be inescapable that Iraq was the kind of situation when American force should *not* be used in the future and that analysis of similar situations should be viewed with a skeptical eye.

The War in Afghanistan

The wars in Iraq and Afghanistan share little in common except that both were largely outgrowths of the American reaction to 9/11 in different ways and for different reasons, and both occurred in the eastern part of the Middle East. The war in Iraq was largely a concoction created by conservative defense intellectuals associated with the Bush administration, and it bore little obvious relationship to the 9/11 terrorists or their motives, unless one accepted the unproven assertion than Saddam Hussein and Al Qaeda were somehow coconspirators. Its conduct and conclusion (to the extent that it has ever completely ended) had little connection with terrorism, although such a link was alleged by its neocon apologists. Historians will scratch their heads for a long time figuring out what the motivation for the war was and what it accomplished beyond resulting in the overthrow and demise of Saddam Hussein.

The Original Motive: Avenging 9/11
The war in Afghanistan had an inarguably righteous beginning in terms of motivation and American interests. The reason for invading and occupying Afghanistan was directly tied to the 9/11 attacks. There was abundant evidence that the attacks were planned and launched by the Al Qaeda (AQ) terrorist organization, which was a "guest" of the Taliban regime that ruled the country and provided a safe haven for the terrorists to prepare their attack. Many Al Qaeda and Taliban members had been part of the resistance to the Soviet invasion of the country in the 1970s, which was the basis of their relationship. Based in Pashtun traditions that dictate that one provide safety for guests (*Pashtunwali*), the Taliban would not comply with American demands to remand the terrorists to US control. If the United States was to bring the AQ perpetrators (including their leader Osama bin Laden) to justice, this meant the Americans would have to violate Afghan sovereignty, invade, and capture the terrorists themselves.

There was essentially no dispute about whether the mission was righteous or whether it was in the vital interest of the United States to perform it. There were, however, two problems that emerged in the execution of the mission. First and most importantly, it failed in its primary and only publicized mission. The Al Qaeda terrorists managed to escape (with the assistance of local tribesmen) into the Tora Bora mountains and across the frontier into Pakistan, an American military ally in the Central Treaty Organization (CENTO). With the terrorists effectively beyond American reach, the original, and totally justifiable, mission failed. When it did so, it effectively voided the main rationale for the invasion in the first place. The United States, probably after issuing a stern warning to the Taliban that it would return in force if Al Qaeda returned, could have left Afghanistan physically. It would have been a less-than-successful mission, but at least a bounded one.

That, of course, did not happen, because the United States had accumulated some Afghan geopolitical baggage in the process. At the time of the American intervention, Afghanistan was in the middle of one of its periodic civil wars between the Taliban and a coalition of other tribally based groups known as the Northern Alliance, and the American intrusion into the country effectively cemented the basis for two developments that contributed both to the American war and its relationship with the Afghans. Since the Taliban were the Afghan protectors of the Al Qaeda terrorists, the Taliban became de facto opponents of the Americans and the United States was drawn more deeply into collaboration with the Northern Alliance. In this case, the "enemy of my enemy" in fact became my friend. This congruence of interests made the United States the informal ally of the anti-Taliban coalition represented by the alliance. At the time, there was little basis for collaboration or alliance otherwise.

This relationship may have been understandable given the circumstances of late 2001 and the pursuit of the terrorists, but it was also geopolitically unfortunate and reflected the lack of any real understanding of Afghan history and politics. Particularly, it reflected a lack of understanding of the crucial role of the Pashtun tribe in the dynamics of Afghan politics. In essence, the result was to put the United States on what ultimately turned out to be the wrong side of the conflict and thus help ensure the long duration of the effort. This mission was not out of any inherent kindred interests or friendship with what became the Afghanistan we promoted and supported until July 2021.

Historically, the Pashtun tribe is the majority group in Afghanistan. They are factionalized along geographic and confessional lines. The major cleavage is urban-rural. Afghanistan is overwhelmingly a rural country, and the Pashtun dominate in these rural, or tribal, regions. Rural Pashtuns tend to be very conservative, and their characteristics include tribal and sub-clan independence, a suspicion of central governments, which are associated with the capital in Kabul, and a deep and abiding hatred for and resistance to physical outsiders (which can include virtually anybody who is not Pashtun). The rural Pashtuns, many of whom fled to Pakistan when the Taliban subsequently fell from power, only to return in opposition in 2003, are very suspicious of more urbanized Pashtuns, who are associated with the capital of Kabul, which became the government of Afghanistan with American help.

It is not clear how acutely aware of these cleavages the Americans were when they decided to invade the country in late 2001 to pursue bin Laden or, more importantly, when they decided to stay in support of the Northern Alliance after that mission failed. An arguable case can be made that the United States should have packed its bags and left after the original mission failed, warning the Taliban we would return if Al Qaeda was allowed to return. If such an option was discussed (which it almost certainly must have been), it is not discussed in the public record.

Prior to 9/11, relations between the two countries were distant, and there were few very important interests and ties the two shared. The major cash crop of Afghanistan was (and remains) the cultivation and the sale of opium poppies, from which heroin is derived, making the country the eastern terminus of the "French connection" of heroin supply to the United States. Opposition to communist occupation and rule was a goal of both the Americans and the Afghans, but there was never a positive tie with the Taliban other than some opposition in the United States to the treatment of women by the religiously conservative group, a policy they have apparently loosened since their return to power in 2021.

The United States instead ended up aligning itself with the Northern Alliance, led by urban Pashtun Hamid Karzai but with support from various other non-Pashtun factions hated by the Pashtuns. This Karzai-led alliance, with American and NATO help, was able to seize power and to banish the Taliban across the Pakistani frontier, where they regrouped and from which they returned. The Americans committed two errors that guaranteed their unpopularity to much of the Pashtun base in the country and aligned themselves with the urban Pashtuns and other non-Pashtun tribal groupings. The result was to place the United States in opposition to some basic Afghan values, including resistance to foreign rule, support of a strong, Kabul-based government that quickly became distinguished as one of the most corrupt in the world, and the ally of a generally unpopular regime. How this combination was supposed to produce an outcome that supported American objectives has never been clearly or comprehensively articulated. It is thus not surprising that, after the American withdrawal, US officials continued to assert that the United States could not abandon the Afghans completely because it endangered "American interests."

The fact that Afghanistan was the launch point for the terrorist attacks represented a real American problem that needed addressing, but was the twenty-year intervention an appropriate method to ensure that Afghanistan did not become the source of future terrorist activity after bin Laden and his cohorts escaped across the border into Pakistan? It is not at all clear that the mission was tasked in this manner or that the difficulty of achieving it was appreciated. Mostly, the problem was that the United States did not recognize the problems it was embracing when it aligned itself with the Northern Alliance.

The problem was that whatever the Afghans thought of the Taliban, their aversion to foreign occupation meant the American continued presence was itself a source of friction, and that aligning ourselves with a corrupt regime that included non-Pashtuns reinforced the conceptual hole we were digging for ourselves. This was a geopolitical problem that made a Taliban government more attractive than it would otherwise have been. To many, we were the problem as much as or more than we were the answer. The simple fact was that many Afghans wanted their country cleansed of outsiders and run by Pashtuns, and the United States was a barrier to achieving either goal. That was a recipe for failed policy.

To make matters worse, it was also probably avoidable. Did the United States need to occupy Afghanistan and side with one contestant in the civil war to achieve its goal of preventing the return of Al Qaeda to Afghan sanctuary? The answer is almost certainly negative, and the alternative was expressed but rejected at the time. That alternative was for the United States to substantially leave the country after it failed to capture Al Qaeda but to warn the Taliban (or whoever the government might be) that if the terrorists returned, we would attack the terrorists with airpower and do our best to destroy them. The Taliban may not have liked that possibility, but if it had been juxtaposed with the alternative of the twenty years' war and occupation that followed, it would likely have seemed more palatable than what happened, and it was certainly a bargain that would have been accepted by Karzai, because it would have allowed him to gain and maintain power without the physical presence of foreign occupiers. During the American disengagement in August 2021, there were some hints that such a relationship might be possible in the new period of Taliban rule. The strength and viability of Taliban rule is itself a matter of some question, but regardless of whether they remain in power, the United States has freed itself from any direct responsibility for what happens next. The possibility of further radicalization of rule always remains a possibility, but one can only hope the United States will not react the way it did in 2001. Foreign military boots on the ground in Afghanistan are simply not the appropriate remediation for what may ail Afghanistan.

Conclusion: The Past in the Future?

The experience of the United States applying force to solving world problems since Vietnam has been a mixed bag. The highlights include participation in the Persian Gulf War, even though propping up the anachronistic Saudi regime (the major beneficiaries of the war) can be questioned on other grounds. Al Qaeda's leader was brought to "justice" a decade later, putting an ending to that part of the problem. The only real blemishes were the two major applications of force in Iraq and Afghanistan, both of which were arguably unnecessary (especially Iraq) and neither of which were ringing successes politically or militarily. The arguable lessons of both campaigns are that they exemplify the kinds of conflicts the country should avoid in the future: commitments to conditions and outcomes marginal to core American interests in places and circumstances where successful results were problematical. The arguable problem is that they represent kinds of problems and temptations that involvements are likely to see in the future. Figuring out a strategy for how to approach these problems in the future and determining successful strategies for dealing with them is a major military and geopolitical task for the future. It is an exercise in trying to answer the question posed in the title: where and when *should* America fight?

The IF Factor, or some construct similar to it, can capture the essential questions that must form the foundation in assessing the application of a successful strategy. It requires an accurate estimation of the challenges ahead in a complicated, changing environment. First and foremost, the United States needs clearly to determine what its interests are in possible venues for employing its forces in advance of doing so, and that requires a level of thinking and knowledge of situations that has not always been present, and this is particularly true in the volatile political environment that has marked the contemporary international arena.

The "action" in these kinds of national security calculations has clearly shifted to Asia. Particularly compared to the historical context, Europe is now militarily tranquil for the most part. The Ukraine war, discussed extensively in these pages, is a notable exception. Latin American concern is largely confined to migration northward, and Africa is primarily consumed by internecine troubles on the continent. Asian potential conflict has been concentrated in the Middle East and East Asia. The issues are quite different and of varying quality and severity in the two subareas. East Asian conflict centers, of course, on China, but it is conditioned by a nuclear balance that inhibits escalation of conflict between the United States and the PRC. The DPRK has been the center of controversy, but political changes and potential internal problems in China from demographic and other sources could upset that somewhat (see my *Cases in International Relations*, seventh edition, for a discussion) and change the situation. Conflict in the Middle East has swirled along historical religious and geopolitical lines that have particular salience, because of the terrorism problem that underlies, directly or indirectly, American interest and involvement in the two countries featured in this chapter. Because the area has attracted the most recent, most extensive, and longest American military excursions, an examination of Iraq and Afghanistan has been introduced as context for a possible future answer to the question of where and in what circumstances to utilize American force.

What exactly was the United States seeking to accomplish in either Iraq or Afghanistan? It is a question the answers to which were almost entirely concocted (at least based on the public record) in Iraq, and once Al Qaeda had eluded capture in Afghanistan, the need to stay was not compelling beyond a general desire to keep Al Qaeda from returning. Were these reasons adequate to spill American blood and treasure in places where the United States had historical disinterest that could hardly have justified the extent of actions taken?

And where did the calculation of achievability fit into the calculations? Both American adventures were to some degree knee-jerk responses to the 9/11 shocks. The United States would never have contemplated intrusion into the Afghan civil war had the Taliban government not protected and refused to hand the perpetrators over to the Americans, and there was a suspicion that Saddam Hussein was conspiring with Al Qaeda that formed at least part of the public rationale for involvement there. In both cases, the reasons clearly were insufficient to justify what turned out to be the nature of the task the United States undertook, although these kinds of problems continue to pop up from time to time and tempt American attention. It is a tentative, even controversial conclusion, but both Iraq and Afghanistan were mistakes, and a lasting lesson has to be that they counsel a calmer, better informed examination of the situation at hand before the United States again commits its forces to what could be future open-end commitments.

Both conflicts—and likely places the United States may be tempted to act again in the future—share the commonality of presenting the United States with the task of facing unconventional forces employing the strategies and techniques of asymmetrical warfare in the future, and the American record in such conflicts since Vietnam is not encouraging to the point that it represents an arguably negative element to the calculation of the feasibility of military success in these kinds of conflicts. Since they are the kinds of possible involvements that may well dominate the landscape of potential American military temptation in the future, the rest of the book will examine this problem. One of the answers to when America should fight, after all, is when it can achieve its interests by doing so—win, in other words.

Bibliography

Ansary, Tamim. *Game Without Rules: The Often-Interrupted History of Afghanistan*. New York: Public Affairs, 2012.

Bacevich, Andrew J. *America's War for the Greater Middle East: A Military History*. New York: Random House, 2016.

Bailey, Beth, and Richard H. Immerman. *Understanding the U.S. Wars in Iraq and Afghanistan*. New York: NYU Press, 2015.

Barfield, Thomas. *Afghanistan: A Cultural and Political History*. Princeton, NJ: Princeton University Press, 2013.

Barnett, Roger W. *Asymmetrical Warfare: Today's Challenge to U.S. Military Power*. Washington, DC: Potomac Books, 2013.

Belasco, Amy. *The Cost of Iraq, Afghanistan, and Other Terrorist Operations Since 2001*. Washington, DC: Congressional Research Service, December 8, 2014.

Central Intelligence Agency. *CIA World Factbook, 2020–2021*. New York: Skyhorse, 2020.

Chandrasekaran, Rajiv. *Imperial Life in the Emerald City: Inside Iraq's Green Zone*. New York: Alfred A. Knopf, 2007.

Coll, Steve. *Directorate S: The C.I.A. and America's Secret Wars in Afghanistan and Pakistan*. New York: Penguin, 2018.

Draper, Robert. *To Start a War: How the Bush Administration Took America into War*. New York, Penguin, 2020.

Ewens, Martin. *Afghanistan: A Short History of Its People and Politics*. New York: Harper Perennials, 2002.

Gallagher, Brendan R. *The Day After: Why America Wins the War but Loses the Peace*. Ithaca, NY: Cornell University Press, 2019.

Goldberg, Jeffrey. "After Iraq." *The Atlantic* 301 (January/February 2008): 68–79.

Haass, Richard. *Wars of Necessity, Wars of Choice. A Memoir of Two Iraq Wars*. New York: Simon and Schuster, 2009.

Isikoff, Michael, and David Corn. *Hubris: The Inside Story of Spin, Scandal and the Selling of the Iraq War*. New York: Three Rivers, 2007.

Jalil, Ali Ahmad. *A Military History of Afghanistan: How and Why They Fight*. Lawrence: University of Kansas Press, 2017.

Johnson, Robert. *The Afghan Way of War: How and Why They Fight*. Oxford, UK: Oxford University Press, 2011.

Jones, Seth G. *In the Graveyard of Empires: America's War in Afghanistan*. New York: W. W. Norton, 2009.

Lee, Jonathan L. *Afghanistan: A History from 1620 to the Present*. London: Reaktion Books. 2019.

Malkasian, Carter. "How the Good War Went Bad: America's Slow-Motion Failure in Afghanistan." *Foreign Affairs* 99, no. 2 (March/April 2020): 77–91.

O'Hanlon, Michael. *The Art of War in an Age of Peace: U.S. Grand Strategy and Resolute Restraint*. New Haven, CT: Yale University Press, 2021.

Packer, George. *The Assassin's Gate: America in Iraq*. New York: Farrar, Straus, and Giroux, 2005.

Polk, William R. *Understanding Iraq*. New York: Harper Perennials, 2005.

Pollack, Kenneth M. *The Threatening Storm: The Case for Invading Iraq*. New York: Random House, 2002.

Rhodes, Ben. "The Democratic Renewal: What It Will Take to Fix U.S. Foreign Policy." *Foreign Affairs* 99, no. 5 (September/October 2020): 46–83.

Ricks, Thomas E. *Fiasco: The American Adventure in Iraq*. New York: Penguin, 2006.

Sadat, Kosh, and Stanley McChrystal. "Staying the Course in Afghanistan: How to Fight the Longest War." *Foreign Affairs* 96, no. 6 (November/December 2017): 2–8.

Shahrani, M. Nafiz. *Modern Afghanistan: The Impact of Forty Years of War*. Bloomington: Indiana University Press, 2018.

Snow, Donald M. *Cases in International Relations*. 9th ed. Lanham, MD: Rowman & Littlefield, 2022.

———. *The Case Against Military Intervention: Why We Do It and Why It Fails*. New York and London: Routledge, 2016.

———*The Middle East and American National Security: Forever Wars and Conflicts?* Lanham, MD: Rowman & Littlefield, 2021.

———. *The Middle East, Oil, and U.S. National Security Policy: Intractable Problems, Impossible Solutions*. Lanham, MD: Rowman & Littlefield, 2016.

———. *National Security*. 7th ed. New York and London: Routledge, 2020.

———. *What After Iraq?* New York: Pearson Longman, 2009.

Tanner, Stephen. *Afghanistan: A Military History from Alexander the Great to the War Against the Taliban*. Boston: Da Capo Press, 2009.

Tomsen, Peter. *The Wars of Afghanistan: Messianic Terrorism, Tribal Conflicts, and the Failure of the Great Powers*. New York: Public Affairs, 2013.

U.S. Marine Corps. *Afghanistan: Operational Culture for Deploying Personnel*. Quantico, VA: Center for Advanced Operational Cultural Learning, 2009.

Weston, J. Karl. *The Mirror Test: America at War in Iraq and Afghanistan*. New York: Vintage Books, 2016.

CHAPTER FOUR

Russia and Ukraine in 2022

The Face of Modern Mayhem?

It has been a principal burden of the preceding chapters to establish that the conduct of warfare has changed fundamentally since World War II. The shift has been both geographic and substantive: war is no longer regularly conducted in the places and by the means by which it was historically fought. Not only has the organization and ways in which war is fought changed, but so have its participants and the reasons that warfare is conducted. The idea of warfare as an interstate phenomenon conducted by the forces of the most developed sovereign states for geographic or political purposes has decreased; states still fight, but it is different states than it used to be, and they fight for different reasons and in different ways than previously. Military force still has the purpose of changing some situations from the advantage of one group to that of another, but how and where it is conducted are not the same as they used to be.

Most post-1945 military planning was based on an extrapolation of World War II, and such a war could still break out—most likely accidentally. Thus, it represents a contingency for which states must prepare, but it is not the only or even arguably the most likely contingency for which those forces are maintained. Things have changed; nuclear weapons epitomize those changes.

Parts of the post–WWII scenarios for another global conflict still exist. Although they are no longer communists, the Russians remain the state with the most overt pretensions to superpower status with the United States (although one can argue they have lost their leading aspirant status to China).

The 2022 conflict over the relationship between the Ukraine and NATO discussed in this chapter demonstrates that their pretension remains. The Russians face a probably impossible task of asserting hegemonic status in central Eurasia, but they (notably Vladimir Putin) are trying desperately to cling to their Cold War mantle as a superpower. Their threats to the Ukrainians and NATO-US responses across the cold, winter-swept Eurasian frontier represent what has become the equivalent of the great-power rivalry of the second half of the twentieth century. The evolution and management of this crisis provides us with some insight into how changes have occurred in traditional great-power conflict. Both sides prepare for conventional war and issue veiled, vague threats about the consequences of noncompliance with their demands while mobilizing forces they have essentially no intention of placing in the kinds of harm's way that could lead to uncontrolled escalation. The dynamics reflect the impact of nuclear weapons on the structure of violence: nuclear powers may threaten one another and puff out their geopolitical chests, but they do not let matters get out of hand to the point that some advertent or inadvertent occurrence causes the crisis to devolve to nuclear exchange.

A paramount result is that the primary locus of probable future war is no longer between traditional enemies on the European continent, although there are occasional exceptions like the current brouhaha over Ukraine. International disagreements between European contestants and their allies are relatively rare and mostly confined to the transition of states that were formerly parts of the Soviet Union such as Ukraine or the Baltic states to more independent status. The likelihood that these disagreements might escalate to direct confrontation and war between Russia and the West are reasonably remote, because no one on either side is anxious to find out what happens if nuclear-armed foes clash. This is especially true of the potential combatants themselves.

There have been two basic dynamics that have created this change in warfare. One "culprit," of course, has been the impact of nuclear weapons. Most of the traditional participants in modern warfare were the traditional "great" powers in Europe and North America. These countries are the ones who either themselves possess or are aligned with nuclear weapons states. Those states' military plans are inhibited by the realization that any violent clash between them could escalate to nuclear war by processes that are not fully known and could cross the nuclear threshold and endanger human civilization. Odd though it may be to phrase this way, but war between those antagonistic states is no longer acceptable behavior, because it is potentially self-destructive, an inhibition that should be remembered when predicting the trajectory of possible great-power clashes. In contemporary dialog and speculation, the only big power conflict that seems possible to some involves the United States and China clashing, but the same inhibiting effect of nuclear weapons almost certainly precludes such a war breaking out. In fact, the physical distance between the two current superpowers is such that it would almost certainly have to be a clash of nontraditional sources such as nuclear-tipped rockets and missiles, making it virtually inevitable that a nuclear clash would destroy both.

This inhibition and aversion results from fear of the consequences of direct war between nuclear powers. It does not arise because the powers no longer have the kinds of differences or harbor the same animosities they had before nuclear weapons changed the rules of interaction. Communism and anti-communism provided the reasons for disagreement and conflict in 1945, and they could have led to post-1945 war between the major powers that was widely expected in the latter 1940s. What changed was not a flood of comity between the traditional combatants or the renunciation of war (and especially European-style conflict); it was fear of what that war could become. The rivalries and hatreds remained and were still present (and in some cases even intensified), but it was fear of the consequences that provided—and continues to provide—a sufficient uncertainty to prevent the recourse to war. Nuclear weapons did not make the reasons and motivations to fight disappear; instead, the quite rightful fear of the consequences provided that inhibition. Competition could, and sometimes did, activate the military motivation and thus preparation for war; fear of the possibilities dampened those emotions. To say that nuclear weapons dissuaded positive war decision may be praise by faint damn, but it apparently worked: we are all still here. In the latter 1940s and early 1950s, many people doubted such a "happy" evolution.

This dynamic extends to the second change, which is where war does and can occur, between whom, for what reasons, and how. One of the most obvious implications of a nuclear-inhibited prohibition on war was that the motives and dynamics leading to conflict—which did not disappear—would have to find new venues and rationales that allowed the competing sides to act out their animosities without fearing that doing so would deteriorate into direct, possibly nuclear, combat between them. Decolonization of the Afro-Asian world provided the context and rationale for the resulting movement of great-power rivalry and interaction away from Europe to Africa and Asia, where the situation and ways to resolve it were markedly less lethal than the situations encountered in Europe.

The Ukrainian crisis of 2021–2022 helps define the ways that warfare has changed in both the purposes for which it is employed and the outcomes for which it is undertaken. It points to the inhibiting possibilities that the recourse to violence between nuclear possessors imposes on its possessors. Nuclear weapons, to simplify, create two contradictory changes: they simultaneously multiply the potential deadliness of conflict of war between possessors and their colleague states to unacceptable levels, and they produce greater inhibitions in those who possess those arsenals. By making warfare so potentially catastrophic, they have made the likelihood of the decision to engage in war less likely. In this sense, it is at least arguable to maintain they demonstrate that nuclear deterrence makes the world a less violence-prone place, or at least that the possibility of escalation makes the recourse to violence more dangerous than before.

The Balkan situation is not of the same order of magnitude in a global sense of danger as the war-producing situations of the twentieth century. For Americans, violence in Eastern Europe is more familiar and was part of the Cold War competition for some reasons apparent in the current confrontation in the Ukraine. Since Ukraine is located between traditional European powers like Germany and Poland and Russia, it has always been important to Russia, which has long evidenced an obsession with Ukraine's political situation and especially political relationship with them. When the Soviet Union dissolved, the political bond between Russia and the Ukraine shifted toward Ukrainian autonomy from Russia, a condition that Putin and his regime find intolerable and seek to modify. The current crisis along the Ukrainian-Russian border is a reprise of a long history of conflict between Ukrainians and Russians in a different context. Historically, Ukraine was a buffer against invasions eastward. Now, it is also a symbol of continued Russian great-power pretense.

Russia and Ukraine have, by virtue of geography, always been rivals. Ukraine's location between the West and Russia assures that Russia will always have an interest in protecting itself in this traditional invasion route into the Russian motherland. Geography curses Ukraine and makes it a geographic victim in international power politics. It is a medium-sized power: it has a physical area about the size of Texas and had a population of about 44 million in 2019. Like so much of Europe (including that of Russia), its population is projected to shrink to about 37 million in 2050, leaving the Ukraine as a vulnerable buffer between the traditional powers of Western Europe and Russia (the Russian population, once over 300 million as the Soviet Union, is now about 140 million and shrinking). The road eastward to Russia runs through Ukraine (and depending on route chosen, past the site of the world's worst nuclear accident site at Chernobyl). Who exercises interest or control of Ukraine thus has potential importance to any political entity seeking to move from west to east or east to west across Europe. That location is the curse of this medium-sized power, which is condemned to be a pawn in the calculus of any state or group of states seeking to expand or reinforce its status. The competition between Russia and NATO over who will exercise influence within the Ukrainian state today is just the latest version of a geographically determined competition in which the Ukrainians are the effective pawns.

During the Cold War, American policy was officially neutral regarding relations between the two competitors. The Ukraine was a state within the Soviet Union, a status that disappeared when the Soviet state dissolved. Freed of its bonds as a formal part of the Russian empire, Ukraine developed a more independent stance vis-à-vis post-Soviet Russia, a change that has most recently included a flirtation with NATO. This initiative toward the West is both a threat and an affront to Russia; it potentially threatens the physical separation of Russia from the West. To make matters worse from a Russian vantage point, the Western threat is most clearly associated with the continuing vitality of NATO and the admission of several former Soviet satellites to membership and other forms of association.

In this context, it is not difficult to understand the Russian attempt to create and maintain a pro-Russian political leadership in western Russia and Ukraine. Advocacy among some Ukrainians to associate their country formally with NATO is like poking a stick in the eye of the current Russian leadership and thus defines the current kerfuffle from a Russian viewpoint. As we will discuss later in the chapter, the situation is particularly irksome to Vladimir Putin, who has effectively tied his not insignificant concern for his legacy to the restoration of Russia as the dominant power in that part of Eurasia. An independent, and especially hostile, Ukraine endangers that status. The Ukrainian situation is thus important because it is a continuation of a Cold War irritant that challenges Russia's role as a superpower. If not opposed, the Ukrainian flirtation with NATO vividly demonstrates the diminishing role of Russia in the world. Given Putin's apparent determination to restore Russia to great-power status during his remaining tenure in power, the reasons for the current conflict thus begin to take shape and direction.

Defining Parameters in 2022: The Ukrainian Case

The conflict between Russia and Ukraine is an important example of how contemporary international violent behavior has been affected by the military situation in a world of nuclear weapons. These weapons do not necessarily have a direct, overt impact on those relations or on the potential military or current situation, but the extent to which the Ukrainian quest for self-determination places them at odds with Russia gives the situation a lingering Cold War flavor that has added a significant NATO-Russian overlay, raising Cold War questions about whether the situation could deteriorate into direct East-West military conflict, possibly beginning quite conventionally but with the possibility it could expand based on how events unfold. As the crisis unfolded during winter 2022, the prospects of a major transformation to a nuclear power confrontation may have been slight. The outcome of the conflict may be important to the Russians and Ukrainians, but it hardly rises to the point where either side is willing potentially to put world existence on the line. Thus, in this case, the conflict in Ukraine may be important to both parties, but not to the point of allowing it to escalate totally out of control. Simply put, the Russian-Ukrainian conflict is not worth an inadvertent escalation to nuclear exchange, the avoidance of which is a cardinal value of all sides. Could this situation somehow devolve into general war like something that was envisaged in Cold War scenarios? Such a devolution is conceivable in the sense that anything one can think about is conceivable. The likelihood of this happening is very low, and the structure of a military system with nuclear weapons at its core is certainly part of why that is true. The Ukrainian-Russian border is simply not worth the risk, and that takes a lot of options off the table.

The evolving situation demonstrates these limiting dynamics of nuclear weapons. The two principal players in the current conflict are Putin's Russia and the government of the Ukraine, which seeks to distance itself from a historically hostile, even aggressive Russia that has sought to control Ukrainian politics through the threat or employment of renewed Russian military intimidation. The heart of the problem lies in the desire of the Ukrainians to separate themselves politically and otherwise from Russian rule and control. It is a reciprocal relationship: the Russians oppose Ukrainian separatism on the grounds that the more independent Ukraine becomes, the more anti-Russian it is also likely to become. There has always been a Russian or Ukrainian minority on the other's soils, and both have strong nationalist roots. The Russian minority has been in control when Russia could exercise power over the territory of Ukraine, but the Ukrainians enjoy some autonomy to rule themselves. Whenever these desires (Ukrainian autonomy, Russian control) come into conflict (as they often do) there is an incendiary possibility that can lead to war. The 2022 crisis is just the latest instance of that dynamic.

There is another less well publicized influence that may provide the real motivation for Russian actions: the ego of Vladimir Putin defined largely in geopolitical, Cold War terms. It is commonly recognized (although not always stated), that Russian assertive capability and status as a superpower are approaching a last gasp, which has sizable implications for the myth of Russian sway in international affairs. Russia arguably reached its pinnacle as a world power during the Cold War years, and demographic realities do not favor the Soviets. A large portion of non-Russian Soviet territory seceded at the first opportunity in 1991, and this had two obvious outcomes, both unfavorable in population terms for the Russian/Soviet state.

The Ukraine occupies an unenviable physical position regarding Russian aspirations to be treated both as a dominant member of the European balance and as a Eurasian power. It is the largest buffer state between the Russian state and traditional European powers (its largest contiguous neighbors are Russia to the east and Poland to the west). Its buffer role with Russia has been particularly important to the Russians, because the Ukraine is part of the central route for the invasion of Russia from Europe. World War II was the last time this route was employed, and postwar Soviet/Russian foreign policy has had as a first principle ensuring that the route is closed permanently.

Ukraine is thus a very central part of Russian/Soviet position in the world. Recognizing this, it is probably of more than symbolic importance that the first non-Russian leader of the Soviet Union, Nikita Khrushchev, was a Ukrainian national, and the two countries have had a long and frequently contentious history. Especially from a Russian geopolitical vantage point, establishing a neutral/friendly regime in the Ukraine is close to a core value. Because of Russia's size and history with them, it is also unsurprising that Ukrainian nationalists would seek as much autonomy from Russia as they can achieve. The pro-Western sentiment manifested in the Ukrainian desire to associate itself with the European Union and NATO makes sense from the vantage point of Ukrainians; suspicion, even fear, of such a movement also makes geopolitical sense from a Russian perspective. These adversarial perspectives flare up periodically; 2022 is the latest instance.

The Incendiary Potential of the 2022 Crisis: A Presage to a Larger War?

As the crisis developed during January 2022, it assumed familiar proportions. Those former parts of the old Soviet empire where Russian influence remains the most significant are European facing, have significant European cultural and other preferences, and want, to the extent doing so is possible, to align themselves with the West. The most contentious expression of this desire is for political and thus potentially military relations with NATO, and this sentiment includes support among those former Eastern European states who were members of the Warsaw Pact and even some of the members of the former Soviet Union itself. The Ukraine, which was invaded and partly dismembered in 2014 when the Russians reconsolidated their control of Crimea, is a prime example.

Such desires both threaten and demean the Russians, and they have regularly sought to suppress them. The most threatening possibility from a Russian vantage point is formal association of Eastern European states with NATO, and especially full membership in NATO for former parts of the Soviet state. Such an association is what the Ukrainians have proposed, and the Russian movement of troops to the Ukrainian frontier is evidence of their concern. If states historically part of the Russian security orbit can freely disassociate themselves from their historically dominant neighbor, what does this say of what remains of Russian power and status as the dominant regional power? The Russian action is at least partly a reminder to the Ukrainians (and anyone else who harbors aspirations of independence from Russian hegemony) that these relations have not fundamentally changed. From a Russian vantage point, the major geopolitical function that states like Ukraine fulfill is to provide a buffer for Russia against future incursions from the West. The Soviet Cold War empire provided such a barrier, but it has eroded. From the vantage point of Russia, its actions toward Ukraine are at least partly a way to remind both Ukraine and any predators in the West that the barriers have not disappeared. Russia is still Russia.

In this context, just how dangerous is this latest Russian action? More importantly, does it greatly threaten to devolve into a military confrontation with Russia on one side and NATO-backed Ukraine on the other? As an extension of the Cold War analogy, does the Ukrainian crisis carry within it the possibility of a major military confrontation between East and West with significant escalatory potential? Before the Cold War and the introduction of nuclear weapons to the military calculus in the region, that incendiary potential might have seemed great, particularly if the Ukrainian initiative had gained significant support in the West. Such support exists today and has been expressed as the crisis has dragged out, but does that mean that war is a possible, even likely outcome of the crisis? The answer is, of course, speculative. This crisis has been leavened by the possibility that a crisis could result in Chernobyl on a much greater scale if diplomacy fails. That means there is a much greater momentum to resolve the issues short of major conflict than there might have been in an earlier time. Military possibilities dampen military actions.

The heart of the conflict, of course, is the Russian demand that Ukraine back away from the stated desire of some Ukrainians to join the NATO alliance. The positions on both sides are understandable and will likely be included in the eventual settlement of the current crisis. The Ukrainians have an entirely reasonable interest and desire to establish and reinforce a non-dependent relationship with Moscow, as do other states in the region (e.g., the Baltic states), which have historically been reluctant associates or parts or dependents of Russia in the Soviet Union. NATO affiliation is one way to pursue greater autonomy from Russia. These political communities have every reason not to trust the Russians, who view them primarily as buffer zones where the next Western invasion of Russia will be fought somewhere other than on Russian soil. For Russia, the current crisis is very much an exercise in territorial integrity.

Given Russian history culminated by the Napoleonic invasion and Hitler's assault, creating a buffer zone where a future attack can be confronted short of Russian soil makes ultimate good and defensible sense. A Ukrainian proposal to join the Western alliance (NATO) is hostile and unacceptable to Russian security interests given Russian history and relations between Russia and NATO since the dissolution of the Soviet empire. Talks have been held periodically about Russian membership or special status within NATO, but they have never reached fruition due to disagreement on what the Russian role might be. Ukrainians simply want to be freed of the Russian yoke with international support for their independence. This sets the parameters of conflict: Russia's desire to be insulated from a future hostile invasion from the west versus Ukraine's desire not to be a vassal state of Russia. The problem is that devising a solution that satisfies both parties has been the victim of mutual distrust and animosity. If the solution was easy, it probably would already have been reached.

This creates the problem, of course, of how to offer acceptable assurances to the Russians and the Ukrainians that neither will be subject to threat or incursion by the other or its minions: how does one guarantee security for both? Russian flirtation with NATO has not and probably cannot reach an ultimate positive conclusion. NATO, after all, was initially formed in the late 1940s primarily as an anti-Soviet (read anti-Russian by many Russians) Cold War contrivance, and many members and supporters of NATO believe that is still its primary function. NATO effectively provides a barrier to Russian expansionism and, to many in Eastern Europe, a barrier to a reinvigorated Russian incursion on their freedom and independence. Russia opposes NATO as an anti-Russian construct the purpose of which is to constrict Russian expansion and weaken its security. Its reasons are clear: that is the primary historical purpose of the alliance, and also the activism of the Ukrainians to formalize a relationship ensuring that separation.

Both sides have partisan virtue: the Ukraine (along with other Eastern European countries) wants a formalized guarantee that Russia will not attack them in the future, and membership in NATO is one possible vehicle to provide that guarantee. From a Russian perspective, such a guarantee is not benign: those who seek reliable assurance (such as the Ukrainians) are historical enemies of Russia and have occasionally participated in active anti-Russian behavior such as collaboration with those menacing or attacking Russia.

The problem is reciprocal: the Russian position is a mirror image of how the non-Russian peoples on the Russian periphery feel about the Russians. Very simply, most people on the Russian periphery (and part of the historic Russian sphere of influence) do not trust the Russians and want to be maximally independent of the Russian bear. Is Ukrainian nationalism and desire for guaranteed protection from Russian interference from Russia sincere? Yes. Is it baseless? Of course not. In that part of the world animosities are deep, long-standing, and entirely sincere. In those circumstances, is an arrangement that would guarantee protection for the Eastern European former parts of the Soviet Union potentially attractive? Of course it is! The problem is trying to find a nonviolent way to achieve that goal that provides an acceptable, enforceable agreement that both assures the integrity of Russian soil from a future invasion while simultaneously protecting countries like Ukraine from Russian intimidation or worse. From that vantage point, who must be willing to sacrifice what to form the basis for a viable peace? That is the heart of the geopolitical dilemma.

And Then There Is Putin

There is another, less publicly discussed basis that reflects Russian politics: the role and legacy of Vladimir Putin, which is an international geopolitical concern. In important, largely demographic terms Russia, as already chronicled, is clearly a superpower in decline. The most dramatic harbinger for the Russian future is that the country's population is shrinking both absolutely and relatively in the hierarchy of states. Unless something unforeseen occurs, by the middle of the current century, the Russian population will be less than a third that of the United States at under 100 million compared to an American projection of nearly 350 million. Russia's economy is also in an unenviable situation for future growth. Because it has the world's second-largest petroleum reserves under the Arctic and the frozen tundra of its landmass, the leadership has effectively converted the country into being a "petrostate" where economic activity and prosperity are effectively the hostage of petroleum production and sales. This dependence has produced acceptable results in terms of both financing Russian military power and underwriting citizen standards of living and satisfaction until now, but it is not a strategy that can sustain the Russian geopolitical position indefinitely.

As a world power, Russia is thus in a barely disguisable downward spiral that Putin, through an aggressive foreign policy, is trying to hide. It is not clear whether this situation was entirely avoidable. The debilitating effects of being a petrostate are recognized as a contributing factor to decline and instability in heavily oil-dependent regions of Africa and Latin America, and it is central to the Putin-based Russian equation as well. The problem is that petroleum-generated wealth is a transitory tool of the past that has limited potential for achieving long-term economic success in the future. The Russians have been basing their status and role on oil, and this is not a viable long-term status in a world where the influence of oil is declining. Oil wealth has hidden this vulnerability until now, but it cannot last. Unless Russia can somehow reverse its demographic and economic difficulties, its future is one of inevitable decline that seems impossible to reverse or contain in the medium to long term. Russia's future sway in the international system is in jeopardy, and the regime understands this and is acting aggressively to insulate its future from the inevitable debilitating consequences.

No one is more aware of these dynamics than Russian President Vladimir Putin, who must know he is in a desperate and probably losing struggle to maintain Russia's status as a superpower. Russia reached the pinnacle of its influence in international politics as the Soviet Union, and it has been in a basic free fall since the collapse of the Soviet state. Putin, of course, is the inheritor of this decline and has made the restoration of superpower status the major foreign policy dream of his regime.

Putin at seventy is, however, aging, and the time he has available to accomplish this transformation is circumscribed both by his own longevity and the demographic constraints of a declining population and an economy overly dependent on oil. Unless something changes dramatically, Russia's situation is not going to improve materially, and those restive states adjacent to Russia and historically in the security orbit of Russia are aware of this. A generation ago, Ukrainians would not have seriously entertained open advocacy of formal association with NATO; Putin's actions toward the incipient rebellion suggests that he is reminding those states that Russia is still around and is still the dominant state in the region. It is also a reminder that the Russians are not above enforcing the traditional order by military threats and the use of force.

The amassing of large numbers of Russian troops on the Ukraine border and into Ukraine (over 100,000) was a classic Cold War–era response to the challenge posed by demographics. In a very real sense, the scenario that unfolded in January 2022 was a reprise of 2014, when Russian troops occupied and annexed the Crimean region of what the Ukrainians consider part of their sovereign territory. In that instance, the international community condemned the Russian action and took some mostly symbolic actions to express their displeasure, but the Russians essentially got away with the seizure and annexation, which stand to this day and seem a model for Putin's latest actions, and if he succeeds, possibly the future.

The confrontation has followed predictable patterns of Russian-Western interaction. The Ukraine is on the Russian perimeter, and Russia has claimed primary influence on those areas that are buffers between itself and the European balance of power for a variety of reasons that include geopolitical and status reasons, as well as kinships between some of the peoples involved. The relationship between the Russians living in these historically Russian-dominated states and their counterparts in Europe and in the Mediterranean has always been adversarial: the Russians have claimed primary influence in areas where that relationship is denied by the inhabitants, and the Russians have been powerful enough to retain primary status regardless of the desires of the others, whether they be residents of the Crimea, other parts of Ukraine, the Baltic states, or territories washing on Russia's limited warm-water access to the Mediterranean or beyond. During the Cold War, Russian sway over its "empire" was accepted by the West as simply a part of the international geopolitics. The collapse of the Soviet Union weakened or broke the coercive hold the Russians had on those non-Russian territories on their frontiers. Particularly as Russia has sought to establish a geopolitical presence in the new system and those former Soviet states who were reluctant parts of the empire have sought greater autonomy, the result has been a level of tension that boils over from time to time; the crisis of 2022 is the latest manifestation. The basic question is how important and combustible this kind of tension is and whether it should be the potential cause of American recourse to arms. It is a question worth considering, because Russian antipathy with the West is one of a relatively few phenomena involving the major powers that has the potential to escalate to armed conflict in which the United States could be directly involved.

Trying to answer the question begins by determining what motivates the Russians in the current crisis. Certainly part of the reason for the Russian action is symbolic: it is a reminder to the rest of the world that Russia is still a major power—even a superpower—and that its interests must be honored and respected. Vladimir Putin, after all, is a product of the Soviet era where a Russian sphere of primacy and primary interest was established and expected, and the Ukrainian flirtation with NATO (open advocacy of joining a military alliance formed nearly three-quarters of a century ago as a counterweight to Soviet power and assertiveness symbolizes a rejection of that special status and even potentially involves the addition of parts of the old Soviet empire to the aggregation of less-than-friendly governments on Soviet borders). At a minimum, the Ukrainian flirtation with NATO shows a disrespect for Russian status that no former Soviet veteran of the Cold War competition could readily accept either on geopolitical grounds (having actively hostile regimes literally on their border) or as an implicit admission that Russia has become just another major power that can be treated accordingly as important but not as possessing a veto over international actions. Russian demographics may be headed in the wrong direction; the rumblings from Kiev simply amplify a change in status, and one cannot expect Putin to embrace or, to the extent he can avoid it, tolerate these trends. Is he acting because the time he can without invoking the nuclear card is closing for him?

The War Worthiness of the Ukrainian Crisis: Before and After the Impact of Nuclear Weapons

Does the current confrontation between Russia and Ukraine rise to the level where war between Russia and the West represents a viable possible avenue, an acceptable way of settling an international disagreement about the status of Ukraine in Eastern Europe and East-West politics? Before the addition of potential nuclear conflict between the participants, the answers to that question were very different than they are today. Alterations of the map of Europe by force, after all, provided the proximate causes leading to world war twice in the last century. The process leading to World War I in the Balkans is a prime example, but that occurred in a situation where the recourse to war did not include calculating the possibility that such actions could devolve into Armageddon. In the nuclear age, the question of escalation brings two adversaries with nuclear capability into potential direct conflict. How does that change alter the contemplation of war—on both sides?

One can overstate and oversimplify the comparability of the pre-nuclear and nuclear cases. Mutual nuclear possession by Russia and America now spans almost three-quarters of a century, after all, and since both sides peered figuratively over the precipice of potential nuclear war in the Cuban missile crisis and decided no gains justified the possible dangers of nuclear escalation, the weapons have not been used and the quality of relations between them has moderated. More nuclear states have been added, and in one case (India and Pakistan) new nuclear powers have confronted one another in battle. During that 1990s crisis, some analysts nervously contemplated the possible escalation of that example of the violent conflict between the two in terms of potential escalation, but both sides backed away from the brink and the world breathed a sigh of relief. Kashmir (the focus of the conflict) is and remains a major source of conflict between India and Pakistan, but they have at least implicitly agreed that it is not worth destroying humankind over.

How does the Ukrainian crisis fit into the reasoning surrounding nuclear escalation and the influence of the shadow of the mushroom shaped cloud (an analogy I introduced in a 1978 monograph) influence the evolution and settlement of the conflict over Ukraine and its flirtation with the West? In the last third of the twentieth century (at least before the implosion of the Soviet Union), the perspective and prognosis would have been quite different than contemporary analysis of the confrontation between Russia and Ukraine suggests. Ukraine was not, during most of that period, a sovereign state but was instead part of the Soviet empire; thus consideration of Russian-Ukrainian relations would have been a question of intra-Soviet politics. Any Soviet espousing something like Ukrainian alignment with the West would have been harshly and summarily dealt with by the regime in Moscow. Despite some Western expressions of sympathy with the plight of any dissidents proposing loosening the bonds between Moscow and one of its effective vassal states, the incident would have remained effectively outside international relations as a matter of internal Soviet politics. Losing that control over the former empire has been one of the most difficult, even humiliating, phenomena with which Moscow—and particularly Putin—have had to deal. Given geography, history, and geopolitics, Moscow's threat of armed intervention in Ukraine is not surprising but rather a continuation (or reassertion) of the Soviet historical order.

The Ukrainians, of course, have never been enthusiastic vassals of Russian/Soviet overlordship, but neither have they possessed the temerity to express in quite such defiant, geopolitically confrontational ways in the past. Put colloquially, the fear of the Russian bear used to guarantee enforced Russian domination of Europe east of the Cold War boundary between NATO and the Warsaw Pact. The dissolution of the Soviet Union moved the boundary eastward; much of the Warsaw Pact is now part of NATO, and other parts seek affiliation. The Ukrainians have proposed moving NATO to the long Russian frontier with Ukraine. If Ukrainian interests in NATO are realized, Russia has a potentially hostile military arrangement on its borders and appears to be just another part of the European balance, hardly the status of an unquestionable superpower. That prospect, while arguably inevitable in the long run, is simply too much for Putin and his regime to accept. The Russian buildup on the Ukrainian boundary is, in many ways, a reminder to Ukraine and its neighbors that Russia is still the "big dog" in the neighborhood. The neighborhood, however, has nuclear weapons on both sides as a conditioning and limiting element on how those big dogs "play."

Resolving the Ukrainian Crisis

Vladimir Putin and his calculations about what actions may or may not upset relations among the major states is obviously the key element in the evolution of the 2022 crisis. Both sides, Ukrainians and Russians, have arguably reasonable bases for the positions they have taken. The Ukrainians would clearly like to have the protection of Article 5 of the NATO charter (the heart of which is that "an attack against one is an attack against all" and will be met with unspecified resistance) to back them up and protect them from traditional Russian predatory actions, and Russia has historical geopolitical reasons for wanting the cordon sanitaire represented by non-hostile neighbors—a situation they feel is threatened by anything resembling formal Ukrainian ties to the West. Neither side trusts the other; both suspicions are undoubtedly valid in large measure and thus difficult to resolve in a manner acceptable both politically and geopolitically by both.

In the past, when the escalatory possibilities did not include planetary devastation, there is less question whether Russia would have invaded, successfully overcome whatever resistance the Ukrainians could provide, and returned them to their historic vassal's status and plight. NATO would probably have protested and decried the Russian action and condemned it in international fora like the United Nations. In the end, Russian interests would have been served, and the incident would have been just another example of why being located next to a major power can compromise one's independence. Certainly the Russians would probably not have hesitated to invade, crush the heresy in Ukraine, and return Ukraine to its subservient position as a buffer state between Western Europe and Russia. That may be the ultimate outcome, but it has not unfolded as easily as it once would have. Russia massed forces on the Ukrainian frontier, issued warnings, and made predatory gestures. But when those gestures were not heeded, they did not act decisively, instead blaming the West for provocative attitudes. The Russians clearly want to be accorded the superpower status they possessed during the Cold War; it is not so clear whether the actual employment of overwhelming Russian force is their preferred method to do so in a nuclear world where the use of that force is potentially suicidal.

The Russians thus must have another, less obvious objective in the crisis, and that is the reestablishment (or recognition) of Russia as a global superpower with continued major sway over Eastern European affairs. Whether the designation is pretentious or not, Russia is still the regional hegemon, and both regional states and outsiders must recognize and honor Russian primacy and interests in the region. There may not be a current obvious threat to that status, but the creeping incursion of NATO into the area feeds a Russian paranoia toward the area that has a long history. Due to population declines, Russian demographics may work against its global pretensions as a superpower, but it remains the largest, most dominant state in the subregion and demands that its status be recognized and acknowledged. Adjacent states like Ukraine may see an opening toward greater independence that allows them to associate more closely with the states of NATO, but such initiatives are bound to clash with the Russian self-image of its regional supremacy. The difficult key to an enduring, viable settlement is somehow to craft a political atmosphere where Russia remains secure (which includes a belief in its regional supremacy) and Eastern European states (e.g., Ukraine) believe in their statuses as independent states. Russian troops on the Ukrainian border invading eastern Ukraine does not provide a long-term solution to that problem, but Russia is in increasing need of some accommodation that both protects at least the semblance of Russian superpower status and prohibits future predation from historic rivals.

Russia is thus in a difficult situation. The long-term solutions are not obvious and may not be favorable to their future status. Size has always been Russia's hole card: it is physically the largest country in the world, and its population used to be one of the top three among states. There are no immediate threats to the physical size of the country, although territories on the peripheries like Georgia and Ukraine that are not part of Great Russia per se would clearly like to establish a more autonomous relationship with the center, which Moscow predictably resists. The physical mass of Russia may be subject to some peripheral decay, but internal demographic realities are the real problem. If population projections are accurate, by the middle of the present century, the population of Russia could be only slightly larger than 100 million (some estimates are lower than that). Global population is expected to level off (the US population at mid-century will probably be around 350 million), but the effect will be particularly damaging for Russia. A sizable population mass will no longer be a meaningful contributor to Russian great-power status.

The Russian economic situation is similarly unpromising. In traditional developmental terms, Russia has always lagged the other traditional European states. Its claim to status has been based on its sheer physical size and population. Russia was big and backward, but it was also effectively almost impossible to subdue because there were so many Russians spread over such a large mass. The land mass remains, but the population is shrinking. Moreover, it is not a particularly distinguished population: it remains by many measures a developing country, and one whose future status among the great powers remains questionable.

The only measure by which Russia remains a great power is military, and more specifically nuclear, power. That power is, however, a double-edged sword. It gives the Russians great physical power, but since it has equivalent power arrayed against it, that power is self-limiting. What happens to Russia as it moves into Ukraine? Possibly nothing; Western warnings of dire consequences could prove to be bluffs, or they could not. As the crisis has unfolded, the West, led by the Biden administration, warned of dire consequences but did not specify what they were, beyond aid to Ukraine. The imputation was that they would be primarily economic, an area where the Russians are notably vulnerable (and especially rich members of the Russian elite with huge bankrolls in Western banks). Massing tanks on the Ukrainian border used to be the lingua franca of gaining compliance; things are a bit more complex in a nuclear world. It is now more acceptable for Putin to pose with the Chinese leadership at the Beijing Winter Olympics than it is to saber rattle. Times have changed.

The possibility of escalation of any conflict, including the recourse to armed forces that might have nuclear capability, changes the calculus for everyone involved. An incursion into Ukraine to remind the Ukrainians of Russian dominance is one thing if the costs are a limited number of casualties and condemnation by the United Nations. Such possibilities have limited and arguably acceptable consequences, and the Russians have demonstrated in the past in places like Georgia that they are willing to take their chances in such situations. But the Ukrainian situation is arguably different. A Russian power grab could still trigger a response from the NATO forces arrayed against it, and how that response might be constituted—and what unanticipated or underestimated results might occur—may be different. An invasion of an adjacent state that results in a negative General Resolution in the United Nations is one thing; an occupation in which the possibility of purposeful or inadvertent escalation to nuclear war is quite another.

One can argue that the likelihood of nuclear escalation is very low, possibly negligible in any given situation, but it is not absent altogether. The demands by some Ukrainians for what amounts to full inclusion in the Western alliance are potentially consequential, especially to the Russians. The West has, after all, invaded Russia in the past, the cordon sanitaire afforded by the Warsaw Pact as a buffer to stop a future invasion short of Russian territory has evaporated as NATO has incorporated former parts of that barrier, and the calls from within Ukraine for inclusion in NATO are a direct repudiation of the attraction of the barrier regionally. It is impossible to know exactly how seriously the Russians regard calls from Ukraine to move NATO to the Russian border (the physical effect of incorporating Ukraine into NATO), but it is not unreasonable to admit that this is a matter of concern to them. The movement of over 100,000 Russian forces to the border area may be a slightly hysterical reaction; that Russia finds these initiatives important is a matter of national security.

Look briefly at the demands the Russians had made as of early February 2020 to resolve the crisis short of the use of the forces they have amassed along the border. Basically, there are three components. First, the Russians demand that Ukraine never be allowed to join NATO. That demand is not entirely unreasonable in a geopolitical sense: imagine how the United States would have reacted to a proposal to include Mexico in the Warsaw Pact during the Cold War. Second, the Russians demand that NATO halt additional NATO force deployment near Russian borders; there are already NATO forces in the Baltic states, so this is a matter both of national integrity and national pride parallel to American reactions to Russian presence in Cuba. The Russians really do not need to be reminded physically of their military decline in other than nuclear terms; making Ukraine a NATO ally and thus part of the forces confronting Russia only magnifies that reminder. Third, the Russians demand that NATO forces already near its boundaries be rolled back westward and that there be no increase in Western presence in Eastern Europe. This is a matter both of national defense to provide additional physical protection to the Russian state and to lessen the psychological impact of continued encirclement: they seek a binding guarantee of Russian security from attack from Europe. Both sides have a point: Eastern European states want to feel secure from renewed Russian domination; Russia wants security from European threats.

What is striking about these demands is what the effects would be of accommodating them, and how such an accommodation could be made palatable to both the Russians and the Ukrainians. The fact that the Russians have not unceremoniously invaded Ukraine and crushed Ukrainian opposition—which they largely did in reannexing the Crimea—shows how things have changed. The Russians have implicitly threatened to crush Ukrainian anti-Russian activism by moving their forces to the border, but they have consistently denied any intention of an aggression against that territory (a pledge the sincerity of which is not accepted in Kiev or in most of the west). Will they move at all? The longer they do not, the more likely it is that their credibility will decline in the region and even globally. That is certainly not a perception the Russians nurture or which their reputation as an unquestioned superpower can survive untarnished. The situation cannot remain static indefinitely without making the Russian movement of troops to the Ukrainian border seem like a hollow bluff, a perception Putin is unlikely to accept. What to do?

The nuclear factor helps provide an avenue for settlement with face-saving virtues for all sides. Russia may be an otherwise diminished power today, but it remains a full-scale nuclear power, and their possession of the nuclear arsenal and the nuclear relationship with other similarly armed countries like the United States changes the dynamics of the situation. Imagine the lower status the world would accord Russia if it did not have nuclear weapons.

Would the Ukrainian situation have been solved differently without that backdrop of nuclear weapons? Would, in other words, the Russians have been more likely to have invaded Ukraine if doing so had not raised at least the possibility of an escalatory process in which nuclear weapons might have become involved? The answer is, of course, speculative and subject to change based on the evolution of events. Denying any aggressive intent and at least going through some semblance of achieving a peaceful revolution is, however, good international politics for the Russians to tamp down perceptions they are potential nuclear aggressors. Russia may seethe at the pronouncements from some Ukrainians about effectively extending the NATO geopolitical noose it perceives to be around its neck, but the Russian government is also not anxious to make moves that could brand them universally as the aggressor. More importantly, they are acting increasingly like a country that has concluded that it is unsure that consolidating their influence on Ukraine is worth the possibility of an escalation of the situation. Both sides profess resolve about what they feel is an acceptable outcome, but neither side appears anxious to push their preferences to the brink of actual war with uncertain escalatory possibilities. The Russians may act militantly by increasing forces near the Ukrainian border, but as of mid-autumn 2022, they had not physically invaded Ukraine proper with those forces.

While the outcome of the crisis remains uncertain, the prospects that the Russians will actually employ those massed forces are not as obvious as some of the rhetoric on both sides may suggest. Ukraine 2022 may be the "model" for major-power military interaction in the future. As one scans the geopolitical map, the cleavages that exist today are essentially the same as they were during the Cold War. The United States still leads the coalition of the major European powers, with Russia as the primary impediment to a tranquil relationship. The 2022 crisis, however, also offers some evidence that the fervor and explosiveness assumed during the Cold War may be waning.

The Ukrainian crisis is, after all, containable: assuming Ukraine is convinced to back away from its demands to be incorporated by NATO but instead is treated as a kind of independent dependency that NATO says it would defend outside any formal commitment, the peace could hold. The current crisis may be a kind of last hurrah for Russian global politics (and the crown jewel of Putin's maintenance of some semblance of Russia's continuing status as a superpower). It is Putin's self-legacy based in the traumas that Russia has endured since 1991. Russia and the West do not need to be and probably will never be the best of friends; they can, however, agree not to destroy the world.

Conclusion: The Nuclear Prophylactic?

The Ukrainian crisis appears to demonstrate two apparently contradictory lessons. As the first major military standoff between East and West since 2014, it shows that there is still a potentially incendiary element in the world power balance. The Russians still have the capability to destroy the world, a capability matched by the West. At one level, this mutual possession is irrational; the possession by each is intended to keep the other from obliterating them both, which is the probable outcome if they use their arsenals. At the same time, each side fears that they have to keep their arsenal to prevent the other side from using theirs and destroying them both. Deterrence based on this dynamic truly demonstrates the logic of the insane that has dominated nuclear thinking since the 1940s. It lurks in the background of the current crisis, however.

Moreover, the Russians are willing to brandish their nuclear might in Eastern Europe when they feel it is necessary (Ukraine in NATO apparently demonstrates that feeling of need), and the West led by the United States has shown it will not readily back away from the challenge. In some ways, this crisis is the legacy of two-thirds of a century of animus that has at least a partially irrational base. At the same time, however, the crisis also shows how things have changed. The Russians have massed troops on the Ukraine frontier, but unlike 2014 in the Crimea, they have been slow to move them into Ukraine and consistently have maintained they have no aggressive plans to do so. All this, of course, may be posturing, but it also shows a restraint that has not always been part of relations in Europe and its peripheries.

Is the shadow of mushroom clouds the inhibiting factor? As one peruses the rhetoric surrounding the crisis, the concept of nuclear warfare rarely if ever is mentioned. It remains true that any shooting war between the West and Russia *could* devolve into nuclear exchange, and both sides know it. Moreover, although much energy has been devoted to trying to understand and predict the dynamics of warfare in which nuclear weapons use is a possibility, it also remains true that such thought remains speculative. Perversely enough, that may be a good thing, because it not only inhibits potential combatants but leaves others with expansive world visions more uncertain than they might otherwise be. The net effect, however, has been to make traditional European (including American) military relations different than they might otherwise be. Europe is not at peace, but Ukraine demonstrates that no one wants to take the chance of having it go to war. If nuclear powers cannot fight, the peripheries of the developing world in the form of asymmetrical warfare remain the likely battlegrounds of the foreseeable future, and they are—thankfully—largely nonnuclear for now. The upshot is, of course, at least partially irrational: we can fight in places that are not vital to our interests, but not where they are.

Bibliography

Altman, Dan, and Kathleen E. Powers. "When Redlines Fail: The Promise and Perils of Public Threats." *Foreign Affairs* (online), February 4, 2022.

Brands, Hal. "Does America Have More Rivals Than It Can Handle?" *Foreign Affairs* (online), January 18, 2022.

Committee on Foreign Relations, U.S. Senate. *Strategic Assessment of U.S.-Russian Relations.* New York: Create Space, 2018.

D'Anieri, Paul. *Ukraine and Russia: From Civilized Divorce to Uncivil War.* Cambridge, UK: Cambridge University Press, 2019.

Dawisha, Karen. *Putin's Kleptocracy: Who Owns Russia?* New York: Simon and Schuster, 2014.

Finucane, Brian. "The Unauthorized War: The Shaky Legal Ground for the U.S. Operation in Syria." *Foreign Affairs* (online), January 10, 2022.

Freedman, Lawrence. *Ukraine and the Art of Strategy.* Oxford, UK: Oxford University Press, 2019.

Gage, Beverly. "The Art of War: Can Culture Drive Geopolitics?" *Foreign Affairs* (online), January 1, 2022.

Gorbachev, Mikhail. *The New Russia*. Cambridge, UK: Polity Press, 2016.

Gotz, Elias, ed. *Russia, the West, and the Ukrainian Crisis*. New York and London: Routledge. 2019.

Mandelbaum, Michael. "The New Containment: Handling Russia, China, and Iran." *Foreign Affairs* 98, no. 2 (March/April 2019): 123–31.

Mathews, Jennifer T. "American Power After Afghanistan: How to Right-Size the Country's Global Role." *Foreign Affairs* (online), September 17, 2021.

Menen, Ryan, and Eugene B. Rumer. *Conflict in Ukraine: The Unwinding of the Post–Cold War Order*. Reprint ed. Cambridge, MA: MIT Press, 2015.

Nalbandov, Robert. *Not by Bread Alone: Russian Foreign Policy Under Putin*. Washington, DC: Potomac Books, 2016.

Plokhy, Serhii. *The Gates of Europe: A History of Ukraine*. New York: Basic Books, 2021.

Snow, Donald M. *Cases in U.S. National Security: Concepts and Processes*. Lanham, MD: Rowman & Littlefield, 2019.

———. *The Shape of the Future: The Post–Cold War World*. 3 eds. Armonk, NY: M. E. Sharpe, 1991, 1995, 1999.

Stent, Angela. *The Limits of Partnership: U.S.-Russian Relations in the Twenty-First Century*. Princeton, NJ: Princeton University Press, 2015.

———. "The Putin Doctrine: A Move on Ukraine Has Always Been Part of the Plan." *Foreign Affairs* (online), January 28, 2022.

———. *Putin's World: Russia Against the West and with the Rest*. New York: Twelve Books, 2020.

Toal, Bernard. *Near Abroad: Putin, the West, and the Contest over Ukraine and the Caucasus*. Oxford, UK: Oxford University Press, 2017.

Trenin, Dmitri. *Should We Fear Russia?* Cambridge, UK: Polity Press, 2016.

———. "What Putin Really Wants in Ukraine: Russia Seeks to Stop NATO's Expansion, Not to Annex More Territory." *Foreign Affairs* (online), February 11, 2022.

Tsyganov, Andrei. *Russia's Foreign Policy: Change and Continuity in National Identity*. 4th ed. Lanham, MD: Rowman & Littlefield, 2016.

Yaffa, Joshua. *Between Two Fires: Truth, Ambition, and Compromise in Putin's Russia*. New York: Random House, 2021.

Zurcher, Christoph. *The Post-Soviet Wars: Rebellion, Ethnicity, and Nationhood in the Caucasus*. New York: NYU Press, 2009.

CHAPTER FIVE

Contemporary Warfare and American Force
Conventional and Asymmetrical Warfare in the World

In light of the early 2022 confrontation between the West and Russia over the invasion of Ukraine, what kinds of circumstances may require or tempt the United States to commit its armed forces into harm's way in the near to mid future? Since the Korean war ended nearly seventy years ago, the United States has used its armed might several times, essentially exclusively in the developing world and especially, since 1979, in the Middle East. The messy withdrawal of the country from Afghanistan in 2021 probably signals a capping of American willingness to involve itself directly in the inevitable conflicts that break out in that region. A major conflict in which Israeli security was seriously compromised is the probable major exception, but Israeli nuclear weapons effectively make it the unchallengeable hegemon in that traditional spot.

The traditional venues for the traditional application of developed world forces in large-scale (e.g., World War II–style and intensity) military commitments have become very infrequent. The Russian aggression in Ukraine demonstrates that military forces cannot be dismantled or significantly reduced because traditional threats could always return, as they did in Ukraine. It was the first open intra-European clash in seventy years, and it underscored the continued need for conventional forces to deter, and if necessary, to fight. The short-term recourse to traditional warfare among historical opponents may not be as great as it once was, but it has not ebbed enough to suggest dismantling the forces. In Ukraine, the existence of large conventional—and nuclear—forces served some deterrent purposes and thus reinforced the continued need to possess them. The likelihood that World War III would result in the irradiated destruction of humankind makes its purposive initiation reasonably remote, and all sides implicitly acknowledged this influence on the crisis.

The epicenter of violence is, as it largely has been for some time, in the developing world. This concentration is partly a result of the nuclear inhibitory factor that keeps the traditional powers from fighting one another: the shadow of nuclear weapons and the unwillingness to press disagreements to the point that they could lead to nuclear consequences. In the Russo-Ukrainian crisis, the question of whether escalation to that level was never truly clear: Putin, for all his other aggressive tendencies, clearly understood that the disagreement between Moscow and Kyiv was not so important as to risk destroying the world over (although the dynamics were never stated this way). Since their last global bloodletting in the 1940s, the major powers have come to realize the possible outcomes of allowing their disagreements to get out of hand. Although they maintain deadly capabilities that could destroy us all, they have implicitly agreed that their competitions and disagreements must be bounded below that level. The 2022 instance of Russo-Ukrainian rivalry that featured the preparations for war like mobilization and troop massing may have been reminiscent of the 1940s, but they have to this point (fall 2022) stopped short of a confrontation that could spiral out of control.

The same kinds of physical inhibitions do not exist in situations in the developing world, with limited exceptions: the Afro-Asian (and to a lesser extent Latin American) region has been the part of the world where violence has been concentrated, but where nuclear weapons are not part of the calculus. The most important reason for violence and instability, of course, has been decolonization of the European world empires that dominated the developing world before World War II. European losses and exhaustion arising from the war caused the colonial occupying powers, individually and collectively, to conclude that trying to continue control of these areas was an unaffordable proposition, and the flood of former colonies declaring their independence and asserting statehood erupted in the 1940s and has been an inexorable force ever since.

The basic problem, however, is that there was virtually no foresight or preparation for independence by the colonial powers, who basically bowed to the inevitability of demands for self-determination and acceded to the movements. Largely because decolonization was unplanned, it has been a messy, imperfect process that still exhibits many animosities and hatreds manifesting themselves in violence. Supporting one side or another in specific situations became the "acceptable" form of great-power rivalry in this milieu and resulted in, among other places, the American quagmire in Vietnam and Soviet failure in Afghanistan twenty years before the United States blundered into that country's violent politics.

The area that has been most affected by these dynamics has been the Middle East, which has also been the site of much of the violence and outside interference by the Cold War superpowers, who have competed and fought (often through proxies) in many of the fracases that have ensued. Although the post-Soviet Russians have had to back away except in places like Syria before its Ukrainian aggression, the developing world is the site of much of the world's violence and instability. As such, it has also become the part of the world in which the United States has been most likely to employ military force.

This change has also altered the pattern and methods by which violent conflicts are now conducted in the world, and the change has significant implications for where and how the United States plans for and sometimes employs force. The basic reason this change is important is that the developing countries cannot and do not conduct warfare in the same way that the developed countries do. The European-style warfare that typified the fighting of the last century simply does not apply to warfare between the developed and developing worlds. Western-style organization and ways of fighting are known as conventional warfare, and warring parties in the developing world simply lack the wherewithal to fight that way. The result is that the dominant means of warfare that countries like the United States encounter when they find themselves engaged in the developing world is Eastern-style engagement, or what is called unconventional or asymmetrical warfare in the West.

The distinction is important, because the methods, styles, and determinations of success using one method or the other are distinctly different. Western-style warfare is what is often referred to as "heavy" warfare, which means it is dominated by reliance on large, highly lethal weapons systems like bomber and fighter aircraft, heavy artillery, and massive engagements by heavily equipped forces. These kinds of weaponry are generally unavailable (or only available in small numbers) in the developing world, and direct confrontation between two sides fighting using the two approaches will almost always result in success for the heavily armed combatant. So-called unconventional warfare is premised on the need to negate these advantages in order to have any chance of success. It does this by changing the methods and "rules" of engagement, often to the great frustration of the opponent. This environment is the operative military ground for the United States in much of the developing world, and it presents problems that the United States has not been entirely successful in overcoming. Understanding these difficulties, in turn, affects the attractiveness and even wisdom of some kinds and purposes of military activity by the United States and is thus worth considering when the United States contemplates the employment of its forces in the future.

Fighting in the Developing World: The IF Factor in Application

It is a simple fact that most of the violence and instability in the contemporary world is in the countries of the developing world. Much of that violence has been the more or less direct result of the breakdown of European colonial rule in most of the developing world in a disorderly fashion that did not produce or even promote the orderly assumption and conduct of governance in and between many of the new countries. When the Cold War rivalry became established in the Euro-centered world, the competition between communism and anti-communism moved into the developing world to promote internal regimes and regional balances that would both be stable and promote the interests of one or another of the principal Cold Warriors.

That competition as such, of course, largely came to an end with the collapse of the Soviet Union, although China has moved to replace the Soviets in some parts of Africa and elsewhere. The simple facts, however, are that many developing world areas remain internally unstable and that their instability often spills over into both internal and regional politics and balances. In the thirty-plus years since the collapse of the Soviet Union, their competition has been most active in the Middle East, but it has the potential to spill over into parts of eastern Asia and Africa. The question of importance here is the extent of American involvement in these conflicts and thus the likelihood and desirability of American direct intervention in these areas with military force. In the twenty-first century, the concentration has been in the Middle East, but the Ukrainian crisis and rumblings in east Asia principally involving China and Taiwan suggest that problems could spread widely.

There is absolutely nothing "new" about the phenomenon now called "unconventional" warfare. The origins of this form of warfare, also known as asymmetrical warfare, is Eastern, and its principles and outlines are suggested in classic texts like Sun Tzu's *The Art of War* that raised the question of the *feasibility* of achieving those goals through the application of American armed forces. The situations are often idiosyncratic, making broad generalization perilous, and the resulting contemporary debate is compromised to some extent by the general toxicity of current American politics.

The heart of the debate reflects the realities of the contemporary international system. Given the general peace in the West (at least before Ukraine) and the effective inadmissibility of direct engagement between the traditional Cold War rivals, warfare has shifted to the old colonial world in terms of conflicts within and between former colonies or between those countries and the major powers. These conflicts are often very bloody and difficult, although their conduct and outcomes are not as systemically traumatic as major-power confrontations of the last century like the world wars. Competition for influence in the developing world, however, has become the major form of semi-military involvement and more during the Cold War.

The epicenter of much of this trauma has been the Middle East. Oil from that region is central to concerns about Middle Eastern politics, but rivalries based in denominational divisions (e.g., Sunnism versus Shiism within Islam) and between faiths (Islam versus Judaism) are also important sources. The area is made more difficult by nuclear weapons, which Israel possesses but others like Iran may choose to acquire, and by religiously based terrorism, some of which has been directed at the United States and brings the United States into the midst of violent regional politics.

These sources of conflict and potential violent involvement are emphases of current American (and other Western) security policy, mainly because the West is often the object of terrorist activities. The result is a kind of crazy quilt of interests, concerns, and possible actions in which the United States has and may continue to find itself entwined. The withdrawal from Afghanistan in 2021 (an international event the United States seeks to avoid duplicating in the future) signaled a break of sorts for America from two decades of entanglement in violence there, as well as counseling some reluctance to commit actual combat troops elsewhere. What to do (and not do) in the Middle East and elsewhere in the developing world will be central to American military policy for the foreseeable future. It also means that the United States, in deciding where to become involved personally or not must become familiar with and adept at prevailing in asymmetrical warfare in the Middle East and elsewhere in the developing world.

The contemplation of potential involvements can be usefully organized around the IF principles. The concern must begin with a humbling admission: involvement in developing world conflicts against opponents employing asymmetrical warfare techniques and principles has been difficult for countries practicing the massive style of fighting associated with European-style war. This should not be a surprise, because asymmetrical warfare is designed for negating the ways of fighting associated with the European model. The questions of interests and feasibility of involvement must take place in this context, conditioned by an honest assessment of interests and feasibility, as well as the prospects for achieving the goals pursued in these kinds of wars.

Application of the two IF principles of interest and feasibility is daunting. Most of the conflicts where a country like the United States is likely to encounter a foe fighting asymmetrically are in the developing world. This form of warfare is generally associated with Asia, notably China, and it has been adopted by opposition movements confronting European (including American) opponents through much of the developing world. The reason is simple: developing countries (and movements within them) do not possess the military "mass" (e.g., large stores of weaponry with the kind of lethality associated with Western forces) to confront Western opponents on Western-style terms. Asymmetrical methods seek to reduce or eliminate the advantages of those forces and, in effect, to "level" the battlefield so they have a chance of succeeding. Western, including American, militaries have attempted to adapt to the resulting ways of fighting associated with the asymmetrical method. For a variety of reasons, they have not been totally successful in overcoming the challenges of the asymmetrical warrior.

Doing so has proven difficult, creating a level of frustration about involvement in wars where one confronts asymmetrical opponents. The IF factors capture part of the frustration that results. The kinds of countries where the United States is likely to confront an asymmetrical opponent are places where American interests are not fundamental, even obviously compelling. Operationally, this means that intervention is more attractive if the costs of intervention are low, but integral to the asymmetrical approach is to increase that difficulty and cost to the point that the potential outside intervenor becomes frustrated with the lack of progress and decides that continuation is not worth the continuing, uncertain effort. That dynamic can be seen in places like Afghanistan and earlier in Vietnam. In neither place was the United States defeated militarily; it was, however, frustrated in the pursuit of its goals and eventually concluded they were not worth the effort; neither did it succeed. This determination applies to the feasibility of success: is involvement worth the meager gains one can hope to achieve but of which the opponents frustrate accomplishment? Ultimately, one is forced to ask whether military intervention is worth it. The asymmetrical warrior succeeds if the answer to that question is negative.

Contemplating Involvements:
The Challenges of Asymmetrical Warfare

The first recognized, large-scale encounter with asymmetrical warfare by the United States came in the Vietnam War. Vietnam was not the first time or place that Americans encountered opposition that would now be called asymmetrical, but it was probably the first time that the country institutionally recognized the phenomenon. Americans had themselves practiced the equivalent of asymmetrical warfare during parts of the American Revolution, resistance to white American conquest of the American West by some Indian tribes was asymmetrical, and it is arguable that the American Civil War might have had a different outcome if the Confederates had occupied and defended the Appalachian Mountains asymmetrically instead of contributing to their own defeat by fighting European style. Unfortunately for them (but happily for the Union), they did not.

What exactly is asymmetrical warfare? The first thing to be said about this form of warfare is that it is physically and conceptually different from the style of warfare the United States is most familiar with and comfortable fighting. The differences include the reasons for which it is fought, how those who practice it think and act, and motivation. Asymmetrical warfare is both militarily and conceptually unconventional and distinctive from European-style war, and the differences affect those who employ it and those who oppose it.

The heart of asymmetrical warfare is a mindset that arises from the fact that the asymmetrical warrior always begins from a condition of conventional military inferiority. If that warrior attempts to fight in the manner of its conventional foe, it will lose. The problem for unconventional warriors is how to negate their disadvantages. Adaptability to situations of disadvantage is at the heart of the asymmetrical warrior: adoption of an asymmetrical mindset does not provide the practitioner with a set of strategies and tactics so much as a mindset of asking what it can do to negate the disadvantages it faces and enhance its advantages. Each asymmetrical campaign is different based on circumstances, and thus the planner must be eclectic, searching for and exploiting situations to its advantage regardless of conventional norms about acceptable and unacceptable ways of fighting. For this reason, unconventional warriors are often derogated by their opponents for their "cowardly" methods, and they are underestimated.

Most asymmetrical wars occur in developing world situations where an indigenous force(s) confronts heavily armed opponents with far more lethal, sophisticated capabilities. The opponents of the asymmetrical forces are often outsiders like the United States, and the problem for the asymmetrical warrior is how to neutralize the overwhelming material advantages of the opposition (which normally includes a government force armed and equipped by outside Westerners). If the asymmetrical warrior adopts the rules of engagement preferred by the outsider, it will likely be decimated by the firepower advantages of the intervener. The problem is how to negate those disadvantages to their advantage.

The experience of the United States and Iraq illustrates this dynamic. Iraq attempted to confront the United States conventionally in Kuwait, and its armed forces were crushed in the process. The Iraqis learned from the experience that in any future encounter with the Americans, it could not fight the Americans on their terms without being crushed. When the United States invaded Iraq in 2003, the Iraqis thus went asymmetrical: they offered only enough resistance to make the Americans think they were prevailing decisively, while they regrouped to organize a resistance to the American onslaught. Limited unconventional methods became their tool of resistance in forms like ambushes, car bombings, and suicide self-immolations. The purpose was not to drive the Americans out, which they were incapable of doing, but rather it was to convince the Americans that the costs of occupation were not worth sustaining.

Ultimately, it worked; the Americans did leave without achieving the goals they had set out for themselves, a reprise of the Vietnam experience. There are more potential Iraq (and Afghanistan) situations in the developing world into which the United States may be tempted to involve itself; the experience of the last quarter century is not encouraging in terms of the IF principles: how important was Iraq to the United States? And were we able to achieve whatever goals we had defined?

Not all future temptations for intervention will be like Iraq (or Vietnam), but the experience should be cautionary. At a minimum, they suggest the United States needs to decide if it should devote the energy and resources to develop the capability to prevail in these conflicts and thus achieve whatever objectives it has, or should it retreat from situations that often prove to be intractable and outside its core interests? Are American interests important enough to put American forces' lives at risk? Can they succeed in achieving whatever mission to which they are assigned? Is the expenditure of American resources worth the effort? Where and when, in other words, should America choose to fight?

Assessing the Prospects: The Middle East Quagmire as Rejoinder

The question of worth is particularly poignant in the contemporary world balance. The end of the Cold War relieved American and allied powers of the pressing need to contain a communist expansionism that no longer existed in that guise, although the Russian intrusion into Ukraine offers some parallels. Religious terrorism has to some extent replaced communism as the major system threat, but it is a much more difficult dynamic in some ways. Most of the terrorists are non-state actors based in the Middle East whose goals (to the extent they are coherently articulated) are anti-Western, promoting Islam in one guise or another, and opposing Western influence and especially the United States where they are active. That activity has mostly been confined to the greater Middle East. Currently, the arguably most dangerous if not widely publicized problem surrounds nuclear-armed Israel and potentially nuclear Iran.

It used to be the mantra that American policy in that region had three parts: the protection of Israel from regional enemies (essentially everyone else), the protection of regional oil from interruption, and the exclusion of Soviet influence from the region. These priorities have changed in the contemporary system. As the only nuclear power in the region, Israel has arguably emerged as the regional military hegemon, and much of Israeli concern with the Iranian nuclear program is based in the threat an Iranian nuclear arsenal would pose to their status. Middle Eastern oil, like petroleum generally, remains an important but contracting factor due to shifts away from fossil fuel sources, a problem that affects Russia greatly. The major challenge could become Chinese initiatives to gain access, since China is an energy-deficient country. The Soviet threat, of course, no longer exists as such, but the Ukrainian crisis of 2022 demonstrates that Russia, as what is left of the Soviet Union, has not disappeared as a geopolitical irritant.

The United States retains interests in the area, but they are also changing. Iran, which before 1979 was America's major regional Muslim ally, is now its chief antagonist since the 1979 revolution dethroned the Shah of Iran and replaced him with a militant Islamic regime fundamentally opposed to the United States. The United States, which had been closely aligned with the Iranian regime and the Shah's programs of Westernization, became the "great Satan" to the Iranians, and the United States went from effective ally to fundamental opponent to the largest, and potentially most powerful, country in the region. This change is important, since it has heightened competition and antagonism between the two most powerful regional powers in the Middle East, Israel and Iran. The United States no long stands between the two countries as an arbiter and mutual friend.

The United States has thus been placed in an unadmitted regional quandary. During the roughly quarter century of the Shah's rule in Iran, American policy centered on the country's close relations with Israel and Iran, a relationship that benefited those countries as well as the United States. During some of the Arab-Israeli conflicts, for instance, Iran was the only Islamic country that supplied Israel with energy while the fighting was ongoing, and relations between the two countries was closer than Israeli relations with other Muslim countries.

The Iranian revolution of 1979 shattered that triangular relationship. Stripped of its close relationship with the Americans, Iran was isolated in a Sunni-dominated region, with Israel and its nuclear arsenal looming over them. The new militant regime in Teheran was largely on its own in a hostile environment in which the Americans were now a primary opponent and obstacle rather than a close ally. The result was a growing isolation for the Iranians.

What distinguishes the region from other places where asymmetrical warfare is sometimes conducted has been in the existence of nuclear weapons in the area. Israel is the only nuclear state in the Middle East as of today (2022), but Iran could easily join the list, creating an adversarial standoff between nuclear Israel and Iran in an area where the conflict has remained generally limited until now. Whether the stability and restraint that has developed around nuclear weapons extends to other places in the region is an open question.

Iran is the most naturally prominent and potentially powerful country in the region. It has a population of more than eighty million that dwarfs its neighbors (Israel's population is about 10 percent of Iran's). Saudi Arabia, the closest thing there is to a regional Muslim rival to Iran, has a population of less than half that of Iran, and the Saudis are notorious for their lack of personal assertiveness in military means, preferring to open their oil-sodden wallets to hire others to implement their national security for them. Israel stands out as the major rival and impediment to Iranian power in the region. Because of its nuclear arsenal (unacknowledged but believed to consist of about three hundred warheads: see my *The Middle East and American National Security*), Israel is the de facto military hegemon, a status the Trump administration appeared to embrace and about which the Biden administration has not taken a public stand.

Historically, the Iranians have disavowed any interest in becoming a nuclear weapons power, although they certainly could become one, apparently in less than a year. Iran is the largest country in the region geographically and in terms of population, it has a well-educated, sophisticated elite (partly the result of its long Shah-related collaboration with the Americans), and if it can regain access to the Iranian funds frozen in the United States, it could rapidly become the geopolitical giant of the region—including displacing Israel as the de facto hegemon in the region. The return of an American commitment to a posture of Iranian disinterest in becoming a nuclear weapons state has become a primary rhetorical policy goal of the United States, but it is not clear that it is succeeding. If there is a regional conflict with potential incendiary possibilities, it is that if the non-proliferation agreement between the Iranians and the West is not restored, Iran will move forward with nuclear weapons acquisition. If that process emerges, the question is how the Israelis might act preemptively to prevent an operational Iranian nuclear capability, and the prospects include employing their own nuclear weapons against Iran.

The possible development of a nuclear arms competition between the two most assertive countries represents a novel way that regional peace could be endangered with incalculable effects. The Israelis have had nuclear weapons since the latter 1960s (although they have never formally admitted it), and Iran has been a potential nuclear power for nearly that long. When the United States and Iran were close allies, this was not a problem, since the United States had strong influence over both governments, and each antagonist could reasonably assume the Americans would exercise restraint on the other. When American relations with Iran turned sour in 1979, that dynamic changed, and the Israelis became more antagonistic toward the Iranians, setting in motion a level of tension that is internationally troubling. The Iranians have historically eschewed any interest in gaining nuclear weapons, but rumblings from Teheran suggest that view is weakening. The Israelis were emboldened to act militantly during the Trump administration, although that changed with the removal of Trump and Israeli prime minister Benjamin Netanyahu from office. Before 1979, the United States could act as an arbiter between the two rivals, but the breach in relations between the Americans and the Iranians means there is no out-of-area source of restraint on Iranian antagonism toward the Israelis. Iran has anointed itself as the major promoter of Palestinian independence, and Israel has appointed itself as the restrainer of the Iranians. Any comity that existed before 1979 has dissolved into a competition that could be made entirely more dangerous should the Iranians decide to produce their own nuclear weapons.

The Israeli-Iranian situation is worth raising because it is arguably the only potential nuclear relationship with possible expansion into violent, even nuclear, conflict. North Korean possession of nuclear weapons is a partial exception, but their nuclear forces do not confront a practical opponent: they implicitly argue them as a deterrent against the United States, but their threats (and especially actions) would be so clearly suicidal as to be controllable. Some Israelis, on the other hand, have openly stated that should their country come under imminent threat they might employ their weapons even if the result was disastrous for them, the region, and even beyond.

The United States and Potential Deployments beyond the Traditional Middle East Conflict

Almost all the potential violent situations into which the United States might be drawn (or tempted to insert itself) are in the developing world. The country has not initiated a major deployment of forces since the reactions to the 9/11 bombings, but it has accumulated a not entirely enviable record from the last century, and the prospect of violence breaking out in developing world situations remains a potential scenario the United States must confront and evaluate. Virtually all the scenarios one can envision will be asymmetrical in some ways, and thus it is worthwhile to assess the problems they can create in attempting to apply the IF factors to decisions that might be made. The personal restraint of the United States in the Ukrainian crisis reinforces this dynamic.

The international challenges with possible military implications for the United States have become more diverse and generally less threatening than they were during the Cold War. Regionally, the greatest concentration remains in the Middle East because of the residual value and necessity of carbon-based petroleum energy to so much of the globe and the unresolved aspects of the Arab-Israeli conflict based on the plight of the Palestinians. The historic commitment of the United States to Israeli security has overridden other considerations in that region. At the same time, the shadow cast by nuclear weapons hangs over the region. There are sources of some instability in the Far East, where Chinese aspiration to something like superpower status unsettles their relationship with the United States and its neighbors, and African instability and potential for destabilization remains a partial spillover from the destabilization caused by terrorist-based organizations.

All the threats that could result in destabilization are amorphous, with few concrete threats that unambiguously demand American military responses. Unexpected events like Russia's renewed aggression in Ukraine have made making planning for establishing standards for involvement difficult. After 9/11, the locus of conflict moved decisively into the Middle East, and the major operational threat the United States had to deal with was suppression of Middle East terrorists who opposed US policy goals in the region. That emphasis led the United States into and out of direct involvements in Iraq and Afghanistan.

It has also meant that the Americans have encountered significant asymmetrical warfare challenges in the area that have complicated, made more difficult, and frustrated American military plans and execution. Iraq and especially Afghanistan stand out. Both, but especially Afghanistan, confronted American forces with problems that the United States had run up against in a different setting in Southeast Asia: fighting against asymmetrical opponents in a hostile environment. The United States did not exit either experience bathed in the glory of unquestionably successful endeavors. These are arguably the kinds of efforts the United States either should avoid in the future or master asymmetrical approaches to warfare and adapt to the problems it creates. These problems may be most prevalent in the Middle East, but they are also present elsewhere in the developing world. In its encounters with these kinds of opponents, the United States has not been conspicuously successful, which almost certainly will cause future potential opponents to consider and sometimes to adopt the approach.

Asymmetrical Warfare 101

In most cases, asymmetrical wars occur in the developing world and at least begin as contests between a national government (quite often headed by the group that led the independence movement by which the country achieved independence) and a dissident group, often ethnically defined. The issue dividing the government under siege and the insurgent group seeking to overthrow it, of course, is who should rule and how. During the Cold War period, support for the government and its opposition often took on communist–anti-communist dimensions, although such affiliations and their meanings were often somewhat obscure. That affiliation base, however, often meant that groups were supported by the Cold War parties: frequently, that meant American support for the anti-communist postindependence government and Soviet/communist support for the insurgents.

This structure is instructive of the predicament created for the United States in IF terms. Because the United States was not a major colonial power, it did not have inherent postcolonial interests in the independence dynamics, but Soviet or Chinese interest in promoting opposition to postindependence governments sanctioned by the retreating colonial power transformed these internal, often parochial disagreements into Cold War confrontations over whether the communists or noncommunists would prevail.

In most cases, the successor government to colonial rule had the initial advantage: it inherited the governmental structure and whatever armed capability the new government possessed. Most of the new states were multinational (composed of people with differing regional or ethnic loyalties), and governance was often chaotic, conflictual, and violence prone. When conflicts formed and broke out, new governments tended to turn to the West for assistance, whereas insurgencies lacked the resources to do so and turned to the Soviet Union and China for assistance. The United States was sometimes drawn into these fracases, almost always supporting the new government in power.

These circumstances defined the environment in which modern asymmetrical warfare emerged. As suggested, asymmetrical warfare is not a new phenomenon at all, but is instead a kind of mindset in which a physically inferior force can attempt to become militarily competitive with a larger, better equipped foe that it cannot confront and defeat in conventional warfare. The term *asymmetrical warfare* reflects this problem. Asymmetrical warfare is defined as the situation where one side fights in one way (normally "conventionally" in a European sense), and the other (asymmetrical) side rejects the rules of conventional warfare and adopts alternative ways of fighting that hopefully enhance its chances of prevailing in a conflict it would almost certainly lose if it fought conventionally. The asymmetrical warrior must change the rules of engagement to have a chance of prevailing. The only alternative may be defeat or, worse, extinction.

The basic idea and motivation for asymmetrical warfare is as old as the earliest encounters between human groups in situations that were less than friendly. When one side has a sizable, and apparently insurmountable, advantage over the other in terms of military power, the weaker side has limited alternatives. One option is to flee, if that is possible, or to surrender, and another is to stand and fight, hoping for the best. If the enemy is overwhelmingly more powerful, none of these responses is likely to be attractive and can be ultimately self-destructive. Only a radical alteration of the rules and methods of combat can give the weaker power a chance of prevailing, even of surviving.

This scenario describes the dilemma of a developing world military force when it faces a modern Westernized military machine like that possessed by the United States. Although the asymmetrical warrior is disadvantaged in terms like firepower and mechanization (e.g., he normally lacks modern lethal tools like military aircraft or weaponry like tanks), he has advantages that can be exploited if he ignores or bends accepted means of fighting. Developing world conflicts, for instance, are typically fought in places that are deficient in characteristics like transportation assets (e.g., road grids that can accommodate the movement of tanks and other armored vehicles) on which European-style armed forces rely. Vietnam, for instance, was fought in large measure in the mountainous jungled terrain of the Southeast Asian peninsula, where heavy American equipment had difficulty operating, necessitating operations by troops on foot through difficult, hostile terrain. The asymmetrical warrior will seek to exploit these circumstances and force the European-style force to fight in ways it does not want to fight and that put that opponent in environmental circumstances that work to his disadvantage.

The use of ambushes is an example. Primitive environmental conditions lack the kinds of infrastructural development that facilitate the movement of highly mechanized, lethal capabilities possessed by symmetrical warriors like the United States, and in primitive environmental situations, can result in daunting, and certainly frustrating, circumstances for developed country militaries.

It has taken the Americans a while to recognize this problem. When the United States was ramping up its Southeast Asian effort, then President Lyndon Johnson derogated the challenge by referring to Vietnam as a "pissant" country, presumably suggesting that defeating the insurgency in South Vietnam would be an easy task. This assessment, of course, did not adequately account for the asymmetrical response of the opponent and particularly how that opponent could manipulate a hostile, unfamiliar environment to frustrate the Americans.

Confronting and defeating an asymmetrical warrior is much harder than originally conceptualized when the Americans marched off to war in the early 1960s. The reasons are geopolitical in both the senses that have been introduced. On the one hand, American interests, while not altogether absent in these situations, are generally not so great that they create a long-term sustainability for combat in a situation where the fighting is expensive and the results do not indicate clear progress toward "victory," the exact meaning of which is often not clear. Asymmetrical conflicts tend to occur in places that are physically challenging for a developed state to prevail, and that is one of the major reasons that potential opponents of the United States have modified the basic philosophy of asymmetrical warfare to their special circumstances when the United States may be involved. Vietnam is the prototype of this phenomenon; Afghanistan is the latest instance.

Asymmetry and the IF Factor

What vital interest did the United States have in a noncommunist Vietnam the population of which did not seem overwhelmingly interested in the outcome for which the United States was fighting and sacrificing? The United States concocted various arguments for why there were sufficient reasons for the commitment, and none of them stuck. The prevailing domino theory argument was that if the communists were successful in Vietnam, the other Southeast Asian countries would topple to communist regimes, and there was no end to how long and far those dominos might fall. It never truly captured American public support. Vietnam was, after all, seven thousand miles away.

The problem with that explanation centered on those literally thousands of miles of open oceans between Vietnam and the United States. It was inconceivable to most Americans that those dominos would keep falling until they reached the California coast. In the long run, the domino theory eventually proved true but irrelevant to the United States: the Southeast Asian peninsula countries did fall to communists, and it had no visible impact on American security. As the American body count mounted toward its eventual 58,000 count chronicled on the Vietnam Wall on the Washington Mall, the answer to why the United States was there came to be answered increasingly negatively. Another way to raise the question of interests is to ask at the outset what the dire consequences of failure will be; in the case of Southeast Asia, the answer was hardly any consequences at all. Had that question been realistically debated in 1962, the American post–World War II military experience might have been very different.

The other question is that of the feasibility of success of any action that might be contemplated. If an interest is important enough potentially to be pursued by the recourse to force, can it be done successfully? The answer in Vietnam begins by recognizing that there were very few (if any) American core, survival-level interests so fundamentally threatened that the country had *no choice* but to go to war. The problem was the only direct, encompassing threats to American survival come from the possession of nuclear weapons by potential opponents, and nobody on the Southeast Asian peninsula had those weapons.

The feasibility question is further complicated by the unspoken assumption that success in developing world conflicts is somehow easier than it has proven to be. On paper, the balance of military capabilities between the United States and any developing world government or insurgency overwhelmingly favors the Americans materially, and one of the implications of traditional analysis is that these "pissant" opponents should be no match for the Americans and that their violent interaction will naturally lead to American triumph.

This conclusion is almost certainly true if the opposition agrees to confront and fight the United States (or other Western power) on the terms and by the rules of Western-style warfare. American military interaction with Iraq illustrates the point. When Iraq invaded and subdued Kuwait in 1990 and seemed poised to move into Saudi Arabia to gain control of their oil fields and refineries, the Americans formed the core of a resistance to Iraqi aggressiveness and led the coalition that stopped Iraqi progress, confronted and decisively defeated an Iraqi military organized along Western lines, and sent it fleeing in defeat back home the next year. Was it a victory for the West, or an abject defeat for an Iraqi armed force that inadvisably had adopted the organization and rules of Western warfare but were not as good at it as the Americans?

The answer, of course, was that Iraq may have attempted to emulate the Americans, but they failed to match American proficiency and capability in this style of warfare. They tried, in other words, to fight the way the Americans wanted to fight, they were not good enough to compete that way, and they lost. The lesson was clear to the Iraqis and other potential American opponents who watched the Iraqi defeat: do not confront the Americans on their own terms, because you will lose if you do. Fighting the Americans on their own terms (symmetrically) is futile; the only way you have a chance is to change the rules in such a way as to give yourself a chance—fight asymmetrically.

When the United States invaded and conquered Iraq in 2003, the Iraqis had learned this lesson and did not confront the Americans in traditional, symmetrical warfare: instead, they largely stood aside after making a token defense and let the American offensive succeed. Their resistance was unconventional and did not start until the Americans were in charge. As is typical in these situations, the Americans eventually tired of the frustrations of the ensuing, inconclusive occupation and left in 2011. Who won? Iraq, a classic artificial state, remains less than stable; they did survive the Americans. Was that the meaning of asymmetrical warfare in this instance? Will the United States confront the same kind of outcome if it tries an Iraq-style operation elsewhere in the future? Or has the United States been sufficiently chastened by the experience there (and in Afghanistan) that they would be extremely unlikely to repeat it?

A large part of the answer to that question depends on how (or if) the United States adapts to the likely repetition of asymmetrical responses *in situations where American vital interests are not unambiguously at stake*. The emphasis on this question is not coincidental for at least two reasons. One is that this is the form of opposition the United States and other developed countries will confront in the developing world in the future. Second, the United States has not developed a "counter-asymmetrical" strategy that renders recourse to asymmetrical opposition futile. The lesson from Vietnam to Afghanistan is that this approach to dealing with the Americans works better than the alternatives available.

The broad purpose of the asymmetrical warrior is to minimize the advantages of the opponent and to maximize the advantages it has. The major advantage of a military power like the United States is in firepower, the amount of mayhem it can bring to the battlefield and concentrate on the opponent, and its associated characteristics include mechanization and mobility: vehicle-carried forces, intense firepower, and the ability to concentrate and maximize its lethal advantages. The asymmetrical force, on the other hand, is likely to be deficient in terms of mobility and concentrated force: its forces, for instance, quite often must travel on foot and carry only hand-held rifles and the like as weapons. If these kinds of forces meet Western-style opponents in some form of open space (the preference of the symmetrical warrior), asymmetrical warriors do not stand a chance. They can only "level" the battleground by creating conditions that neutralize the advantages created by the symmetrical force's superior firepower.

The style of warfare preferred by the most developed country was developed in and for European fighting, where the terrain is generally amenable to mechanized movement of forces and there are adequate open spaces in which to locate and attack the enemy. Modern forces rely on relative independence from the natural environment, preferring to fly over or drive through it, locate concentrations of opposition warriors, and "service" them with maximally deadly concentrations of lethal fire. Its purpose is to decimate the opposition to the point that it cannot continue.

The asymmetrical philosophy concentrates on avoiding that fate. In conventional terms, the asymmetrical foe is easy to underestimate, particularly when that force and its physical characteristics are placed side by side with those of a country like the United States. On paper, the contest is decidedly one-sided, with the advantage to the heavy, developed side, and it is consciously or subconsciously easy for the symmetrical warrior to assume that the "pissant" insurgents will be easy prey. It is the burden of the opponents they face to convince them differently; changing the odds of victory and defeat is the task of asymmetrical approaches to warfare.

Asymmetrical Warfare Is Not Easy

Asymmetrical warriors are not without advantages of their own. Some are physical, including fighting on home terrain, which means the asymmetrical warrior is more familiar with and probably understands better the optimal places to engage an enemy and where to avoid such contact if possible. Many developing world environments where violence occurs are in underdeveloped and physically challenging locations. Southeast Asia, which is a prototype of sorts for the kind of environment in which a power like the United States is most disadvantaged, is exemplary. Much of the countryside is mountainous, dominated by heavy, jungle-like growth—or both. The terrain is underdeveloped in terms of transportation amenities like the kinds of roads necessary to accommodate military vehicles, meaning much of the effort to locate and target the enemy had to be carried out on foot looking for an enemy who used terrain and vegetation either to avoid detection or to make the terms of contact more amenable to guerrilla fighters with light armaments. Tanks, armored personnel carriers, and the like, which are the standard means by which European-style fighters move from place to place and locate the enemy for elimination, were simply not available. Finding the open fields that are the legacy of the European tradition was simply impossible; trekking on foot through steaming, heavily vegetated physical terrain was impossible. This environment was familiar territory for the insurgents; it was hostile to the European-style fighters, and the result was an advantage the opposition exploited.

There was a strong political element as well. In Vietnam (and Afghanistan), there was disagreement about whether the outside intervenors were dedicated to a solution that the local population supported. The asymmetrical warrior normally has the initial advantage of being locals, and thus they are part of the general population, while the intervening party may have difficulty identifying with the people of the country and their interests. An outsider may think it is liberating an oppressed people—a heroic mission. The natives may think they are interlopers of whom they are suspicious simply because they are outsiders. This factor was undoubtedly a problem the Americans faced when occupying an Afghanistan that is historically famous for its suspicion of and dislike for outsiders.

The result of trying to "liberate" people in another country from oppression is frustrated by the intervenor's ignorance of the country, including the chauvinistic hatred the population may have for outside "liberators" who "free" them but then leave them alone afterward. Part of the disillusion that Americans felt with Vietnam and in other places where they have intervened is the lack of apparent enthusiasm and gratitude the liberated population has for their efforts.

The result is often to create unrealistic expectations on the part of the intervening party both about how it will be received (as a liberator or as an invader), and when the effects are not gratitude, disillusion with the effort that sours support for the enterprise. Since he lacks the ability to defeat the intervenor in combat, this psychological impact is exactly what the asymmetrical warrior wants because what he *can* do is undermine support for the intervenor in that intruder's home country and thus cause the intervenor to lose domestic support for his effort.

The Dynamics of Defeating Intervention

The asymmetrical warrior and the outside intervenor enter clashes with different criteria for success and failure reflecting both their situations and their capabilities. Clashes between groups that adopt asymmetrical warfare and conventional forces are themselves asymmetrical—both sides fight by different rules and employ different means. The frustrating experiences of the United States in Vietnam and Afghanistan help frame and explain the differences.

Outside interventions usually occur in developing world countries. The issue at the heart of the contest is over who should govern, and it is framed in terms of which domestic side, the government or their opponents, will provide a more desirable outcome for the citizenry. During the Cold War, the differences between the two sides were usually stated in communist–anti-communist terms, a contrast that often reflected the needs of the contending sides to gain assistance in their endeavor rather than any deep-seated philosophical differences.

The Vietnam war was of this nature: the South Vietnamese government was supported by the United States versus the communist insurgency in the north supported by China and Russia. The issue was whether the war would conclude with a communist or anti-communist predominance on the peninsula and was articulated as a matter of geopolitical significance that drove a Western objective (the domino theory) of defeating the communists to prevent the spread of global communism. With minimal outside physical assistance (other than arms), the North Vietnamese and their southern allies were winning that contest, and the large purpose of American intervention was to prevent communist success. To achieve that outcome, the United States had to act decisively to defeat the insurgents. It had to win to win: as long as the Vietnamese communists were active, there was a problem. The difficulty was that the opponents were natives of the peninsula, and the Americans were outsiders. The Americans (and South Vietnamese) could prevail only by vanquishing the enemy.

These differences created contrasting objectives. The United States and the South Vietnamese could only prevail by destroying the insurgency, because if the insurgency continued, victory could not be asserted. The problem for the National Liberation Front (the communist political designation) was more compact: since they were the intruders, the problem they posed was different. If they continued to exist (not lose), they were a problem that grew as the opposition became increasingly frustrated by its own lack of progress: the insurgents' mission was to win by not losing. If they succeeded in avoiding defeat, it was only a matter of time until the intervenors tired of the effort and left. They were correct in that assessment. Roughly the same thing happened in Afghanistan.

A common thread in both cases was an apparent misunderstanding on the American part of the dynamics of the contest. In Vietnam, the United States conceptualized the war primarily in Cold War terms, as a contest about turning more of the world's map red or blue, which was the kind of interpretation that was necessary to gain American support for intervention in a war half a world away that otherwise did not clearly involve American interests.

The Cold War overlay was present in the war (the Communist supporters of Ho Chi Minh versus the anti-communist South Vietnamese), but that was not the point from an indigenous vantage point. The war was more about the removal of Chinese absentee landowners and thus reform. The American geopolitical emphasis was simply beside the point to the Vietnamese fighting the war, and when the Americans tired of their role and sought to disengage, it did not lessen the resolve of the indigenous population to achieve its goals. They would keep fighting until the Americans left and they could unify the country. The war simply meant more to the asymmetrical warriors than it did to the outside intervenors, and that is a common dilemma in these kinds of wars.

Prolonged American presence in Afghanistan also largely missed the point of why there was an ongoing war there. The initial American motivations were, of course, justified by the US government demanding that the Taliban regime in Kabul remand the Al Qaeda leadership to American custody. The Taliban, which had hosted the terrorists since the mid-1990s, refused. The American invasion pursued Al Qaeda, but that effort ultimately failed because the terrorists managed to escape over the Tora Bora mountains into Pakistan with the assistance of mostly Afghan Pashtun sympathizers in the area. The operation was righteous, if unsuccessful, to this point. What followed arguably was not and entrapped the United States in the twenty-year occupation that ended in 2021.

After the effort to capture the Al Qaeda leadership failed, the United States had several options. One was simply to leave Afghanistan. Possible actions included bringing pressure on the Pakistani government that became the de facto hosts to capture and turn them over, an effort they rejected. A second was to conduct an offshore or Iraq-based air campaign against the terrorists from carriers in the Persian Gulf or from Iraq. The third was to stay in Afghanistan to prevent Al Qaeda from returning and hopefully to break their support within the Afghan population. The United States essentially chose the third option, which included trying to keep the Taliban from returning to power and throwing its support behind anti-Taliban forces in the country. Aided by NATO allies, the United States chose the third option. It was a mistake born of a lack of understanding of the political and physical situation in the country.

The problem was that the decision placed the Americans in alliance with an insurgent movement that wrested power (with American and allied help) from the Taliban and took control of the government. That government, led by Hamid Karzai, never had the unquestionable support of Afghan people. It was instead a coalition of various ethnic groups in different parts of the country, and that was its fatal flaw. The history of Afghanistan is dominated physically by the Pashtun tribe, which formed a majority in the country until American support for Karzai caused many to flee into Pakistan. Many Pashtuns allied themselves with the Taliban, whose membership was almost exclusively Pashtun.

The history of Afghanistan is clear regarding the importance of the majority Pashtun. At least since Afghanistan emerged as a sovereign state around the time of the American Revolution, they have dominated the country, and Pashtuns have exercised political power and whatever level of stability might exist at any point in time. There was Pashtun support among the rebels that overthrew the Taliban and installed the Karzai regime. There were Pashtuns in the government (Karzai was an urban Pashtun), but there were also members of other ethnic groups, and many Afghans never trusted the government because of that adulteration. The Taliban became the representatives of the Pashtun tradition, and the government became the symbol of distrusted, even hated others. The result was that the Taliban gained most of the Pashtun support. The United States was involved in a two-decades-long, futile war that ended with the Taliban in power in 2021.

In retrospect, both interventions were probably unwise and should not have been undertaken, certainly not for as long as they were. Were American interests in Southeast Asia sufficient to justify over 58,000 American service members dying in South Vietnam? The answer probably is that the commitment might have been justifiable if the worst predictions from the domino theory were true, but they were not. The simple fact is that Lyndon Johnson was convinced that American force could easily overwhelm the "pissant" asymmetrical effort of the natives. That assessment was wrong; the outcome was visibly more important to the asymmetrical warriors, and they were fighting on home ground with everything at stake. In Afghanistan, the United States underestimated the determination of the Pashtuns and spent two futile, unsuccessful decades seeking to create a political order the Afghans never embraced. In both cases, the United States failed. The Vietnam

Wall is the testimony to 1960s hubris; the political chaos at the Kabul airport is the legacy of the twenty-first-century repetition. Were American interests in Southeast Asia worth so many American lives? Was whatever the United States sought to accomplish in Afghanistan worth several trillions of dollars and a smaller loss of life? Put in a slightly different way, were American interests and the feasibility of achieving them worth the efforts expended?

Conclusions

The Russian invasion of Ukraine represents an additional piece to the mosaic that is represented by the contemporary use of violence. The issues dividing the two countries were relatively straightforward: should NATO membership be extended to the modern Russian border through Ukrainian membership in NATO? The Russian response was an emphatic and unequivocal no.

Although issues were not sharply articulated, the underlying question was the legitimacy of an independent (and potentially hostile) Ukrainian state on Russia's western border. Ukraine itself poses no direct military threat to Russia, although its efforts to establish an independence from Russia was certainly a slap in the face of Russia. And this dynamic is magnified by Ukrainian interest in NATO and the EU. Ukrainians who pushed hardest for these ties had to know that Putin would resist their advocacies in some way. Whether they believed he would react with an invasion is debatable.

The Russian action pushed the world closer to major war than it had been "in seventy years," in the words of American Vice President Kamala Harris and others, and this was the first major power incursion into a neighboring sovereign European state since the Russians forcefully seized and annexed the Crimea—also a part of Ukraine—in 2014. The physical actions in terms of a military buildup on the Ukrainian frontier were reminiscent of the preludes to major military actions in the past, and they were followed by a physical invasion of the country. Putin pursued a traditional military objective that states have pursued through history, but he did it differently, in a manner that produced condemnation and disapproval but not a direct military response from the world beyond sending additional military accoutrements to Ukraine to help it defend itself and instituting stiff economic sanctions against Russia. In an earlier era in Europe, this crisis could have started an inexorable slide to wider war, but it did not. What was decisively different this time?

Historians will have to unravel the complex dynamics that led to the evolution of and motivations underlying the conflict, but two factors stand out in the direct shadow of the war. The first is the Russian condition. The

Russians have a long ambiguous relationship with Europe and the international system. Russia is, after all, the largest physical territory in the world, and until its population began to shrink dramatically after the breakup of the Soviet Union, was among its most populous and powerful. They were one of the two world superpowers, a thermonuclear giant that stood toe to toe with the Americans on most geopolitical indicators. Since 1991, the Russian state has declined and shrunk. Putin's actions may have been little more than a reminder that Russia has not gone away. His apparent activation of his nuclear arsenal may similarly have been a reminder that his country is still a premier nuclear giant.

The Cold War was, after all, the high point of Russian power, and it is a status from which they retreat with great reluctance. The most striking characteristic of the Russian condition currently, however, is decline. It remains a nuclear superpower, but essentially all the other trendlines project as negative. Its population is in irreversible decline. The Russian economy is heavily dependent on petroleum energy production and sale abroad, and that is also the basis of much of the prosperity the country enjoys. Given climate change and the resultant decline of petroleum as a resource, that dependency is not the ideal recipe for continued prosperity and preeminence. It is not clear what alternative basis for continued prosperity and economic strength the Russians have. To the east, it is arguable that China has already passed Russia as a world power and as the leading rival of the United States; the signs of Russian equality with the United States in areas like population are negative and possibly irreversible. If one occupies Putin's desk in Moscow, these prospects cannot appear bright. Arguably, Russia's future is now, a kind of last hurrah. The further into the future one looks, the more Russian competitive prospects appear to dim.

The Putin factor dominates the Russian picture. There are three obvious sources of concern intimately tied to the Russian president that help explain his aggressive behavior toward Ukraine. There is a new international order forming in which Russia is likely to emerge as a significant power, but not as a superpower due to demographic and economic factors. The capture of peripheral parts of Ukraine is about as challenging an action as Putin is willing to take. He is reluctant to engage in acts of military assertiveness that might lead to direct confrontation with the United States and the rest of NATO. Putin made a point throughout the crisis to avoid rhetoric and actions that might lead to military confrontation with the United States with inevitable escalatory potential. He announced the activation of his nuclear forces. But going beyond that is avoided assiduously in a nuclear-armed world. In the Ukrainian crisis, it meant that hostile actions were confined to rhetoric and non-military (primarily economic) sanctions. Nobody wants to run the risk of triggering a spiral to nuclear war, and as long as that rejoinder dominates great-power interactions, there are two major implications for war and peace. First, the dangers of major, systemic violent conflict will be minimal, since no one wants to test the limits of deterrence (an observation that is also particularly relevant for conflicts between the United States and China). Second, it means that actual instability and violence will continue to levels of restraint for the United States based in interests (e.g., places not worth fighting over) and feasibility (e.g., the US track record in developing world conflicts). Putin tested the boundary of systemic violence; his actions were traditionally violent, but they were also constrained. Ukraine may have been a fluke to everyone but the Ukrainians. Most conflict remains in the developing world.

Bibliography

Allison, Graham T. *The Essence of Decision: Explaining the Cuban Missile Crisis.* New York: HarperCollins, 1972.

Barnett, Roger W. *Asymmetrical Warfare: Today's Challenge to U.S. Military Power.* Washington, DC: Potomac Books, 2013.

Berkowitz, Bruce. *The New Face of War: How War Will Be Fought in the 21st Century.* New York: Free Press, 2003.

Biden, Joseph S. Jr., and Michael Carpenter. "How to Stand Up to the Kremlin: Defending Democracy Against Its Enemies." *Foreign Affairs* 97, no. 1 (January/February 2018): 44–57.

Blanchette, Jude, and Benny Lin. "China's Ukraine Crisis: What Xi Gains—and Loses—from Backing Putin." *Foreign Affairs* (online), February 22, 2022.

Bremmer, Ian. "Putin Won. But Russia Is Losing. *Time* 191, April 2, 2018, 41.

Clark, Ronald W. *The Greatest Power on Earth: The International Race for Nuclear Supremacy, Earliest Theory to Three Mile Island.* New York: Harper and Row, 1980.

DaVargo, Julie, and Clinton A. Grammich. *Dire Demographics: Population Trends in the Russian Federation.* Santa Monica, CA: RAND Corporation, 2007.

Dawisha, Karen. *Putin's Kleptocracy: Who Owns Russia?* New York: Simon and Schuster, 2014.

Friedman, Thomas L. "The First Law of Petropolitics." *Foreign Policy* (May/June 2006): 28–36.

Galula, David. *Counterinsurgency Warfare: Theory and Practice.* Westport, CT: Praeger, 2006.

Giap, Vo Nguyen. *People's War, People's Army.* New York: Praeger, 1962.

Gorbachev, Mikhail. *The New Russia.* Cambridge, UK: Polity Press, 2016.

———. *Perestroika: New Thinking for Our Country and the World.* New York: Harper and Row, 1987.

Isikoff, Michael, and David Korn. *Russian Roulette: The Inside Story of Putin's War on America and the Election of Donald Trump*. New York: Twelve Books, 2018.

Joffe, Julia. "Putin's Game." *The Atlantic* 321, no. 1 (January/February 2018), 68–85.

Kaurin, Pauline M. *Military Ethics and Contemporary Warfare: Achilles Goes Asymmetrical*. New York and London: Routledge, 2016.

King, Charles, and Rajon Menon. "Prisoners of the Caucasus: Russia's Invisible Civil War." *Foreign Affairs* 89, no. 4 (July/August 2010): 20–34.

Kolesnikov, Andrei. "Would Russians Embrace War? Why an Attack on Ukraine Might Erode Putin's Support." *Foreign Affairs* (online), February 9, 2022.

Kotkin, Stephen. "Russia's Perpetual Geopolitics: Putin Returns to the Historical Pattern." *Foreign Affairs* 89, no. 3 (May/June 2016): 2–9.

Lukyanov, Fyodor. "Putin's Foreign Policy: The Quest to Restore Russia's Rightful Place." *Foreign Affairs* 95, no. 3 (May/June 2016): 2–9.

Malkasian, Carter. *The American War in Afghanistan: A History*. Oxford, UK: Oxford University Press, 2021.

Pelyakova, Alinh, and David Fried. "Putin's Long Game in Ukraine: How the West Can Protect Kyiv." *Foreign Affairs* (online), February 22, 2022.

Snow, Donald M. *Cases in National Security: Principles and Applications*. Lanham, MD: Rowman & Littlefield, 2019.

———. *The Middle East and American National Security: Forever Wars and Conflicts?* Lanham, MD: Rowman & Littlefield, 2021.

———. *The Necessary Peace: Nuclear Weapons and Superpower Relations*. Lexington, MA: Lexington Books, 1987.

Stent, Angela. "The Putin Doctrine: A Move on Ukraine Has Always Been Part of the Plan." *Foreign Affairs* (online), February 10, 2022.

Sun Tzu. *The Art of War*. Translated by Samuel B. Griffith. Oxford, UK: Oxford University Press, 1963.

Toal, Bernard. *Near Abroad: Putin, the West, and the Contest over Ukraine and the Caucasus*. Oxford, UK: Oxford University Press, 2017.

Trenin, Dmitri. *Should We Fear Russia?* Cambridge, UK: Polity Press, 2016.

CHAPTER SIX

The Briar Patch of Intervention in a Complex Environment
The Developed World

One way to assess where and when the United States might be tempted to use force in the contemporary world is to examine where threats to the peace might exist and provide the potential magnet for US involvement. As the discussion to this point has suggested, two contingencies have popped out in the contemporary system. Developing world instability has been a "constant" of sorts, as conflicts within and between developing world countries continue to break out, often with possible consequences that could affect American interests. Occasionally, these conflicts directly involve the United States, and the question becomes what degree of American interests are engaged and what kinds of actions the United States should be prepared for and willing to commit to affect the outcomes. These conflicts are examined in more detail in chapter 7.

Although most of the violence in the system is concentrated in the developing world and has its source in internal or limited regional disagreements, some of it has spread to more traditional locales, thereby tempting more direct American attention. Given the American stature as a superpower and a dominant military force globally, one of the concerns that inevitably arises is whether American interests are sufficient to consider or use military force to affect the outcome in more or less conventional conflicts. The recent past has seen the emergence of what appear traditional conflicts: violence pitting two countries against one another. Possibly because the events, locations, and dynamics of these have been idiosyncratic, American responses have varied significantly. The United States, for instance, invaded Iraq for reasons that were not entirely clear at the time and still are not. Getting into Afghanistan initially made sense; staying for so long did not so clearly make sense. Russia invaded Ukraine and the United States essentially resuscitated the Nixon Doctrine (the idea that we will give rhetorical support, material military aid, and diplomatic backing, but not troops in other people's instability) in response.

There is a significant difference between the circumstances surrounding the articulation of the Nixon Doctrine in the 1970s and its unacknowledged revival in 2022. When Nixon laid out what became his namesake doctrine, the context was the end of a very unpopular Vietnam War. The doctrine was essentially a promise to 1972 prospective voters that under his watch the country would not repeat that enormously unpopular adventure. In essence, the Nixon Doctrine promised there would be No More Vietnams (the mantra of the anti-war movement). The concept has lain moribund for nearly a half century, but it has been symbolically revived in concept in American assistance to Ukraine in 2022. In the early 1970s, the dynamic was anti-war sentiment; what bounds American response today is the fear of nuclear escalation.

The 2022 Ukrainian confrontation implicitly revived Nixon's principle when Putin announced early on during the Russian aggression that he had ordered that Russia's nuclear arsenal be placed on a heightened state of readiness. Ukraine lacks these weapons, so the threat was not directly aimed at them. When it was part of the Soviet Union, part of the arsenal was deployed in Ukraine, but in 1994, as part of the terms of the final breakup of the Soviet state, those weapons were surrendered to Russia. Ukraine's major symbolic connection in nuclear matters is as the site of the Chernobyl nuclear accident, so the Russian motive could not have been to deter a Ukrainian threat or use of weapons they did not possess. Putin's motives in raising the nuclear contingency were directly aimed at deterring a nuclear strike on Russia that no one had threatened. The fact that the announcement was made in the first days of the invasion suggests, however, a possible implicit admission of the instability of the Russian regime, its leader, or the strength of the Soviet state, which had a much more difficult time invading and subduing the Ukrainians than was largely expected, which was apparently surprising to the Russians.

These kinds of international violence create one frame around the kinds of international situations and challenges the American military may confront in the future. They are very different from developing world asymmetrical wars, and it is difficult to develop an orientation regarding when the United States should fight that adequately encompasses both asymmetrical wars and the return of more opponents in traditionally based conflict. Both situations present a different kind of problem to the United States. They are of different orders of magnitude both as American problems and in their impact on the world order, and each requires a different military and geopolitical posture and attitude.

The Russian invasion of Ukraine rocked the peace in Europe that has prevailed for three-quarters of a century since the end of World War II and, most ominously, returns the shadow of the mushroom-shaped cloud to international calculations, which hopefully will prove aberrational. The hope must be that the crisis will be settled at least partially because the prevailing fear of nuclear escalation has produced the outer boundary of superpower interactions since both arsenals reached potential civilization-ending proportions. There is less chance there will be a nuclear outbreak of instability in the developing world, raising into consideration the calculations of into which of these events (if any) the United States might involve itself and how it can do so in a more satisfactory way than has been the case in the past several decades.

The two situations are discrete in terms of the criteria of the IF principles. Avoiding a direct military confrontation with Russia that could somehow devolve into nuclear war is clearly in the highest interest of the United States (and everyone else). Basic to that importance is the calculation of achieving goals: the consensus underlying peace has, after all, been based mostly in the fear that war could destroy us all. That fear has underlain the peace and Russia has, at least until the Ukrainian adventure, also been guided by this prospect. In February 2022, Putin announced he had ordered Russian nuclear forces to some unspecified level of active status as the Russian advance in Ukraine was bogging down. Developing world internal conflicts, of course, do not have the escalatory potential of superpower interactions, but are more frequent. These two polar extremes of international violent activity and potential represent the most likely sources of situations in which American military involvement could occur.

Dealing with the Modal Threats

The problems for American security posed by the very different threats from Russia and in the developing world share some common roots and causes. The major common element is that both are leftovers from the Cold War period. The Soviet-American conflict was, of course, the heart of American national security concern from the late 1940s until the collapse of the Soviet Union in 1991. The great source of commonality was competition between the two powers directly for world leadership, and this competition extended into the developing world. As the Cold War evolved, competition for loyalty and fealty toward one or another in the Afro-Asian world became a placebo for direct conflict that could conceivably escalate to nuclear exchange. It was a relatively "safe" form of military interaction. It was generally limited to supplying and underwriting one side or another in internal situations where the success of one side or the other was annoying or mildly damaging to the superpower whose allies did not prevail, but those outcomes were not so important to either that failure or success likely had any escalatory real potential.

Communism versus anti-communism was the common theme of this competition. The major element was political and military competition for support. The heart of the direct competition was centered in Europe and featured the Iron Curtain that divided the communist and noncommunist states. As an extension of the European geopolitical competition of the twentieth century and earlier, it centered militarily on preparations for the next world war that was widely feared, as already noted. The symbol of the gravity of that confrontation was nuclear weapons. Nuclear "saber rattling," as it was sometimes known, was the shibboleth of the common fear of war. Particularly since the demise of the Soviet state, nuclear threats and fears have receded as the European order has adjusted to new realities.

Putin's late February 2022 announcement of upgraded nuclear readiness has revived the nuclear dynamic as part of international concern, as well as reintroducing war to a Europe theater enjoying seventy consecutive years of peace. The question is whether that introduction is simply an aberration or a reactivated obsession in international geopolitics. The answer to that question is tightly focused on Russian leader Vladimir Putin and why he undertook this major breach of the European peace.

The competition in the developing world is related to this system dynamic. The Cold War was, at heart, a contest for which system, Western-style democracy or Soviet communism, would dominate the international order. The lines were clearly drawn in the traditional Euro-centered world by the late 1940s, which happened to coincide with the movement to end colonialism in the developing world. The new countries that emerged from this process became the battleground onto which the communist–anti-communist competition was contested.

These two dynamics, Russian attempted resurgence and developing world violence, are at the heart of the environmental challenges to the United States and operationally define the question of when the United States should think about using force for the foreseeable future. They are very different contingencies in terms of the problems they pose, their military contexts, and the degree to which they pose problems answerable in terms of the IF criteria. As a result, each must be examined independently—major power conflict in this chapter and developing world conflict in the next.

The Russian Invasion of Ukraine

The Russian invasion and occupation of Ukraine is a reminder that conflict among major powers has not disappeared completely and that concerted attention must still be directed both to suppressing conflicts between major powers (especially when the potential combatants are nuclear-armed) and, as in the case of the latest Russian adventure, trying to contain and end the bloodletting, especially if there is any danger that it might spread to other places. The conspicuous supporting unity among Western powers in the face of Putin's aggression in Ukraine represents, among other things, a major symbol of common Western resolve that has not always been evident in dealing with conflicts among major powers. The apparent role of nuclear weapons in this situation is ambivalent: raising them by heightening their readiness levels reminds us that they are still the ultimate part of the military condition and that at least some leaders like Putin may see utility in nuclear saber rattling and reminding opponents of the potential consequences of interfering with Russia's actions, although in unspecified ways. The uncertain impact will be explored in the rest of this chapter. Developing world asymmetrical conflict will be described in chapter 7.

The Return of Major Power Conflict: Why Did Putin Do It?
The second invasion of Ukraine by Russia since it occupied and annexed Ukrainian Crimea in 2014 was a puzzling geopolitical move to most Westerners. European relations with Russia had been relatively peaceful since the dissolution of the old Soviet Union, as the Russians struggled sequentially with the breakup of empire, political realignment within the power structure, and more recently with Putin's attempt to redeem Russia's premier power role in the world largely through economic means centering on Russian oil. The three elements in this process are, of course, related to one another, and each plays some role in the Ukrainian situation. Partly because the brutal invasion represents the first overt breakdown of peace (or at least the absence of war) in Europe since 1945, and partly because its outcome will almost certainly contribute to the trajectory of Russia's likely declining role as a world power, it is worth speculating on in some detail.

The invasion was, in many ways, difficult to explain. It surprised most Westerners, who had become comfortable with the apparent stability and peacefulness of the international order and were thus nonplussed by Russian saber rattling and the rumbling of Russian tanks into Ukraine. Because of the closed nature of the Russian system (reflecting Russian history generally), the total motives will likely remain obscured long after the Russians return home and Ukraine is returned to some semblance of normalcy (a process that will be generously aided by the West, quite the opposite effect that Putin wanted). About the only outcome that is reasonably easy to predict is that, in the long term, Russia will likely suffer more than it benefits from the experience. At a minimum, its label as a pariah state has more than been reinforced.

The entire phenomenon centers on why Putin authorized what he did. We will likely never know entirely, because the Russian president and his actions and motivations have remained shielded from direct observation. Thus, we can only speculate on what dynamics *may* have underlain the enterprise, which in turn may help institute the foundation of systemic safeguards that will make a similar action less likely in the future.

Only Putin and those around him know exactly what the dynamics were, and those advisors are unlikely to acknowledge the details publicly. There will not be a rush of tell-all memoirs after the fact pouring from publishing houses in Russia like the flood of interpretations of the Trump experience after he left office. Thus, the explanation that follows may be spot on, and it may not be. It is offered as one possible construction of motives and realities.

The nub of the explanation centers on Putin and the outcome he bequeaths to Russia as his part of his enduring legacy. Putin's vision may best be summed in his statement during the 1990s that the dismantlement of the Soviet Union was the worst event of the twentieth century; it was certainly the greatest blow to the Russian pretension to superpower status, a position that Russians, sitting on the edge of Europe, had coveted for centuries.

When he emerged as the champion of a revived Russian place in the world based in a reassertion of something like Soviet status, he revealed his worldview and his hope for Russian resurgence. But his vision had to be realized in the context of the inevitable, demographically and economically defined decline of Russia. Putin thus saw his country's downward spiral that almost inevitably would get worse and for which he would be assigned (rightly or wrongly) some or most of the blame. It was not a legacy with which any leader would want to be identified; it certainly was not a niche in history that the KGB Cold Warrior could willingly accept.

Putin has consistently seen himself as the anointed vessel for arresting and reversing his country's decline in an international environment that he believes to be intent on further marginalizing Russia's great-power status. No political leader wants his or her legacy defined as having presided over his country's decline, and Soviet/Russian prestige and influence plummeted during the 1990s. When Putin achieved and consolidated power after the turn of the century, Russia's stature in the international order had deteriorated and showed little indication of reversing its decline. That fate was unacceptable to Putin and those in Russia who have supported him. Ukraine, a reluctant, unwilling part of the Soviet empire, broke away from the former Soviet "paradise" and became increasingly independent and antagonistic. That made them a potential target for Russian ire, and more specifically, the retributive instinct of the former KGB agent in Moscow.

Putin's emergence from the political chaos of the 1990s symbolized by the hard-drinking Boris Yeltsin gave voice to the humiliation many Russians felt, and that emotion helped propel Putin into power. The contrast between the leaders was great. Yeltsin was a florid veteran of the Kremlin wars and hardly cut a heroic physical visage compared to Putin, who at about fifty years old was in conspicuously good physical condition and exuded a vigorous contrast to Yeltsin, and Russians seemed to embrace this invigorated image of the former KGB operative. Moreover, Putin radiated energy and ambition for Russia, which he demonstrated in actions against former Soviet republics like Georgia and in 2014 against the Crimean section of Ukraine. Putin clearly intended a more aggressive approach than Yeltsin, and that included, to the extent possible, the reestablishment of Russian suzerainty over breakaway former Soviet republics, and specifically those bordering upon or important to a reinvigorated, secure Russia.

The Russian invasion, to the extent we know why he ordered it, appeared to be an attempt to reestablish Russia's regional sway in the area surrounding its borders. It was not always an easy or commodious process, since the Russians had alienated the people in many areas. As the Soviet Union expanded, one way the Russians sought to justify and solidify their hold on areas, many of which were—and still are—hostile to the Russians, was to colonize areas they had incorporated with Russian immigrants. When the Soviet Union dissolved, many of these native Russian-speakers found themselves in new independent states like Georgia and Ukraine, where they were not especially welcome and did not integrate well with local ethnic populations. In 2014, Russia invaded Crimea, which had a predominately Ukrainian native population but also a largely imported Russian population, and the Russian rationale for intervention was at least partly to guarantee their protection. (It also secured Russia's only warm-water port access to the Mediterranean Sea and beyond.) Part of the official rationale for the invasion of Ukraine was to protect equivalent Russian populations in Donetsk and Lugansk.

Protecting Russian immigrants in Ukraine was the "high road" motive for the invasion. It is almost certainly true that Putin did not want a suppressed Russian minority in Ukraine as part of his legacy, but it was his predecessors who created much of this problem by encouraging the movement of native Russians from the motherland to the areas being annexed as part of the growing Soviet empire. The purpose then was to Russify these conquered areas to justify the growing Soviet empire. When the Soviet state dissolved and was reduced to a struggling Russia, many of these immigrants stayed on, often in enclaves near the Russian border, rather than returning to Russia. Continued advocacy of the safety of these populations in Ukraine is an official part of the Russian case for war; creating a buffer zone between Russia and what is left of Ukraine after the war is another.

Putin is both a megalomaniac and a Russian nationalist. Part of his motivation is grounded in Russian nationalism: he both wants his native country to thrive as a preeminent power and does not want to be blamed by the historians if it does not. The two motivations are undoubtedly intertwined in his thinking and his actions against Ukraine. There is probably not a great deal that Putin (or any other Russian leader) can do to prevent the demographic and oil-based economic strictures the country faces. Given Russian predilections apparently shared by Putin, expansionism and saber rattling have essentially always been attractive for a country that has been outside the general European system. The invasion of neighboring countries that provide a buffer between Russia and Europe is consistent with how the Russians have tried to position themselves in European politics. Countries like the Baltic states and Ukraine wedged between mainstream Europe and Russia have always been subject to pressures from both sides, normally more violent and ham-handed by the Russians.

It is clear Putin and those Russians who support his vision have the largest stake in how the war ends. The Western worst-case scenario suggested as fighting dragged on was that subduing Ukraine and probably annexing its eastern provinces was part of a larger game plan to restore as much of former Soviet territory to Russian control as possible. A "fitting" legacy for Putin would be to preside over the effective reconstruction of as much of the Soviet Union as possible as part of Russia. That is the sort of grand outcome that Putin clearly would cherish as the core of his legacy.

It is an ambitious goal, and one it is difficult to imagine that Putin can achieve or even likely approach. Parts of the European Soviet Union—notably the Baltic states but extending beyond them—have integrated enough with the West through institutions like NATO that a Ukraine-style assault on them would trigger Western responses far more clearly spelled out in Article 5 of the NATO Treaty, a status to which Ukraine aspires. The NATO bond spelled out in the NATO treaty is that in the event of an attack on a member (or members), the organization has an obligation to act to right the wrong committed. Member states are not required to employ armed force, leaving the nature of the response purposely vague. The Article 5 commitment is unspecific because the treaty would not have been ratified by the US Senate had there been an automatic response, on the grounds that doing so would have effectively taken the war-making power away from the Senate and transferred that authority to NATO, a forfeiture the Senate would not have accepted, thereby torpedoing NATO membership by the United States.

The Article 5 provision has been controversial, but is also useful in some situations, of which Ukraine is an example. It means that if an opponent engages in military action against a NATO member, the organization is required to contemplate and presumably to take some form of action. A potential aggressor does not know what NATO might do, because since armed retaliation is one of the possible responses, it is a contingency the potential peace breaker must consider. Precedent is not helpful; the only time Article 5 was invoked was in a resolution supporting the United States after the 9/11 attacks.

The shadow of NATO hangs over Russia and Putin. Post-Soviet Russia flirted with NATO membership, but the negotiations broke down in the 1990s over Russian insistence on a special status akin to America's. Today, Russia views NATO as an essentially anti-Russian structure, and one under which the Russians—and especially Putin—chafes. NATO was formed to counter the Soviet offensive threat to the West. Today, the Russians see it as a threat against them, and the closer membership gets to Russian soil, the more troubling it becomes. To Russia, NATO is its primary security problem and threat; and the idea of Ukraine joining NATO and becoming a part of that threat is very real to a country like Russia for which relations with other countries is often a choice between adversaries and vassals. When NATO turned the Russians away, animosity and threat were rekindled.

The Russians have always placed Ukraine and Georgia in a special category of states the neutrality (at a minimum) of which they believe is vital to their own security. As Putin has consolidated power, the neutrality of these states has been a paramount element of Russian relationships with the former Soviet republics and with the West. The growing power of Putin and a more assertive Russian posture in the world have helped give rise to increased concern about renewed Russian aggressiveness. This in turn has given rise to desires for greater protection from a resurgent Russian bear, and in Ukraine, the open advocacy of NATO membership was a product of that concern. It also apparently crossed the line of acceptable postures for the Russians.

Encirclement was a minimal Russian problem when the member states of the Soviet Union surrounded and effectively shielded Russia proper from those hostile others. One consequence of the end of the Cold War was to strip away that protection as former Soviet states broke away and declared their independence from the Russian yoke. The former communist states and regions have gradually aligned themselves and their politico-military futures with the West, and that conversion has resulted in a Russia that has significant potential hostile neighbors on its boundaries. Ukraine is among the largest and most contiguous examples of this change, and when Ukrainians began to voice interest in NATO, Russian reactions were predictably negative. They turned violent during the winter of 2022. The goal of the Russian action, as best one can know from afar, was to push the West further away from Russian soil, and Putin was almost certainly influenced both by those concerns and with the credit he would earn from the Russian people for protecting them from the hostile others. It was not an entirely surprising response. Whether correcting the situation required a massive commitment of Russian forces who engaged in brutal attacks against Ukraine is debatable; for the Russians (and clearly for Putin), it was justified. Whether the ends will prove to have justified the means is a different matter. How history judges Russian actions will depend on the judgment about how the Russians dealt with this aspect of their NATO problem and what precedent that may have for the future. Will the experience be chastening, or will it encourage Russia to apply the "Putin Solution" elsewhere on the Russian periphery?

The American Response: Aggression and Nuclear Weapons

The American response to the crisis—roundly condemning and levying extensive sanctions on Russia but specifically eschewing any intent to allow the United States to become militarily engaged—demonstrates how international military activity has changed in the post–Cold War nuclear weapons age. The most prominent element has been the very conscious design and implementation of responses to minimize or eliminate the possibility that American and Russian troops might unintentionally physically engage one another in combat that could escalate to war between them. The reason is very clear: to reduce the likelihood of a spiral that could lead to the use of nuclear weapons as part of the conflict. Economic sanctions have replaced armed combat as the American (and allied) weapon of choice in the current conflict. This precedent may be the most important long-term consequence of the war beyond the fate of the Ukrainian people.

As the invasion evolved, it was clear (if unadmitted) that the Russian action was a strategic failure—in effect a reprise of the Soviet invasion of Afghanistan that helped bring down the regime. The Russians clearly believed the invasion and subsequent occupation would be essentially easy, given the sheer size and lethal capabilities of the Russian armed forces he had massed on the Ukrainian border. The conceptual plan was a kind of "shock and awe" show of force to intimidate and quickly overwhelm the Ukrainian resistance and allow a speedy completion of the conquest in a short time, hopefully before world opinion could galvanize in opposition to the action. The strategic intent was clear: to present the world with a strategic *fait accompli* that burnished Russian prestige and power globally and provided a reminder to other former Soviet republics of the consequences of trying the same thing. In Putin's mind, the result would be a renewed world respect for, even fear of, Russia. As the war proceeded with hints of what a European-style asymmetrical resistance might look like, these optimistic views faded.

The struggle did not work out that way, for reasons that analysts will continue to study for some time. Russian power was not vindicated, as the Ukrainians withheld the imposition of Russian dominance for a variety of reasons, from faulty, overly optimistic Russian planning to the poor performance of its troops and equipment in the field. Russia did not physically lose the war, but they certainly did not win it in the decisive manner one would have expected given the differences in size and military capability. Instead, it offered some hint of what a Western-style adaptation of asymmetrical warfare might look like, a contingency that the Russians had clearly not anticipated. An unstated reason for the invasion had to be to reestablish the stature of the Russian military machine. It failed to do so.

Putin's arguable purpose of reminding the world of the potency and prowess of Russia as a world power was tarnished by its military performance. Its intended result was to remind the world that Russia is still a world force to be reckoned with. It was a clear failure: what should, by conventional standards, have been a walkover was anything but that. The tarnish extends to Putin himself: there will not be statues of Vladimir Putin erected in Moscow and elsewhere celebrating his strategic victory over Ukraine after he is gone; Russian history will almost certainly lay the blame for a botched effort on him. Afghanistan was Russia's first encounter with what we have described here as unconventional, asymmetrical warfare, and it failed. The Soviet Union responded to that defeat by collapsing; what will Putin do? The question includes to what ends he will try to resort to avoid that conclusion, and how far Russia will follow him.

The more subtle and, in some respects, more consequential lesson of this clash was how the lethality of contemporary—especially nuclear—forces affected the war's conduct on both sides, but especially by NATO. The possibility that the confrontation could, under the wrong circumstances, escalate to nuclear exchange was always implicit in the evolution of the crisis and national, and especially American, responses and policy decisions.

The United States took the public leadership in shaping the NATO response. The basic decision facing the alliance was the physical and conceptual nature of that response: would it be primarily military, featuring forceful actions the United States and its allies would take to defend their erstwhile suitor, or would it be in some other form? The situation could not be ignored because of the devastating effect wrong decisions might have had on the likelihood that the situation could escalate out of hand to the threat or actual use of nuclear weapons.

The decisions in turn had to be calibrated in terms of their effectiveness and the impact they would have had on global perceptions of Western backbone in the face of a challenge. One option, and the choice ultimately implemented, was to approach the problem non-militarily, using economic sanctions against Russia to cause damage to the Russian economy and strain the lives of the Russian people, while at the same time providing needed assistance to the Ukrainian resistance in military and humanitarian ways. These plans and actions consciously eschewed any actions that might bring American and Russian troops into direct military confrontation. Sending American (and other NATO) forces into Ukraine would inevitably bring them into contact with Russian invaders, entail combat casualties on both sides, and raise markedly—and possibly inevitably—the prospect of escalation that might include the nuclear option. Avoiding that contingency was clearly the top American priority.

The greatest fear was that a decisive military solution carried with it the possibility of escalation to nuclear exchange. The dynamics of such a possibility occurring, as emphasized earlier, are unknown and unknowable short of an actual confrontation, and it has been a cardinal, if implicit, tenet of the nuclear arms race to avoid finding out definitively—knowledge only an actual nuclear confrontation could provide. Although Putin did elevate the readiness of his nuclear arsenal at one point, the Americans refused to escalate the situation with the direct application of force to dislodge the Russians. The reason was simple: the use of force could escalate the action, possibly to the nuclear level, and no one, most prominently the Americans, was willing to take the chance. As the situation evolved with Russian failure to defeat the Ukrainians as its most obvious characteristic, the question of how Putin would react to failure had to be raised: could he accept an Afghan outcome knowing its effect on Russia? Or might he choose to escalate the conflict? This set of choices was the most frightening aspect of the war's evolution.

The result was a war of economic sanctions rather than a conflict of arms conducted by NATO members opposing the invasion as a step short of raising the violence. The implicit assumption underlying this determination was that the conventional defense of Ukraine was not worth the risk of a civilization-ending nuclear conflagration. Instead of using bullets to influence what the Russians did, economic strictures were put in place to constrict Russian activities in ways about which the Russians chafed but that gave them no reasonable excuse to redirect their violence to the United States and the NATO allies. It was not the war of John Wayne World War II movies when there were no nuclear weapons; it may be the only kind of warfare in a nuclear age involving nuclear-armed opponents.

This reorientation of the calculus of war changes the way states think about when and how they can threaten and employ force. At one level, it becomes a factor in the decision to make war: a nuclear-armed country contemplating war that may create an adverse reaction from other nuclear countries must include an assessment of the likelihood its actions will create that form of response from the other side, what that reaction may be, whatever risks it believes that reaction may be, how it can counter those reactions, and whether the costs of doing so justify the risks and hoped-for gains. Such considerations have always been part of the calculus of war, but they have historically been calculable in military terms. The response to the Russian invasion of Ukraine alters those calculations in ways that were not entirely anticipated by the Russians, but if they succeed, they will be repeated in the future. If they fail, nuclear muscle boundedness may move the conduct of war from the traditional battlefield to the checkbook.

In essence, the extensive economic sanctions imposed by the Biden administration and joined by the NATO allies had the purpose of bringing the war's consequences directly to the Russian people in terms of economic pain. It has crippled the Russian economy greatly in ways that will only fully be understood after the war is over and recovery on both sides proceeds. Ukraine will have a badly scarred country that the international community will almost certainly act decisively to repair. Russia may be allowed back into the world economy, but with provisions designed to prevent a repeat of its performance in Ukraine.

The most fascinating, potentially consequential outcome will be on the effects on Russia itself, and the prospects are ironic and dangerous, to say the least. Putin started the war to neutralize and prevent Ukrainian flirtation with NATO and the EU, but one of the other effects that undoubtedly also motivated his decision was to enhance his, and Russia's, stature as a world power. It is probably impossible to separate these two motives—one intensely nationalist, the other equally egotistical—altogether, but it is possible to raise and tentatively assess the question of whether Russia and its leader are better or worse off for the effort. The tentative answers suggest that Putin and his associates miscalculated the situation and how it evolved, and that the result, akin to the Soviet Union's failed invasion and occupation of Afghanistan, was disastrous for the Soviet Union. Putin knows this. What might he contemplate to avoid a similar disaster? How the West handles this question may be the most important effect of the war.

Is Ukraine Russia's Vietnam—Or a Reprise of Afghanistan and Iraq?
Regardless of the eventual outcome of the conflict initiated by Russia against Ukraine, it will clearly not be a victory for Russian arms or its conduct of power politics. The massing and unleashing of Russian armed forces on a country with a fraction of its population through a massive attack demonstrated the historical brutality of the Russian style of war and elicited more outside sympathy and support for the Ukrainians than probably would have been the case had the action been more measured and less heavy-handed.

The Russian invasion was apparently intended as a shock-and-awe operation that would quickly demoralize the Ukrainian resistance and allow a rapid occupation of the country. The apparent model was Soviet occupation of Georgia in 2008; but Russian forces entering Ukraine were greeted by a more determined resistance on a larger scale, and they appeared not to have been prepared for it. The analogy of Georgia was mistaken; Afghanistan may have been the more prescient comparison. In addition, their military forces performed at less than peak efficiency, prolonging the resistance that apparently was unanticipated and revealing the Russian military "machine" as much less formidable than the Russians and the rest of the world presumed them to be. Overthrowing the Zelensky government proved to be a far more formidable task than they must have envisioned in prewar planning, and the execution of their plan was clearly flawed. The memory one may have of the Russian "onslaught" is aerial photography of the miles of Russian forces apparently stalled on their way to the capital of Kyiv. When their presumable initial plan failed, they resorted to the relentless shelling of civilian centers. This time, however, their actions were captured by global media and broadcast in real time around the world. It cannot have been the kind of coverage that the image-conscious Putin hoped for or envisaged. Additionally, the demographics of Russia's shrinking and aging population appeared to have created manpower problems when the Ukrainians mounted a much more spirited defense than they apparently anticipated.

The post-Ukrainian analysis will likely be dominated by two questions. The first will be why did the Russians invade in the first place? Their stated explanation was because of the threat that Ukraine would be admitted to NATO and the EU, thus firmly implanting another Western presence along the Russian border and meaning, in the worst case, that Russia could itself be attacked directly from hostile territory. They feared losing their protection from European attack, a long-standing obsession of much Russian security policy. This threat was not apparent outside Putin's inner circle, and it seemed more of a contrived excuse than an honest threat from a carnivorous cabal supposedly poising itself on the Russian-Ukrainian border ready to invade Russia. It seemed contrived, and it will continue to be questioned unless the Russians can somehow explain it convincingly, which they are unlikely to do. To most in the outside world, it looked like familiar Russian thuggery at work: Russia being Russia.

Second, was there another way to accomplish this goal that did not require the heavy, ham-handed, application of Russian force? From a Russian perspective, this is not an easy question to answer. Russia is ringed by hostile neighbors, most of which it has earned and who were reluctant partners in the Soviet Union relieved to see the Russians go. Russia has sought to squelch anti-Russian actions and sentiments in the old empire, in effect to reestablish Russian influence, even control, and it has worked in places like Georgia, Chechnya, and even the Crimean region of Ukraine. Resistance in Ukraine to a Russian return has been qualitatively stouter than in other places partly because Ukraine is physically larger and more populous than the other places Russia has attacked. Putin and his generals may have underestimated the problem of invading and toppling independent Ukraine, thinking it would be somehow easy. Whose fault was that? Putin's? His generals? What will be the long-term consequences of this clumsy, apparently mishandled operation? The Russian action was almost certainly motivated by a desire to remind the world that Russia, negative demographic trendlines notwithstanding, was still a major force with which to be reckoned. Is that the takeaway the world will remember?

This action, as best one can tell without direct and reliable access to internal Kremlin decision making, is that it has clearly been Putin's war, and it will likely be remembered as such. It was not the kind of walkover success that Putin and his associates expected, and it will hardly be remembered as a success of Russian arms or diplomacy. Many of the details do not resemble what happened to the United States in Southeast Asia over a half century ago, but the outcome may bear a strong resemblance. Neither country, after all, was clearly successful in Afghanistan either.

Ukraine was not Russia's Vietnam in any direct, symmetrical way. The United States was asked by the South Vietnamese government to enter its civil war, while Russia hardly had that kind of invitation. If there is an analogy, however, it was that Russia clearly believed that the Ukrainians would not resist or would not offer a spirited, effective resistance. The Ukraine was, to borrow LBJ's depiction, viewed by Russia as a "pissant" country like Vietnam was supposed to have been. Those depictions were wrong in estimating the importance of the fight to the Ukrainians, just as the United States underestimated how important their cause was to the Vietnamese.

The resistance in Ukraine was initially not as well organized as the opposition to the American-backed regime in Vietnam in the early 1960s, but it proved to be a good deal more tenacious and determined than the Russians anticipated, and the Russian forces proved less formidable than Putin undoubtedly hoped and was told they would be. The comparison of forces reflects the difference in importance of the outcome to the two sides. The apparent difference between the two conflicts is that public opinion in the United States was crucial in causing the United States to leave. Whether Putin can suppress opposition that has arisen in Russia and elsewhere is a crucial factor in how the Russians' Ukraine aggression ends.

The result may well prove to be that the experience will be a hybrid of the American experience in Vietnam and the Russian experience in Afghanistan. In both cases, the superpower underestimated and probably misunderstood what they were getting into. The United States clearly misunderstood the political and military situation in Vietnam, conceptualizing what was a civil war over who would govern Vietnam as an outside Cold War contest and thus misapprehending how they should approach a communist takeover that they thought could be brushed aside by beating the "commies." The Russians apparently underestimated both the depth and strength of Ukrainian nationalism and resolve and hatred of Russian domination and thus presumed they would meet little resistance. Both superpowers were wrong in their assessments. The result was ignominious for the United States, and the same possibility exists for Russia. The United States was able to recover from its mistake; it is far less likely that the Putin regime can survive if it does not subdue the Ukrainian resistance. In that sense, the outcome is critical to both Putin's tenure and his legacy. Vietnam drove Lyndon Johnson from the presidency; Ukraine could have a parallel effect on Putin.

There are two possible outcomes of the Ukrainian War, and they affect Russia's future far more greatly than the American failure in Vietnam affected the United States. Russia aims to cut the politico-military ties between Ukraine and the West. Putin's regime must achieve at least the strong semblance of this goal to prevent Ukraine moving decisively toward the West and thus avoid losing the resulting peace. The Russian invasion and brutal prosecution of the war is making achieving that goal in an internationally tolerable manner increasingly difficult, if not impossible. When the war was just a possibility and not a bloody reality, could Russia have negotiated Ukrainian neutrality and abandonment of NATO membership? Doing so would have been difficult, but can the war accomplish that end? Given virtually united global condemnation of their action, the mission seems increasingly unattainable.

The other possible outcome is Russian failure, on the battlefield, within the theater of world opinion, or both. The Ukrainian situation is not the same as the Georgian experience. In that case, the Russians achieved their goals because the world did not care sufficiently about Georgia to act politically to reverse the outcome. Georgia was an obscure place that the world hardly noticed. A Russian military triumph, occupation, and forced Ukrainian acquiescence in abandoning their NATO ambitions will not be the same. The Russian invasion has made the case strongly that Ukraine needs NATO protection from Russia. The world effectively forgot and thus implicitly forgot Georgia. The brutality, destruction, and refugee flow in the Ukrainian case ensures the world will not forget this time.

Russia will almost certainly emerge from this war as the geopolitical, and even possibly the military, loser, and the Ukrainians will be regarded as martyrs and heroes. The West, and notably the United States, has played a restrained role in this process. President Biden quickly eschewed any American intent or willingness to intervene with armed forces. It was a not-so-implicit acknowledgement of the restraining role of nuclear weapons on conflict between nuclear-armed powers. China is the only other country that has a superpower-caliber arsenal, and they avoided any overt role in the crisis or its resolution. If there was any question about whether China had eclipsed Russia as a world power, the Chinese role in this war may have removed it.

Ukraine and the IF Factor
Putin, dragging an unenthusiastic Russian population behind him, sought to impose a nineteenth-century power politics solution to the Russian dilemma of decline and their historical vulnerability to invasion on Ukraine. The effort clearly had geopolitical and personal appeal to Putin both to burnish his own legacy and to return Russian prestige to something like its Soviet-era level, and he could not pull it off. There is ample irony in the evolution of the crisis. Putin used his armed forces to rein in an increasingly independent, even hostile Ukraine in a traditional, nineteenth-century

balance of power way. It failed in the absence of direct military confrontation between the Russians and NATO (including the United States). Economic sanctions and world disapprobation were the weapons of choice, and when combined with Ukrainian heroism and Russian ineptitude, they carried the day. Among other things, one of the dynamics that helped cause this to occur was the "F" part of the IF Principle: feasibility. Hopefully, the lasting lesson of the Russian invasion of Ukraine will be to cause a rethinking of the role of force among major powers in the nuclear age. The accoutrements of traditional war and calculations will not disappear, but they can fade into the background, a position they had occupied in the twenty-first century until early 2022.

Large power involvement in military actions like the Russian intrusion into Ukraine will probably prove to be an aberration in contemporary global military affairs with which the United States must deal and for which it must prepare strategically. Russia will be chastened for a while by its lackluster performance in the invasion of Ukraine, and the war almost certainly activated the process of a transition from Putin to some other leader. Who that may be is not clear at this point, nor is any changed direction of the new leadership in its dealings with the rest of the world's countries. The war did, however, reinforce the idea that the economic instrument of power has superseded the military instrument as a way to approach big power confrontations, thanks largely to the existence and danger posed by nuclear weapons. Unless something mitigates the potential horrors of nuclear war, war between the major powers may have virtually disappeared as a major policy option.

The IF Factor works in contradictory ways in this construction. There were clearly adequate Western interests (both American and especially European NATO) to address the Russian attack on Ukraine. Given the blatant, ham-handed nature of the attack (a historic Russian specialty), the United States and NATO could not avoid some significant response without compromising NATO as an effective geopolitical force. Had there been no NATO response, there arguably would have been little credible reason for anyone (like the Russians) to take NATO seriously in the future: the organization would have been rightfully viewed as a paper tiger whose protestations could safely be ignored, and this taint would have affected the United States. Who would have been deterred from taking hostile actions that the United States rhetorically opposed if the Americans did not act to help a democratic country seeking to join and enjoy the protection of the North Atlantic Treaty Organization?

The question was what else could the United States and its allies have done that did not raise the possibility of nuclear weapons use? There has not

The Briar Patch of Intervention in a Complex Environment ~ 149

been a direct military confrontation between heavily nuclear-armed foes in the nuclear age, although some would argue that the Cuban Missile Crisis of 1962 came close. The Russian invasion of Ukraine was the first instance where the nuclear superpowers faced one another, if indirectly, and they managed to avoid escalation to mutual incineration.

How? The answer to that question turned out to be changing the rules of engagement. If heavily nuclear-armed countries could not confront one another but had significant differences that historically could have led to armed conflict, then there had to be a different way to achieve these kinds of goals. The option chosen by the United States and its NATO allies was the application of the economic instrument of power. It was a method that suited the West, because Europe and North America wield considerably more economic strength than does Russia, whose economy, tied as it is to petroleum, was particularly vulnerable to economic coercion. Additionally, the path from economic sanctions to nuclear exchange is considerably less clear than from conventional fighting to the use of those weapons. Economic "warfare" may have helped to win World War II, but there were no nuclear weapons then (at least until the very end).

It was not a totally satisfying or comforting change to those in the middle of the fray. Although they never admitted to their disadvantage, the Russians know they could not compete successfully at economic "warfare": Russia has never been an economic power. It is, in world comparative economic terms, a "banana republic with oil," not an advanced twenty-first-century economic power. If the world power map adopts economic power as its primary means of allotting status, the Russians lose. Presumably, they understand this, and thus cannot favor a change in the definition of national power away from the sword to the bank account. It was also of little solace to the Ukrainians, who were pummeled mercilessly by Russian military attacks. The application of the economic instrument will help them in their postwar rebuilding and recovery from the Russian attack, but it was of little comfort to them during the war itself.

The United States and its allies had little choice but to respond somehow to the Russian invasion. There were clearly adequate US and European interests endangered by a Russian victory that could move their influence closer to the heart of Europe. President Biden and those around him, however, concluded early on that the military instrument of power was not the proper mode of countervailing power, and they opted for a means of resistance that ultimately would bring greater pressure on Russia to stop without actions with potential nuclear consequences. The disadvantage of this approach is that economic strictures can take longer to take hold and can prove inadequate. The advantage was that there is no known direct path from economic strictures to nuclear conflict. The case for what was done resonated in the West; it obviously was less satisfactory to the Ukrainians who desperately needed the war to end.

This raises the second criterion of the IF Factor, feasibility. The standard asks if it is possible to achieve the intended objective: is it possible to attain or secure whatever interest is at risk? The nuclear factor adds the further criterion of achieving the goal with acceptable costs. In this case, that means avoiding an escalation of hostilities to the point that nuclear exchange becomes a potential consequence of proposed actions. It has been the consistent American position that the United States will not do things that might draw the United States into direct military conflict to the point that violence between American and Russian forces could occur and possibly escalate to direct combat that could, in the worst case, include nuclear munitions. That fear was a prime driver of American policy throughout the war.

The Biden administration was adamant on this point, and it had the support of most of the American population and allied governments. The Zelensky government understands this reluctance, but it presented feasibility problems for them in attempting to repel the Russians. The United States has been generous in supplying the Ukrainians with weapons and economic and other assistance, but the limits of that aid are that its provision cannot bring the Americans into potential direct combat situations with the Russians. The result was that a de facto form of the Nixon Doctrine became the operational limitation for American aid against Russian nuclear forces. That inhibition does not extend to dealing with developing world conflicts in places like Iraq or Afghanistan that do not have these weapons. In this case, feasibility is tempered by the need to keep assistance non-suicidal. It means the resort to war between nuclear powers becomes greatly circumscribed, even functionally unthinkable.

Conclusion: The Legacy of Ukraine?

If great powers can no longer settle their differences by recourse to arms between them, then what methods are feasible for achieving their vital interests when they are challenged by another nuclear power? This is not the first time that this concern has been raised. As the Brodies chronicled over forty years ago, major innovations in warfare tend to be treated apocalyptically when they enter arsenals and seem less so as time goes by. That said, the violent unleashing of nuclear power is a quantum change in the death and destruction possible in war and one that will provide the boundary for acceptable warfare for some time. The questions are how the world adapts to that reality.

The Ukraine invasion has been a kind of test case that suggests one possible limit. Although the introduction of new weapons technologies has historically often been treated as apocalyptic and fundamentally transformative, the nuclear threat provides an objectively instructive example of how unrestrained war could lead to the end of civilization as we know it. This might or might not happen should a nuclear weapon(s) be introduced into warfare. We truly have no empirically based understanding of the nuclear escalatory process, because it has never happened before. Knowing the possibilities of catastrophe should these weapons be used, the only prudent approach has been to try to ensure that no one tests the hypothesis. The possible catastrophe is too great to want to know the answer to the escalatory question, and the result has been a consensus surrounding deterrence for the past seventy years.

The Russian invasion of Ukraine has posed the first real test of the durability of nuclear abstinence, because it is the first time a major nuclear weapons possessor has engaged in war and been opposed by another nuclear possessor. The result seems to vindicate the durability of the deterrence concept. Early in the crisis, Putin mentioned the nuclear option, but was met by a horrified global reaction and he backed away from it. At the same time, Putin clearly invested a great deal of his personal commitment to the task of somehow bringing Ukraine to heel in a military campaign the difficulty of which he clearly underestimated. Backing down from his threat without destroying his legacy as an epic Russian hero made the reinstitution of peace particularly difficult but a necessary prophylactic to soften the blow of failure.

Russia announced four conditions for ending the war early in its conduct. All are derivatives of the most basic Russian objective, which was to force Ukraine to denounce any present or future intention to join the West through membership in NATO and the EU. Putin clearly based his position on a combination of historic Russian security (ensuring that Russian territory would not be threatened by hostile neighbors) and on his personal, ego-driven obsession with being remembered as the leader who assured Russian security in a hostile environment, not as a weak leader who allowed its fatal compromise. Which of these reasons was paramount in his decision to invade Ukraine is almost beside the point, since they apparently merged in Putin's mind. Referring to the invasion of Ukraine as Putin's war is by no means a misnomer.

The heart of Putin's demands was Ukrainian neutrality in East-West terms. This aspiration translated into specific demands. First and most rhetorically, it called on Ukraine to cease military action against Russia. The demand was, of course, rhetorical since Ukrainian military activity was a direct response to a Russian military action against them. The other demands were more substantial, dealing with Ukraine's geopolitical place in the area and Russian sway over Ukrainian territory. First, the Russians demanded that the Ukrainians amend their constitution to "enshrine neutrality," a euphemism for abandoning the flirtation of some Ukrainians with NATO and the EU. Second, it demanded that Ukraine acknowledge the Crimea, Ukrainian territory seized by Russia in 2014, as "Russian territory," effectively sanctioning the Russian aggression of that year. Third, it demanded that Ukraine recognize Luhansk and Donetsk, small provinces along the Ukrainian border with large Russian minorities (most of whom were settlers dispensed to the areas by the Soviets), as independent states. The effect of all these actions was to reinforce the cordon sanitaire between Russia and Poland by neutralizing Ukrainian territory that served as a buffer between the two. One can argue the merits of any of these demands, but they at least provided a base of issues to negotiate and potentially to resolve in a manner acceptable to both sides.

What are the long-term effects of the war and its resolution? It is premature to judge those in detail, but two can be projected. First, the Russians will not escape this episode as clear winners whose power status in the world is enhanced: Russia's armed forces were held largely at bay by a much smaller, and on paper weaker, opponent. The Russians clearly believed they would brush aside any Ukrainian opposition in a matter of days, and they were wrong for reasons the Russian government and the world will have to sort out. Have the Russian forces deteriorated to the point that Russia is a nuclear paper tiger capable of destroying the world but incapable of defending its interests with nonnuclear forces? The juxtaposition of the concepts of nuclear weapons and overall weakness seems incongruous, but it may be accurate. Can Russia project military power in the world without a possible reprise of the Ukraine experience? If Russia remains outside the international mainstream, its interests and those of other major powers will continue to come into conflict; how will they be resolved if Russia concludes (which they could well) that they cannot guarantee the sanctity of their borders (clearly their number one priority) with conventional forces? Will they conclude their policy must change and that they must embrace the international order, or will they become more withdrawn and antagonistic? How will the rest of the international system treat them if they reconcile or withdraw further into their nationalistic shell?

A large part of the calculation revolves on the question of post-Ukraine leadership in Russia. If there is one clear loser in this geopolitical incident, it is Vladimir Putin. He authorized the Russian invasion in the clear expectation of a smashing victory that would elevate his global and regional stature, and that did not occur. Strapped by crushing sanctions and unsuccessful on the battlefield, Russia's stature has been diminished, not enhanced, and Putin bears the major responsibility for this occurrence. Will the seventy-year old dictator fade slowly or rapidly from the scene to pose for statues that almost certainly will not be sculpted, and by whom or how will he be replaced? How will Russia respond to its apparently diminished status in the world? The answer will largely determine the long-term systemic effects of the conflict.

The second effect is on the pattern of warfare itself. This war was the first time a major Cold War military power became entangled in a war in Europe since 1945, and the fighting was neither decisive nor did it spread more widely in the world. Once again, most of the credit for this absence of horizontal (war spreading to more combatants) or vertical (conventional or even nuclear weapons introduction) can be attributed to nuclear weapons, but dependence on the very weapons one most fears does not create a comfortable or comforting situation. Ukraine will be rebuilt with generous Western support and Russian power will be devalued in the world, but the real question is what longer-term impacts the war will have.

The answer(s) to that second question may represent the long-term contribution of Ukraine to the question of when the United States should contemplate using force in the future. The West (notably the United States) did not respond to the Russian action with a personal military response, instead choosing the basic Nixon Doctrine of sending aid but not troops to the fray. The United States avoided the possibility of nuclear escalation in the process, but it was less than the Ukrainians needed to expel the Russian invaders decisively. Is that the precedent for the future? And what signal does that send to future aggressors? What, for instance, will the United States do if China threatens to or physically invades and reannexes Taiwan, threatening possible nuclear use in the process? It is a question that has not been addressed publicly for some time. It may have to be given the Ukrainian outcome. At the heart of the question is whether economic "warfare" can successfully substitute for the clash of arms to resolve the most difficult, fervid conflicts between states.

If the resolution calms these disagreements between Russia and the West, then the primary tasks for potential American employment of force moves back to the developing world, where involvements have effectively resided since the Cuban crisis. The developing world does not present the same geopolitical difficulties it did a half century ago, and there is little reason to believe that the same kinds of economic actions that were applied to Russia are relevant elsewhere. The problem of dealing with those conflicts remains the same as it was—coping with variants of asymmetrical warfare.

Ultimately, the legacy of this war was how reasonably to ensure that a situation like this does not recur. This conflict was, after all, the first time in which nuclear superpowers were on opposing sides of a shooting war outside the developing world and, as such, it was an introduction to the tensions and uncertainties such a confrontation entailed. The real lesson to be learned is how to avoid a reprise that might have a different, and far worse, outcome.

Bibliography

Art, Robert A., and Kenneth N. Waltz, eds. *The Use of Force: Military Power and International Politics*. 7th ed. Lanham, MD: Rowman & Littlefield, 2009.

Ashford, Emma, and Joshua Shifrinson. "How the War in Ukraine Could Get Much Worse." *Foreign Affairs* (online), March 11, 2022.

Bearden, Milton. "Putin's Afghanistan: Ukraine and the Lessons of the Soviets' Afghan War." *Foreign Affairs* (online), March 24, 2022.

Biden, Joseph S. Jr., and Michael Carpenter. "How to Stand Up to the Kremlin: Defending Democracy Against Its Enemies." *Foreign Affairs* 97, no. 1 (January/February 2018): 44–57.

Bremmer, Ian. "Putin Won, But Russia is Losing." *Time* 191, April 2, 2018, 42.

Brodie, Bernard, and Fawn M. Brodie. *From Crossbow to H-Bomb: The Evolution of Weapons and Tactics of Warfare*. Revised and Enlarged Edition. Bloomington: Indiana University Press, 1973.

Central Intelligence Agency. *The CIA World Factbook, 2021–2022*. New York: Skyhorse, 2021.

Committee on Foreign Relations, U.S. Senate. *Strategic Assessment of U.S.-Russian Relations*. New York: Create Space, 2018.

Dawisha, Karen. *Putin's Kleptocracy: Who Owns Russia?* New York: Simon and Schuster, 2014.

Fix, Liana, and Michael Kimmage. "What If Russia Loses? A Defeat for Moscow Won't Be a Clear Victory for the West." *Foreign Affairs* (online), March 4, 2022.

Gorbachev, Mikhail. *The New Russia*. Cambridge, UK: Polity Press, 2016.

Isikoff, Michael, and David Korn. *Russian Roulette: The Inside Story of Putin's War on America and the Election of Donald Trump*. New York: Twelve Books, 2018.

Joffe, Julia. "Putin's Game." *The Atlantic* 321, no. 1 (January/February 2018): 68–85.

King, Charles, and Rajon Menon. "Prisoners of the Caucasus: Russia's Invisible Civil War." *Foreign Affairs* 89, no. 4 (July/August 2010): 20–34.

Kolesnikov, Andrei. "Will Putin Lose Russia? His Grip on Power Rests on Fantasy and Fear." *Foreign Affairs* (online), March 9, 2022.

Mandelbaum, Michael. "The New Containment: Handling Russia, China, and Iran." *Foreign Affairs* 98, no. 2 (March/April 2019): 123–31.
Remnick, David. "The Weakness of the Despot." Interview with MSNBC (online), March 14, 2022.
Snow, Donald M. *The Necessary Peace: Nuclear Weapons and Superpower Relations*. Lexington, MA: Lexington Books, 1987.
Stent, Angela. *The Limits of Partnership: U.S.-Russian Relations in the Twenty-First Century*. Princeton, NJ: Princeton University Press, 2015.
Toal, Gerard. *Near Abroad: Putin, the West and the Contest over Ukraine and the Caucasus*. Oxford, UK: Oxford University Press, 2017.
Trenin, Dmitri. *Should We Fear Russia?* Cambridge, UK: Polity Press, 2016.
Tsygankov, Andrei. *Russia's Foreign Policy: Change and Continuity in National Identity*. 4th ed. Lanham, MD: Rowman & Littlefield, 2016.

CHAPTER SEVEN

Coping with Asymmetrical and Conventional Forms of War
The Challenge for American Expeditionary Forces

One of the more fascinating yet generally unmentioned or unrecognized aspects of the Russian war in Ukraine was its similarity militarily to asymmetrical conflicts. This was especially evident in terms of the problems the war posed for the combatants and how they adapted to them. The major difference was the nature of contestants: European-style Russian forces opposed by Ukrainian regular and irregular elements. By any static measure of military might, it was an asymmetrical match between a twentieth-century superpower (although one, in what became obvious as it progressed, was in substantial decline) and a much smaller neighbor with far more limited resources. The Ukrainians, many of whom were irregulars who volunteered in response to the invasion, did not fight in the same way as have insurgent and other irregular movements in the developing world, but neither did they fight in classic European style. At the same time, the Russian military performed poorly, making comparisons between structural asymmetrical and traditional war risky.

The war on Ukraine may well be an aberration in the modern conduct of war. It was European in terms of its location and the basic way both sides approached it. Both the Russian armed forces and their smaller Ukrainian counterparts were organized for traditional European-style warfare, not the kind of irregular, guerrilla-style war fought by insurgents in the developing world. The major similarity was that, like much asymmetrical war, traditional European constraints on who was attacked and how were broadly ignored in the savage way the Russians assaulted Ukrainian population centers.

The Russian aggression against Ukraine was carried out by a thoroughly European state against another similar state, but it was conducted virtually as an unconventional war in terms of the ferocity and savagery by which it was conducted. Among other things, the war was fought within the framework of Russian nuclear weapons as a conditioning factor. The war could have escalated into nuclear confrontation and even conduct, an outcome the avoidance of which has been the most basic value of America and presumably virtually anybody else worldwide. The American adaptation to this environmental factor was novel and effective: those supporting Ukraine did not respond with a traditional recourse to arms in Ukraine, which might well have created a major confrontation with the Russians. Instead, NATO responded with suffocating economic sanctions that brought pressure on the Russians to negotiate without unduly roiling potential nuclear escalatory waters. Is that the future model for conflict resolution when the potential combatants are nuclear-armed? If so, what does it portend for the future of military force employment?

The dynamics and problems the Russian attack and conduct of hostilities create are distinct from those associated with asymmetrical war in the developing world. The venue is different, the combatants are different, and how they fight is different from traditional European-style warfare.

A (arguably *the*) major difference is the nuclear factor. Potential conflicts between states that possess nuclear weapons are qualitatively different from conflicts between countries that do not. Differences prominently include the possibility of polluting the globe with potential life-threatening levels of radiation. That prospect may be remote in almost all instances, but it is potentially apocalyptical enough to create special inhibitions on the conduct and purposes for which nuclear weapons possessors can contemplate or conduct war.

The legacy of the Russo-Ukrainian conflict may well be forged in the context that it featured potential nuclear combatants on opposite sides of the war. Putin raised this potential dynamic directly when he issued vague edicts raising the readiness status of Russian nuclear forces early in the conflict's evolution, and the United States and its NATO allies implicitly acknowledged it with their virtually total conduct of the conflict with economic "weapons." In the roughly six decades since the Cuban missile crisis, this was the first confrontation between the major nuclear rivals. The Russians ended the Cuban crisis by turning its Cuba-bound missile-laden ships around, but it reminded all concerned of the need for vigilant efforts to avoid planetary extinction.

Nuclear-influenced conflicts remain limited prospects statistically, but they are still highly dangerous in potential effect. Since it has never happened, we do not know what happens if a nuclear weapon is used in anger. Ukraine was the first instance since Cuba where that possibility reemerged, and what the parties did to avoid escalation may be the most important lesson of the war in the long run. Putin inserted nuclear weapons into the conversation, but he did not follow up that introduction. One wonders why. Did the Russian military somehow intervene? Did calmer voices surrounding Putin prevail?

Beyond the problem of Russia, the scenario is bounded. Several nuclear states (e.g., Great Britain and France) are NATO members, and China is a rival of the United States but shows no indication of tendencies toward nuclear aggressiveness. North Korean possession is problematical while the current leadership is in power. Only two major potential nuclear hot spots exist. India and Pakistan are both nuclear-armed, but their 1998 conflict demonstrated they confronted the potential catastrophe of prospective nuclear use and have quieted conflict since they confronted its prospect. The other problem of note is Israel and Iran: Israel has a nuclear arsenal and Iran has the potential to build weapons. The incendiary potential arises from what regional nuclear hegemon Israel might do if Iran acts to arm itself with these weapons. *Both* states are impetuous enough to raise concerns over an exchange in the most unstable part of the world (see chapter 3 of my *The Middle East and American National Security* for a discussion).

The nuclear variable does not come particularly into play in most of the developing world. Conflicts there tend to be internal and factional along ethnic or religious grounds, and since the implosion of the Soviet Union, these instabilities have not been exacerbated by the largely artificial patina of the contest between communism and anti-communism. The current situation thus boils down to two different kinds of situation where the United States might feel it is necessary to respond with armed force to affect the outcome in a way that is compatible with American interests and important enough to activate the nuclear option in some fashion. One is the Russia-Ukraine scenario—conflict in the traditional European theater that interrupts the nonviolent nature of European politics and in the process threatens American interests. The other contingency is violence outside the European theater, the legacy of developing world politics.

The two scenarios create opposite problems. Maintaining the integrity and prosperity of Europe is a core American value and essentially always has been. The United States acknowledged this importance twice in the twentieth century in the world wars, and the premier commitment of the country to European security is at the core of American policy. Unfortunately, most of the possible threats are large and so vital that the nuclear option remains at least theoretically on the table in the event of a European-based conflict. Such threats are infrequent but the most controversial. The European case is both compelling and problematical. The war between Russia and Ukraine is the first major test of the durability of peace. That said, preparation for European-style war is the contingency for which the United States has most meticulously prepared and involves forms of engagement most compatible with the American military tradition.

The developing world differs from the European theater in two fundamental ways that bear on the national security problem for the United States. First, American interests, while substantial in some cases, are not as compelling in most of them as are European-based problems, making the question of direct involvement with armed force more questionable. Second, most of these kinds of conflicts are in physical situations different from the environment in which American military doctrine has been honed.

The problems associated with the two types of conflict are thus distinct enough to be approached separately, as the text has to this point. Beyond the physical nature of fighting and prevailing in conflicts of one kind or the other, there is a physical and intellectual conundrum that overlays the enterprise: the most important American interests are engaged in situations where overt conflict is least likely but potentially most consequential. The conflicts that are most frequent, on the other hand, occur where American interests, while often substantial, are less vital but the consequences less potentially cataclysmic.

"Traditional" War: Russia and Ukraine

Is the Russo-Ukrainian war the face of modern fighting involving traditional powers? One of the most fascinating aspects of the evolution of the Russian aggression against Ukraine was how it was conceptualized and approached by both sides. In systemic terms, what was noteworthy was that the war represented the first time that the old Cold War superpowers came into direct contact with one another in a situation where their mutual military engagement against one another was possible, if not necessarily likely. It thus represented the closest that members of the historically dominant European balance had come face to face in potential military conflict since the Cuban Crisis, and it revived interest for the first time in over a half century in what the dynamics of the remnants of the East-West conflict were. What did the powers need to do to minimize—hopefully even eliminate—the possibility that they might face one another across a battlefield in which the fighting could possibly devolve to nuclear confrontation?

It was not the first time the two powers had been on opposite sides of an international shooting situation. In Syria, for instance, support for the Assad regime had put the Putin administration at odds with the West, but this occurred in a regionalized conflict in which the stakes were not enormous for either side and escalatory possibilities were thus remote. Ukraine, by virtue of its geographic location in the center of Europe, is different, and those differences were magnified by the savage manner in which the Russians conducted their part of the hostilities—especially the targeting and destruction of urban centers with long-range missile and artillery attacks. Most of Europe thought warfare of that ferocity had become obsolete, even anachronistic, in "civilized" Europe. Russia conducted a scorched earth attack unseen in Europe for a long time, adding to the level of outrage directed toward Moscow by all but its most loyal or obsequious supporters.

The Russian aggression came seemingly out of nowhere. An increasingly democratic Ukrainian political system had produced increasingly anti-Russian sentiments since the Russian seizure of the Crimea in 2014, and the interest in seeking NATO membership was less than a carefully guarded secret within Ukraine. There was no apparent groundswell within NATO to act upon this sentiment positively, although some Western political groups were sympathetic to the Ukrainian side. Ukrainian armed forces had not made provocative movements toward the Russian frontier, and although the Russian immigrants imported to the Donbas region by the then Soviet Union were not universally happy, neither was there evidence of their oppression that warranted the massing of large numbers of Russian forces on the Ukrainian frontier. As the buildup continued, the world reacted by asking "what are the Russians doing and why?" The answer was not consensually clear to anyone outside the Kremlin walls.

Although they have not (and probably will not) admit it, the Ukrainian resistance clearly surprised the Russians as much as it did the outside world as did the quality of the Russian effort. The performance of Soviet forces in Afghanistan forty years earlier possibly should have warned the Moscow leadership that its military machine was not the world-class force they believed it to be. The Russian Federation is, after all, the modern face of the Soviet empire. Even though its population is shrinking, it still has between three and four times the population base of Ukraine, and based on sheer mass and numbers, its forces should easily have dispatched the Ukrainians as they had in 2014 in the Crimea. They did not attain their goal. To Putin's chagrin, nobody outside Russia considers their campaign to have been a military success.

Ironically, this war in Eastern Europe may have the effect of convincing others with grievances against Russia that decisive war in Europe is impossible without possible escalation to nuclear exchange. Given the possible consequences of such an escalation, these weapons may thus indirectly contribute to greater European security. Almost everything that has occurred in the Russian aggression has worked to their disadvantage.

How the postwar settlement is crafted will affect whether the war contributes to stability or instability in Europe and around the world. A basic thrust of American-led actions to pressure Russia into abandoning its actions was to isolate them from the political and economic institutions of the international system. The Russian economy was damaged by these sanctions, and what the West does in the war's wake will have long-term effects on that economy and those who live in it. Whether the postwar actions will be to reconcile with Russia (mainly reintegrating the Russian energy industry into the world system) will undoubtedly affect the Russian people's postwar support for the Putin regime or its successor. Putin's legacy will be tarnished and his power presumably shaken.

How will the victors, and possibly especially the Ukrainians, respond? Clearly, the reconstruction of the Ukrainian infrastructure will be the major task of the postwar settlement. The primary vessel will be a very large influx of international assistance into rebuilding that country. What, if anything, will be Russia's contribution and role in that process? Will Russia emerge from the war as an international pariah? Will the victors seek to reconcile and integrate Russia back into the international order? Or will they treat them as unrepentant miscreants? The answer is not clear, but it will certainly contribute to the stability of the postwar peace. Russia's action shattered the seventy-year European peace. Where does Russia fit into its reconstruction?

Then there is the territorial question. Annexation of the Donbas region was, in essence, the goal of the invasion, but it was obscured by their wretched performance in the war. No one outside Russia wants to reward Putin for his reckless attack, but the Russian people must somehow be reconciled to the outcome and return in chastened fashion to the international fold. No one other than the most zealous supporters of Putin will be able to think of the war as anything but a miserable demonstration of Russia's diminished stature in the world, but that does not necessarily translate into a public humiliation. Russia is still the world's largest physical country, and bringing it back into the global fold must be a pillar of a more secure future. The question is how.

The West showed remarkable unity in opposing the Russian invasion, and everyone wants to see the peace of pre-invasion Europe restored as one of the pillars of international order and relative tranquility. A reconciled Russia and a correct, if not congenial, relationship with China are pillars of an orderly global geopolitical environment. The United States successfully navigated a potentially dangerous threat to the peace in Ukraine by leading a coalition of states using the economic instrument of power as their primary "weapon," and it worked, at least in this case. Beyond Europe, the developing world, where the United States has done its fighting since World War II, is the primary battleground for the country in the future, as it has in the past. What does that mean in terms of where America should fight—and how—in the future?

The crisis and war are interesting and instructive in at least two ways. The first is why it occurred in the first place. The trigger appears to have been the mounting sentiment in Ukraine to join the Western associations of NATO and EU. Both proposed affiliations roiled the Russians as evidence that Ukraine sought to join what they perceived as the hostile encirclement of Russia by the Western democracies, a holdover from the Cold War. It was symbolically and physically important because of Ukrainian geography (a 1,944-kilometer-long border with Russia, and territory on the Sea of Azov that is occupied by Russia and is a major part of Russia's warm-water access to the world's oceans) and demography (a population of over 44 million). Putin and his Russian colleagues thus had some legitimate concerns about Ukraine. Still, there was no immediate, internationally obvious reason for the invasion—other, possibly, than for Putin to demonstrate the power of the Russian state and its continuing claim to superpower status. The second, and clearly related, observation was how badly Putin overestimated the potency of his forces and how easily they could subdue the Ukrainians. Their inability to act successfully against the Ukrainians will almost certainly affect Russian relations (notably the credibility and implementation of threats with other former Soviet states) for some time to come.

One of the most fascinating aspects of the entire episode was how the West, led by the United States, was able to use the economic, rather than the military, instrument of power against the Russians, effectively neutralizing Russian military power without any form of military activity beyond supplying and refurbishing military equipment for the Ukrainians. There was no military confrontation between East and West that could have raised tensions and threatened a broadening of the conflict, despite some early peripheral loose talk about the prospects of World War III. Russia was, after all, the last antagonist of the European-based Cold War, and if it could be dissuaded by non-military threats, that represents a major change in the dynamics of European geopolitics.

If the end of the Russian-Ukrainian war changes traditional Russian tensions with the West, what comes next? Some of the dynamics will be determined by the evolution of postwar relations: what have the two sides learned and how will the result affect their relations? A major dynamic will be the effect of the war's outcome on Russia itself. The war bared the deterioration of Russian nonnuclear military pretense as a world power. An oblique example was the Russian raid on Chernobyl, in which Russian military vehicles drove through grounds (notably the famous Red Forest), stirring up and infecting themselves with lethal radiation, and this apparently occurred without warning or attempts to stop the lethal rampage by the Russian military. It should never have occurred, but it did. It is hard to imagine such an egregious breach of intelligence and discipline would have occurred during the Soviet days, but it did in Ukraine. An interesting residual will be how Russian opinion—especially among the families of soldiers who suffer the effects—will be manifested. The Russia-Ukraine War is going to change Russia and the geopolitical balance in Europe and beyond. The question is how.

Asymmetrical Pasts and Futures?

American post–World War II intervention in developing world violence has passed through two distinct phases and is currently between periods of activism. The first phase, of course, occurred in the period between the end of the second global conflict and the end of the Vietnam War. It was marked by major involvements in Korea and Vietnam, both of which were struggles that, from an American viewpoint, mostly surrounded the evolving balance between the communist and noncommunist worlds. The Vietnam War marked the end of American activism in that phase, and the interim ended with the collapse of the Soviet Union in 1991.

The second phase of American activism was spurred by the terrorist attacks against American soil in 2001. During this period, the signal instances of American military activism centered on American intervention in Iraq and Afghanistan in the Middle East that had been hotbeds of the terrorist movement. That phase ended when the United States withdrew its active military presence from Afghanistan.

The 2022 Russian aggression against Ukraine may signal the emergence of a third distinct phase of American involvement in contemporary world violent politics. Since the country withdrew from the "endless wars" in Iraq and Afghanistan, it has retreated from direct involvement in violent situations where circumstances did not appear to demand its presence in terms of the vitality of interests. The Middle East is currently in a virtual lull in violent behavior, partly created by the condominium between Israel and several of the Gulf petroleum monarchies and by cessation of the Syrian civil war. The major, if largely avoided, source of conflict in that part of the world revolves around the nascent Iranian nuclear program and what an Iranian determination and movement toward completing its fabrication of nuclear weapons might portend.

The Israeli-Iranian situation over the Iranian nuclear program is possibly the most volatile, dangerous potential confrontation in the world today. The Ukrainian war has captured headlines because of the blatant nature of Russian aggression, its bloodthirstiness, and the degree of Ukrainian resistance. The main source of global interest, in addition to alleviating Ukrainian suffering from the savage Russian attacks on civilian targets, is how peace can be restored in a manner that saves at least minimal face for the Russians while restoring Ukrainian sovereignty and helping to rebuild its ravaged land.

The major source of instability and violence will, however, remain in parts of the developed world with differential levels of interest to the United States. Since the turn of the twenty-first century, the emergence of international terrorism concentrated American energy and effort in the Middle East, with sidebar deployments to smaller conflicts in places like Kosovo and Haiti. The "highlights" of these involvements have been in places like Kuwait, Iraq, and Afghanistan, all of which now occupy a reduced place on the American agenda but could require American attention in the future.

The Russian invasion of Ukraine has offered a change in the location and pattern of violence, but whether that change is fundamental or idiosyncratic depends both on the outcome of the war and especially on how Russia responds to its poor military performance and its failure to reestablish its buffer zone with the West in Ukraine. What may prove to be a more interesting and consequential effect of the war is the way force is employed in the future. Russia invaded Ukraine with a large, thoroughly conventional armed effort. Its apparent purpose was to overthrow the Ukrainian government, replace it with a puppet regime that could be largely controlled by Russia, and thus reestablish its buffer zone from Western pressure and, in the worst case, invasion. The force it sent into Ukraine was much larger than the Ukrainian armed forces and should, on paper, have been capable of overwhelming the Ukrainian resistance, overthrowing the government, and replacing it with a new regime more compatible with Russian values. The effect would have been to allow Moscow to destroy the goal being voiced by some Ukrainians about applying for NATO and EU affiliation, the avoidance of which was apparently central to Russian motivation in the first place.

The Russians failed in their military mission which, on paper, should have been an easy thing for them to do. Why? The Russians have not, of course, admitted the effort was a failure, but to call the war anything but a failure is a clear instance of, in the colloquial phrase, "putting lipstick on the pig." Other discontented former vassal states near Russia will be encouraged by the Ukrainian effort and outcome, just as developing world countries have viewed the failed outcomes of conflicts with former colonial powers. Asymmetrical warfare has succeeded in other parts of the world. Did a European version of the unconventional approach succeed in Ukraine as well?

Asymmetrical Warfare in Europe?

What happened to Russia in Ukraine happened to the Soviet Union in Afghanistan in the 1970s. That failure, of course, occurred during the twilight of the Soviet Union and helped contribute to its collapse in 1991. The Soviet implosion reduced the image of Russia as a world military power, which in turn caused the reemergence of Russian paranoia about hostile encirclement. Ukraine, because of its size, population, and strategic importance (Ukraine does provide Russia warm-water access to the Black Sea and indirectly to the Mediterranean), is a particular danger to Russian security if in the hands of a hostile regime, which the current Ukrainian regime represents. Combined with Putin's desire to reestablish Russian status and power in the world (as well as to polish his own place in the Russian history books), the invasion became a more compelling—and eventually overwhelming—temptation to the Russian leader.

The attraction was, however, flawed by two basic faulty premises. The first, and most publicly apparent, error was the judgment that the invasion campaign would be completed quickly and decisively by Russian forces—a conquest that would only need a few days to conclude. Once the invasion succeeded, a successor Ukrainian puppet government loyal to Moscow would be installed and relations would be reestablished within a framework of Ukrainian fealty to Moscow—an effective reestablishment of its status as a Soviet state like neighboring Belarus.

The second, and internationally more prominent, error of effort was related: an apparently quantum overestimation of the quality and fighting ability of the Russian forces sent to accomplish the military task and a concomitant underestimation of the will and ability of the Ukrainians to resist. The Russians (and most of the rest of the world) assumed the Russian campaign would take only days to succeed because of the material and manpower superiority of Russian forces. That estimation proved fundamentally wrong. A combination of Ukrainian regular forces and irregular volunteers quickly coalesced to confront the Russian advance, and this resistance was apparently not anticipated by the Russian military or civilian commands.

The "war" was supposed to be a walkover that would be complete within days. As of fall 2022, it was still going on, and the only visible Russian successes were the terror bombing of Ukrainian cities in direct violation of war crimes standards, for which Russia will be held to some form of account after the war is over.

Why has the war been such a debacle for Russia? Part of the reason is clearly Russian miscalculation of what the campaign would be like. The Russian buildup was a calculated effort to frighten the Ukrainians into concluding that resistance was futile given the comparative balance of forces and thus the certainty of their defeat that would lead to a token resistance and capitulation. It was a miscalculation on the part of Putin and the Russian military.

As the fighting continued, the quality of Russian forces in terms of manpower, equipment, and morale (including resistance to a draft call beginning in April 2022), and outside assistance to Ukrainians also got in the way. Morale among the Russian troops was apparently not very high, and this was apparently reflected in public support for the war among potential draftees. Although the tightly controlled Russian media suppressed detailed coverage of the situation in Ukraine, the longevity of the fighting was testimony for all to see that the walkover was not turning out the way Putin initially advertised.

An interesting sidelight was apparent reluctance, even resistance, of draft-eligible Russian males to induction as the fighting continued. The key element of international actions against the Russians was stifling economic sanctions that caused real hardship for many Russians, including those males under thirty years of age, who were subject to conscription. It was a dynamic that resembled anti-war demonstrations and other reactions to the Vietnam War among potential conscripts. The simple fact that Russians would protest military service in what was being advertised as a "patriotic war" was some indication of how the Russian people felt about the invasion and the brutal Russian campaign, which government-controlled media attempted to hide and deny.

The other factor may be the basic nature of the Ukrainian resistance. Very little has been publicized about how the Ukrainians have managed to frustrate the Russian effort, but the dynamics of asymmetrical warfare may be helpful in understanding it. The standing Ukrainian armed forces that confronted the Russians numbered a little over two hundred thousand members, a much smaller force that lacked the firepower, armor, and other material advantages the Russians possessed. The Russians were able to destroy many Ukrainian cities and kill many Ukrainian civilians (committing war crimes for which international judgment will be considered after the war), but they did not break the Ukrainian will to resist, a contingency the Putin leadership either discounted or underestimated.

The Ukrainians were also heavily supported materially in their efforts in ways that may offer a strong indication of the future direction of American and other Western security policy in environments where the combatants possess nuclear weapons and escalation to nuclear exchange is both physically possible and to be avoided at all costs. The heart of the international—and specifically American—response was to provide material, including military, aid to the Ukrainians, but very publicly not to allow American military forces into positions where they could become involved in direct or indirect combat with the Russians. It is the twenty-first-century version of the Nixon Doctrine: the United States will generously provide assistance to beleaguered regimes, but unless American vital interests are at risk, it will not augment that assistance with American military forces that might advertently or inadvertently come into violent contact with the enemy and draw the country into the war.

Ukraine may also be a modern European asymmetrical war. It is not a classic Afro-Asian–style unconventional conflict because of both the physical location and circumstances in which it has been conducted and the nature and structure of the contending forces. Rather, the Ukrainian war appears to be a hybrid somewhere between classic European warfare and asymmetrical war. This characterization is particularly true for the Ukrainian victims of Russian aggression. The prewar Ukrainian armed forces numbered about 220,000 troops, and that number, even augmented as it has been by large numbers of volunteers who have poured into the country, was nowhere nearly large enough to compete on paper with much larger Russian forces in a European-style clash of conventional forces. Moreover, Russian contiguity to Ukraine meant it should have been relatively easy to resupply and reinforce its troops, adding to their overwhelming advantage. On paper, it was seemingly futile, even suicidal, for Ukraine to resist. Putin and those advising him apparently reasoned their material advantages and Ukrainian realization that they could not resist successfully would lead to a quick and relatively painless battlefield success. That calculation ignored the Soviet experience in Afghanistan, where a much larger and conventionally superior Soviet invasion force was stymied by Afghan clans aided by the West in what proved to be decisive ways and were forced to withdraw without achieving their goals. The possibility that the experience might be repeated apparently did not occur to Putin (or was dismissed), and there was little preparation for a spirited resistance that did not contest the Russians so much in strictly conventional ways but instead chose a different, basically asymmetrical, approach to resistance that the Russians were apparently unprepared to defeat. The Ukrainians may have had no meaningful alternative to mounting an unconventional resistance, but that is effectively what they did. Although detailed descriptions of Ukrainian strategy and tactics have not been widely available, it appears that resistance has widely adopted tactics similar to those employed by asymmetrical warriors in the developing world—things like ambushes and booby traps. It was a form of resistance that the Russians apparently did not anticipate or prepare for, and it helped contribute to Ukrainian success and Russian failure. Russian casualties have exceeded their losses in nearly a decade of engagement in Afghanistan and as of October 2022 were still growing.

What the Ukrainians did has not been decisive in "defeating" the much larger, better equipped Russian invaders, but it apparently raised questions among Russians about the quality of their forces and dispelled Russian beliefs that its victory would be swift, decisive, and relatively low cost in military and international political terms. In February 2022, for instance, observers were predicting the Russians would overrun Ukraine in a matter of days, and they did not. After roughly six months, the Russians had managed to decimate Ukrainian territory physically and to create very large civilian casualty counts in ways that have led to accusations of war crimes, including genocide, against the Putin regime that will have to be addressed after the fighting ends. They had not, however, succeeded in gaining control of the country or broken the will of Ukrainians to resist their relentless, brutal assault on Ukraine.

The Ukraine War in Perspective

A question that must be raised is, are we witnessing in Ukraine a variant of the asymmetrical model acting as a form of guidance to forces both inside the developing world and, in adapted form, the developed world as well? Admittedly, no comparison is entirely isomorphic. Developing world asymmetrical approaches to warfare are generally adaptations both to the physical environment in which they are fought and the very different nature and levels of forces (especially firepower) available to sides. By contrast, European conflicts are generally symmetrical in terms of means and lethality of the weaponry available. In this regard, the Russian war against Ukraine is more like a developing world conflict in which an outside power has intervened: it is asymmetrical in terms of the comparative size and nature of the forces engaged. The Russian effort has been conducted by conventional Russian forces in numbers that the much smaller Ukrainian forces cannot match quantitatively and against which they are disadvantaged in conventional material terms. Much of this disadvantage was lessened by arms transfers of things like antiaircraft weapons from the United States and other NATO countries.

This situation mirrors the Russian Afghan experience. In that conflict, the Russians had difficulty communicating with all its elements because of the primitive road system in the country, a problem they sought to overcome by employing helicopters ferrying people and information from place to place. Outside provision of antiaircraft weapons from places like the United States to the Afghans made it unsafe for the Russians to move about the country on helicopters, a problem they never totally surmounted and which served as a contributing part of their failure. That the Soviet loss in Afghanistan contributed to the fall of the Soviet regime has to be a fact of which Putin is acutely aware.

Any analogy between the Ukraine invasion and likely occurrences elsewhere in Europe is, of course, conjectural, probably remote. The only major point of geopolitical abrasion in the Western world is at the junction point between Russia and its neighbors as part of Russia's attempt to maximize its geopolitical position by asserting some level of control over non-Russian areas of the old Soviet empire, and there has been general reluctance to accepting that kind of relationship; Belarus is a partial exception. Russian geopolitical restiveness would be less internationally concerning than it is if the Russians did not possess nuclear weapons.

A final, and the most important question is why the Russians failed to subdue the Ukrainians. The poor military performance of Russian forces was certainly a factor, and one consequence is that other restive former parts of the Soviet empire are less likely to be totally cowed from adopting positions at odds with the Russians than before on the premise that the Russians are probably going to be less willing to employ what have turned out to be less-than-effective forces in Ukraine. The war's outcome will trigger soul-searching and critical appraisal within the Russian political system, including the almost certain "retirement" of Putin. Which kleptocrat replaces him will be of great geopolitical interest worldwide. Russia's global regard has been tarnished by Ukraine, and the Russians will be under considerable pressure to seek reentry into international "society" as a more congenial, less aggressive member. How Russia, including its leaders, are treated in the postwar settling of war crimes accounts will play a large part in that reaction.

What does the outcome of the crisis portend for future conflict and, more specifically, for the future use of American force? How, in other words, does the Russo-Ukrainian conflict contribute to answering the core question in the title of this work: when should America fight? The experience the country has had with involvement in the developing world, and more specifically in the Middle East, since 9/11 suggests caution: the United States has been drawn into regional fracases where it has not been spectacularly successful.

In important systemic ways, this war is an outlier; the instructive value for assessing the future of international conflict may be limited. Russia has always been an exception geographically, politically, and ethnically. Its sheer size has always inflated its perceived place in the world: it is impossible to ignore a country that has the physical size, population base (although shrinking, as noted), and thus physical gravitas of Russia. If there was any question whether Russia is consequential in the world's military power map, its possession of very large stocks of nuclear weapons ensures that it cannot be ignored. It has always been the outlier, however, partly European and thus a fringe member of the European order, but with such a large Asian and Arctic exposure to make it not a unique member. It is the only major member of the European system that has never embraced political democracy, instead clinging to authoritarianism, an ideology more congenial for holding together many diverse peoples, including many who would just as soon not be part of the Russian sphere of influence.

Ukraine is one of the countries that falls into the category of reluctant Russian associates. A major source of division underlying the war has been the Russian (read Putin) contention that Ukraine is an integral part of Russia and that their war effort is motivated by a desire to bring the Ukrainians back into the fold. The Ukrainians, of course, reject any kindred relationship, as do most other states in the region.

This contrasting, conflicting vision of Russia's role in the areas on its borders is fundamental to understanding Russian motivation for pursuing its apparent goal of reintegrating a defeated Ukraine back into what Putin considers Russian Europe. It is important because it is precedent-setting for the future. If Russia succeeds in defeating Ukraine and forcibly reintegrating it back into Russia, then the Russians are likely to be encouraged to try the same ploy elsewhere along the Russo-Asian and European peripheries. If the Russian effort is successfully resisted by the Ukrainians, that also sets a precedent for future Russian relations with other places that Russian expansionists would like to integrate (or reintegrate) into the Russian empire. Russian failure would certainly doom Putin to retirement; it would also set the precedent for Russia's place in the contemporary European order.

Thought of in this way, the war has a greater significance to all concerned than would a simple Russian power grab of a nearby, smaller country. Rather, it was a way for Russia to demonstrate to the world that it is still a world-class country with a distinct sphere of interest over which it wields effective control in areas that might impinge on its secure position in the world. This reasoning may seem (and be) more like a country would have asserted in the nineteenth rather than the twenty-first century, but it provides a framework within which to judge Russian motives and to try to determine what would be clearly acceptable and unacceptable solutions. The evolution of the post–Cold War world has, on the other hand, provided indications that this traditional sphere of influence rationale has eroded and that states—even if they are contiguous to or nearby major powers—have more freedom to set their own courses. Set in terms of the dialogue as the war raged, Russia believes in and has tried to enforce its regional hegemony, while Ukraine denies that dependent status. Russia maintains and wants to assert its status as the dominant power in the region; Ukraine denies that claim.

The Ukraine War, the American Response, and When America Should Fight

Did this war and its outcome command adequate importance to the United States to be involved? If so, what does that level of interest justify in terms of American force? Is Ukraine, to borrow from this book's title, worthy of the United States fighting over? It is not an easy or cut-and-dried matter and judgment.

There are three broad possible answers to the question. The first is the outcome in Ukraine is clearly vital enough to American interests to justify a direct military response (sending American forces to fight). Second, the war is a matter of power politics in an area outside the American (but inside the Russian) sphere of interest and thus does not justify a direct American intervention. Third, enough American and allied interests are at stake to justify intervention short of the insertion of American (and presumably other NATO) forces into the conflict by assisting the Ukrainians up to, but not including, the introduction of American and other NATO forces into combat. The Biden administration has rejected the two extreme forms of reaction (doing nothing or militarily intervening with forces) and adopted the "middle" alternative of aiding and supplying the Ukrainians up to but not including the personal commitment of fighting forces.

The United States and the rest of NATO chose the middle solution. The question is why was that option chosen? And was it the proper choice? Answers are tentative because the final outcomes are still in progress, but one part of that answer is that such a war would have been difficult to wage and, if it became protracted with heavy casualties, unpopular in both the United

States and NATO Europe. Should an active intervention have occurred, the NATO allies would certainly have prevailed easily *if* the war remained conventional, but it would still have been bloody and destructive—World War II with much deadlier capabilities on both sides. Second, the confrontation would have raised in the starkest relief the shadow of the mushroom-shaped cloud: it would have been a potentially nuclear war between heavily nuclear-armed foes. What would such a war have been like? Throughout the nuclear age, the answer to that question has been that nobody wants to find out, and the surest way to avoid the possibility is to ensure that Russia and the United States never come literally to physical blows. In the end, it really is as simple as that.

Budjeryn points out a nuclear irony of sorts in this entire situation. When the Soviet Union dissolved in 1991, parts of its nuclear arsenal were physically located in several states of the defunct union (including Ukraine), and the question was what to do with those weapons. Leaving them in several of the resulting states would effectively have been an act of nuclear proliferation, since it would have increased the number of global nuclear weapons possessors. There was also international concern that some successor states would not know how to manage their new possession, possibly leading to different forms of danger.

The solution, devised and negotiated by NATO (including the United States) was to arrange the transfer of those weapons to Russian control, since the Russian state was the clear successor to the Soviet Union and its military capabilities and the only surviving entity clearly capable of managing the arsenal. It was hoped that the Boris Yeltsin regime in Moscow would prove a stable place for the arsenal. Based on this assessment, negotiations resulted in the transfer of all former Soviet nuclear weapons to Russian control. According to Budjeryn, the Ukrainians transferred the 1,500 warheads on their soil to Russia in return for a guarantee of their sovereignty by Russia, the United States, and the United Kingdom. The weapons were transferred out of Ukrainian into Russian hands in 1994.

The irony, of course, is that if this transfer had not occurred, Ukraine would have been a nuclear power, and as such, probably would have been protected from the Russian invasion of 2022 because of Russian fear of nuclear escalation. The only time nuclear-armed states have gone to war against one another was in 1998 when perpetual enemies India and Pakistan went to conventional war briefly, but fear of the escalatory possibility contributed to ending that contest. Indian-Pak fighting has not been reprised. The possession of these weapons continues to act as an apparent deterrent to any military action against a possessor. One can ask if that guarantee nearly thirty years ago created an ongoing obligation on those who signed it in terms of the 2022 war.

It defies the rules of logic to maintain with any certainty that the 1990s decision to remit former Soviet weapons into the hands of Russia is related to the decision nearly thirty years later for Russia to attack Ukraine, and the deterrent effect of nuclear weapons continues to be a rationale for nuclear pretenders. North Korea is the latest proponent of this value in terms of justifying its own arsenal, and it is an intriguing possibility that the failure of Ukraine and other states to retain control of Soviet weapons in the early 1990s would have changed the nature of Russian policy toward other newly independent members of the fragmented union. Such a situation was probably inconceivable in an atmosphere where Western policy was to reinforce the emergence of a new, democratic Russia that was militarily emasculated if those weapons were in the effective hands of neighbors who could only be described as friends of Russia by stretching definitions. Moreover, the fragmentation of control of those weapons to a number of successor states the stability of which was yet to be established seemed a bad idea on both proliferation and stability bases. At least some Ukrainians must today be wondering if they made the right decision agreeing to remand those weapons to a Russia that would invade their country nearly three decades later, undeterred by Ukrainian non-possession of a deadly nuclear deterrent.

If one assumes that the West could not simply ignore the 2022 Russian action against Ukraine, some form of the middle option was the only realistic alternative for the United States and its allies. The form that alternative took was the use of economic sanctions against Russia to cause enough economic pain to the Russian economy and people to convince them to end their invasion. Economic sanctions are a standard option in the diplomatic arsenal and one of the first alternatives considered in crises and confrontations. Their primary advantage is that when they work, they avoid the bloodshed, suffering, and bitterness created by shooting wars; their primary drawback is that they do not always work.

The effectiveness of sanctions was further strained by the dependence of many NATO states on Russian petroleum energy resources. The simple fact is that most NATO and EU states have traditionally relied on Russian oil and natural gas to power and heat their countries, and that they do not have alternative sources to which they can easily turn for substitutes if they need to. The United States has stepped up to increase exports of energy in the form of liquid natural gas, but it is not clearly a quantitative substitute for Russian supplies. Thus, as sanctions were being implemented, they were partially undermined by continued purchase of Russian imports by countries like Germany, with the unintended result of helping to provide economic resources for Russia in its aggression, from buyers who supported the sanctions in principle and opposed the Russian invasion.

The IF Factor and the Ukrainian War

One way to think about American involvement in the response to the Russian war against Ukraine is in terms of US options associated with the interests and feasibility (IF) model. The United States and its NATO allies rejected the more extreme options of full-scale military intervention and doing nothing, leaving the middle option of hopefully decisive but less provocative military assistance to the Ukrainians. The Zelensky government would have preferred more direct, decisive Western assistance to help drive what turned out to be the frustration of the inept Russian attack, thereby limiting the civilian death and physical suffering and destruction that ensued. They also seemed to realize that a (if not *the*) paramount value of the Americans was to keep the fighting at a controlled enough level so as not to threaten an escalation leading to nuclear war while preserving Ukrainian independence.

The Ukrainian/American/NATO coalition and Russian preferred outcomes were clearly inconsistent with one another. Putin argued at the time of initial intrusion that he feared advocacies of Ukraine joining NATO and thus confronting the Russians with a hostile force on its borders had grown to proportions that made forcefully attacking the Ukrainian government an essentially defensive act, a rationale accepted by many Russians but hardly anyone else. Exactly what motivated Putin may not be known definitively for a long time if ever, and his motivations may have included a belief in the nefarious nature of evolving Ukrainian relationships with the Western alliance. In all likelihood, such "fears" were at least partially concocted and admixed with what the Russian leader saw as an opportunity to polish what had become a dubious place as a global power. Ukraine, one can assume, was supposed to be an easy victory; the Russians were wrong in their assumption about how easily they could assert their will and power; they conducted a brutal, atrocious campaign with heavy elements of war crimes that will doubtless be the subject of analysis and controversy for years to come.

For present purposes, the more important question is what the conflict forebodes for the future of large-power military interactions, and more specifically for the United States and how and when it uses force in a conflict environment in which nuclear weapons are an influence. Certainly this environment affected the attractiveness of the two extreme options. Given that Russia proposed to alter the European balance by force, the United States could not ignore the attack or its success if they did not respond. To have done so would have branded the United States as an insincere, ineffectual protector for other European countries, returned Russia to a much more prominent place in European geopolitics (certainly one of Putin's goals in the first place), and thus maximized the impact on a European power balance which is maximally congenial to the Americans: Pax Americana in Europe would have been undercut in the process, a development the United States could not avoid opposing if it wanted to retain its position of leadership in the world order. At the same time, a full-scale military response in which the United States introduced its own forces into positions of danger would have maximized the danger of violent confrontation with the Russians the consequences of which included possible nuclear escalation, the avoidance of which has been a prime American value.

That left the middle option of coming to the aid of the Ukrainians by means that included the provision of military aid in increasing quantities and qualities, but short of any hint of direct military confrontation between the two Cold War principals, and that was the option ultimately chosen and implemented. The option minimized the danger of direct war between the two countries, which was clearly a prime value—presumably of each country, although it was especially important for Russia, since the use of nuclear weapons over Ukraine would have meant that the radiation cloud it produced would have drifted eastward over Russia, carried by prevailing westerly breezes.

The American response was not robust enough for some critics in terms of the violent commitment the Americans did not make. The reasons for the nature of the economic sanctions approach, however, made sense if one analyzes them in terms of the basic criteria of the IF model: interests and prospects of success (feasibility of attaining interests).

What were American interests in Ukraine, and more specifically in terms of the level and quality of American interests in what happened in Ukraine as a result of the invasion and its outcome? Historically, of course, American interests in Ukraine per se were essentially nonexistent when the country was a state within the Soviet Union and not an independent country with which the United States had anything resembling diplomatic relations, meaning that relations with Ukraine were essentially limited to those of American citizens with personal ties to the Ukraine. There were, as a result, no direct or official ties between the United States and the Ukraine.

US formal relations with the Ukraine have evolved since the country declared its independence in 1991 and since Ukraine declared itself an independent state and adopted an independent position toward Russia. Ukraine is a leading agricultural producer of grains to Western Europe, creating some residual ties with American allies in Europe, but little direct relationship with the United States (the 2020–2021 CIA *World Factbook*, for instance, does not list the United States as one of the seven largest trading partners with Ukraine). Relations between Ukraine and NATO/EU have grown more due to contiguity and trade relation as well as democratization of the country and its bumpy relations with Russia dating at least back to the Russian annexation of Ukrainian Crimea in 2014.

The American relationship with Ukraine in and of itself would almost certainly not have been adequate to describe as vital enough to justify an active role in Ukrainian defense had it not been for the brutal, and from a Western perspective, unprovoked nature of the Russian invasion in February 2022. The United States has supported the democratization of Ukraine, even though that development results in another fully democratic government on Russia's border, a development that Russia does not support. Instead, the Russians object to the association political liberalization in Ukraine creates with NATO and EU countries, which the Russians view (probably with good reason) as threatening to the authoritarian form of governance in Russia itself. The Russians cannot, of course, formulate their objections to democratization in these terms, but Putin's Russia is feeling increasingly uncomfortable by the wall of Western-style governments to its west. This creates some dissonance between the Russians and the Americans over political change in Ukraine, but hardly provides an adequate reason for the Russian invasion or the United States and other NATO countries coming to Ukraine's aid in a major way.

As has been argued in these pages, the Westernization of Ukraine is only the cosmetic reason for a Russian action with more strictly—and interrelated—geopolitical bases. At heart, the war on Ukraine is motivated by Putin's desires to re-create as much as possible the old Soviet empire *and* for the Russian people and history books to give him credit for having been the champion of that revival. Very simply put, as Putin's rule in Russia winds down, he wants to be remembered for the Russian return to its pre-1991 status as international superpower, a goal that is likely unattainable but that comports with the Russian self-image. If he succeeds, the status of the Russian leader will begin to be chiseled and placed strategically in Russia; if he fails, there will be no lionization of his rule.

The United States has no vested interest in how Russian history books treat Putin's tenure beyond how his actions to achieve that goal influence the power balance in Europe and thus the continuing stability of that region. Reasserting Russian military prowess has been the tool he has chosen to remind the world that Russia is still relevant and powerful and must be considered a major power in the power equation. This calculation and the actions he has taken to implement it have upset that balance and, ironically, made Russia's quest for increased power and acceptance less, rather than more, probable.

The Russian invasion has been counterproductive in two ways. First, the abysmal performance of Russian forces has shrunk, rather than increased, Russia's global standing as a world military power. Putin clearly anticipated a quick and decisive thrust that would cause Ukrainian capitulation in a matter of days and the installation of a pro-Russian puppet government of the nature of the Belorussian regime into power. This calculation was premised on a very optimistic assessment of the fighting prowess of the Russian armed forces and in a poor performance by the Ukrainians in defending their country. Both assessments have proven fundamentally flawed. Russian military performance has been mediocre at best and has not overwhelmed the surprisingly resilient Ukrainians, and Russia has alienated more others than it has converted. The most important symbol of that failure has been the overtures of Sweden and Finland to join NATO and then accession to membership, an initiative that the Russians/Soviets had successfully opposed and over which they have implicitly threatened military opposition. The only prominent and enduring legacy of the Soviet period militarily are nuclear weapons, which have done more to deter a Western attack on Russia than the other way around. This outcome, if the United States does not overly use it to embarrass post-Ukrainian relations with Russia, will also reverberate to American advantage.

Whether the United States should have done more physically to aid and protect the Ukrainians will be a matter of future debate that will help define the parameters of American military decision in European-style warfare. The core of the American approach to assistance—sending copious amounts of military aid in the form of weaponry to aid in Ukrainian self-defense—was less robust and heroic than a direct insertion of American power would have been, but it was also far less politically dangerous. The calculation of what the United States would and would not do in this situation was clearly based on avoiding a direct military confrontation between the Americans and the Russians. The premise on which that calculation was built was the minimization of any likelihood of direct combat between American and Russian forces, and the underlying premise equally obviously was minimization of direct conflict that, in the worst case, could possibly trigger nuclear confrontation and exchange. Nuclear weapons were proven not only to be a deterrent of direct nuclear conflict between the world's two largest nuclear possessors but also to provide a strong conceptual impenetrable barrier to *any* shooting conflict between them.

The Ukrainian Precedent

Some of the relatively few open critics of the American strategy for aiding Ukraine have suggested the United States should have taken a more physically proactive role in coming to the aid of the Ukrainian state, presumably including at least the possibility of direct American military participation in the Ukrainian defense of their homeland. The implicit assumption on which such suggestions were premised was that it would have been more "manly" and thus superpower-like to have inserted American troops into the fray.

The flaw in that argument is in its failure to assess the qualitative change such a commitment might have had on the nature of the war. Doing so would have likely assured a faster, more complete eviction of Russian forces and the atrocious forms of violence they employed from the Ukraine, and that would have been a more "manly" form of assistance that Ukrainians could only have appreciated. It might also, however, have caused an escalation of the violence to nuclear exchange from which all participants, prominently including Ukraine, would have suffered grievously, possibly fatally. It also may have been the only way to meet the IF criterion of feasibility of total success, but in a decidedly pyrrhic potential form. The question is debatable, but almost no one, including most of the Ukrainians who suffered because a maximal outside intervention did not occur would concur that the decision was regrettably correct.

It is the possibility of what a major, nuclear-armed power in the throes of a humiliating, politically traumatic defeat may do that makes contemplating contemporary war between great powers (the modern version of European-style warfare) fundamentally different from what has gone on before and which, as a consequence, forces countries to rethink whether and/or how it is possible to conduct such war. In IF terms, what interests of the country are sufficiently vital to chance nuclear annihilation? If it is feasible to mount such an effort without nuclear weapons, then one set of answers may be proper; if it is not, the answer is entirely different. The problem is that we cannot know in advance which answer is correct. The ultimate consequence of major-power war is truly to be feared, and it will hover over humankind as long as those weapons form the ultimate expression of national "defense."

Ukraine's unique place in contemporary military affairs is that it is the first potential test of what that impact may be. The most obvious effect is that it has caused the United States and its closest allies to back away from a direct, face-to-face confrontation with the aggressor Russians as they rape and plunder Ukraine. The Ukrainians have been, in effect, bearing the brunt of unconscionable Russian barbarism partially to minimize the danger of systemic annihilation of an independent Ukrainian state—and possibly the world. Is this the new model for American and other military intervention in historically major conflict? Is this follow-on and adaptation of the Nixon Doctrine to the post–Cold War competition between Russia and the other European states consciously designed to avoid direct American combat, and thus represents the model of major conflict for the future?

What does the structure of the conflict suggest for the future? The disintegration of the Soviet Union is the unique destabilizing event of the post–Cuban crisis international system in two senses. First, it is the only time that one of the major powers has acted forcefully to re-create the structure of the Cold War system with great brute force. The annexation of Georgia to Russia in 2014 was a precursor, but the extent of effort by Putin far exceeds what was necessary before—mostly because Ukraine is larger and more difficult to conquer than were the southern fringes of the old Soviet empire (including parts of Ukraine). Second, the war has created a reemergence of the abrasion between the two halves of Europe for the first time since World War II. The possibility of a collision was the signal fear of the late 1940s and early 1950s, which changed the nature of modern conflict when both sides fielded nuclear forces. In one important sense, the way the war was fought in Ukraine was the current legacy of the nuclear revolution.

Bibliography

Altman, Dan, and Kathleen E. Powers. "When Redlines Fail: The Promise and Perils of Public Threats." *Foreign Affairs* (online), February 4, 2022.

Applebaum, Anne. *Red Famine: Stalin's War on Ukraine*. New York: Anchor, 2015.

Ashford, Emma, and Joshua Shifrinson. "How the War in Ukraine Could Get Much Worse." *Foreign Affairs* (online), March 11, 2022.

Budjeryn, Marianne. "Was Ukraine Wrong to Give Up Its Nukes? The Real Legacy of Kyiv's Post-Soviet Disarmament." *Foreign Affairs* (online), April 8, 2022.

Charap, Samuel. "The Perilous Long Game in Ukraine: Compromising with Putin May Be America's Best Option." *Foreign Affairs* (online), March 30, 2022.

D'Anieri, Paul. *Ukraine and Russia: From Civilized Divorce to Uncivil War*. Cambridge, UK: Cambridge University Press, 2019.

Freedman, Lawrence. *Ukraine and the Art of Strategy*. Oxford, UK: Oxford University Press, 2019.

Gotz, Elias, ed. *Russia, the West, and the Ukrainian Crisis*. New York and London: Routledge, 2019.

Haass, Richard. "What Does the West Want in Ukraine? Defining Success Before It's Too Late." *Foreign Affairs* (online), April 22, 2022.

Kissinger, Henry. "Force and Diplomacy in the Nuclear Age." *Foreign Affairs* 34, no. 2 (April 1956): 349–66.

Kolesnikov, Andrei. "Russians at War: Putin's Aggression Has Turned a Nation Against Itself." *Foreign Affairs* (online), April 18, 2022.

———. "Will Putin Lose Russia? His Grip on Power Rests on Fantasy and Fear." *Foreign Affairs* (online), March 9, 2022.

Kuzio, Taras. *Putin's War Against Ukraine: Revolution, Nationalism, Crimes*. Toronto: University of Toronto Press, 2022.

Menen, Ryan, and Eugene B. Rumer. *Conflict in Ukraine: The Unwinding of the Post-Cold War Order*. Reprint ed. Cambridge, MA: MIT Press, 2015.

Milakovsky, Brian. "Putin's Pyrrhic Victory: Russia's Setbacks in Eastern Ukraine Show Why It Can't Win the Wider War." *Foreign Affairs* (online), March 31, 2022.

Miller, Steven E. "The Case Against a Ukrainian Nuclear Deterrent." *Foreign Affairs* 72, no. 3 (Summer 1993): 67–80.

Plokhy, Serhii. *The Gates of Europe: A History of Ukraine*. New York: Basic Books, 2021.

Reid, Anna, *Borderland: A Journey through the History of Ukraine*. New York: Basic Books, 2015.

Ross, Gideon. "The Irony of Ukraine: We Have Met the Enemy, and It Is Us." *Foreign Affairs* (online), March 29, 2022.

———. "Why the War in Ukraine Won't Go Nuclear: The Old Rules Still Apply to a New and Limited War." *Foreign Affairs* (online), April 25, 2022.

Smith, Christopher. *Ukraine's Revolt, Russia's Revenge*. Washington, DC: Brookings Institution Press, 2022.

Snyder, Timothy. *Bloodlands: Europe between Hitler and Stalin*. New York: Basic Books, 2022.

———. *The Road to Unfreedom: Russia, Europe, America*. New York: Crown, 2019.

Snow, Donald M. *The Middle East and American National Security: Forever Wars and Conflicts?* Lanham, MD: Rowman & Littlefield, 2021.

———. *The Necessary Peace: Nuclear Weapons and Superpower Relations*. Lexington, MA: Lexington Books, 1987.

———. *Nuclear Strategy in a Dynamic World: Policy for the 1980s*. Tuscaloosa: University of Alabama Press, 1981.

Stent, Angela. *Putin's World: Russia Against the West and the Rest*. New York: Twelve Books, 2020.

Trenin, Dmitri. *Should We Fear Russia?* Cambridge, UK: Polity Press, 2016.

Urban, Andrew L., and Chris M. McLeod. *Zelensky: The Unlikely Hero Who Defied Putin and the World*. New York: Regnery Press, 2022.

Yaffa, Joshua. *Between Two Fires: Truth, Ambition, and Compromise in Putin's Russia*. New York: Random House, 2021.

Zurcher, Christoph. *The Post-Soviet Wars: Rebellion, Ethnicity, and Nationhood in the Caucasus*. New York: NYU Press, 2009.

CHAPTER EIGHT

Conclusion

Where Will and Should the United States Fight: The Road Ahead

When I published the predecessor volume to this one, my task seemed a bit simpler than this work has proven to be. It was the period between the Cold War and the War on Terror, a bookend period where the international system became orderly—if not peaceful—enough to allow one to summarize the threat and the mission and tasks that would be assigned to the military. That order was, of course, fairly quickly undermined by the attacks of 9/11, and we have been trying to order the conflict environment and how we should respond to it ever since. In a diluted sense, the Ukraine War has served as a junction point in contemporary security affairs. We are still in the midst of the transition; where it will end—and how—are not yet entirely clear.

The Recent Past as Prologue?

The discussions to this point have suggested two separate areas of interest and concern for the national security conglomerate. The two problems are different from the national security perspective as expressed in the two criteria of the IF construct. The peace in Europe has been a bedrock vital interest of the United States for most of the country's history and remains so. The conditions in which that peace has existed have been remarkably benign and stable for most of the postwar period since the Cuban Missile Crisis of 1962. The Russian invasion of Ukraine represents an interruption in that tranquility and has reminded us that all the problems of Europe have not been resolved satisfactorily in the minds of all the participants. At the same time, selective American interest in various parts of the developing world has presented different problems and solutions. Since 1979 (the year of the Iranian Revolution and the Teheran hostage crisis), American adversarial politics has been concentrated mostly in the eastern part of the Middle East, where the United States has reprised memories of unconventional warfare from the 1960s in Vietnam. This has been a mixed bag in terms of the degree of American interests directly involved and in the success of American forces in dealing with those.

Two questions stand out as we peer into the future and assess where events and trends may tempt the country to apply American force to achieve American (and allied) goals. The first question is where these challenges will appear, and it is an important concern for two reasons (where we might fight determines whether levels of interest justify using force).

The second question, which derives from the first, is how will the United States need to prepare to compete militarily to achieve or protect its interests in either venue. From this perspective, the two environments in which participation might be warranted differ significantly. Before the Russian invasion of Ukraine, the traditional European theater had been remarkably tranquil for half a century. The only major upheaval was the implosion of the Soviet Union and subsequent enthusiastic decommunization of the eastern portion of the continent, which created great problems and angst mostly for those elites being displaced and replaced throughout what had been the communist side of the Iron Curtain.

That process has largely been completed, as most of formerly communist Europe gladly threw what passed for Marxism in the operational communist world aside and moved enthusiastically toward inclusion in the Western European democratic system. Only in Russia, where the "revolution" of anti-communism was most difficult and resisted, since so much of its power elite was composed of former communists, did they remain part of the equation. Putin is one of the last vestiges of that transition. The "new" Russia was, however, a shadow of its old communist self, and Putin's aggression against Ukraine may well have been the last death rattle of that system and the structure of competition and animosity it represented. How Russia is treated in terms of the war's eventual settlement will play a large part in whether post–Ukraine War Europe returns to being an international bulwark with which terms of trade are a much greater daily concern than the threat of another European war.

The second arena of concern is the developing world. It is selectively more unstable and is generally of somewhat lower salience to American national security and American military forces than Europe, but it has also been where the United States has found itself deploying and employing those forces in anger in the contemporary world. The locus of American violent concern has changed. When developing world locales essentially served as surrogate battlegrounds for the Cold War competition between the Americans and the Soviets, it tended to attract American attention in East Asia, and specifically in places like the Southeast Asian peninsula, where American military forces were engaged for over a decade until the American withdrawal in 1973. It has moved to the Middle East, which has been America's "battleground" since.

These two different geographical and political settings offer very different geopolitical challenges that are captured in the IF Principle. Europe has always been politically the most important part of the world to the United States, as it was to the world at large at least through World War II. After the demise of the Cold War confrontation with the USSR, it ceased being a major point of political contention as the Cold War differences dissolved and most of the former adversaries clamored to join the greater prosperity of the Western democracies. Russia, unfortunately for it and the tranquility and stability of that order, has largely been excluded (or excluded itself) from much of the growing prosperity and political cooperation of the new order. As noted already, Russia faces large structural problems, including the negative demographics of a shrinking population and an economy overly dependent on energy production.

The result at this point is the continuation of Russian isolation from the general economic and political prosperity of Europe and the comity of the evolving order. Russia is also the only major European country with a huge arsenal of nuclear weapons and thus the potential to be a nuclear war opponent. Avoidance of that contingency is the most basic American interest, and the question is how feasibly to lower or eliminate the prospect of such a war.

The developing world is the other source of instability, as well as being the geographical area where the United States has primarily employed force since World War II. The pattern has, of course, been selective. Almost all deployments have been in Asia: East Asia in the case of the 1950s American participation in the Korean conflict and the long involvement of armed forces in Southeast Asia; and more recent American interest and support for conflicts in the Middle East (e.g., Kuwait, Iraq, and Afghanistan). The East Asian deployments were all part of the Cold War competition with communism that is now concluded as such, although the current competition with Russia can be construed as a continuation of that physical struggle minus its 1950s ideological trappings. American involvement in the Middle East has been historically tied to the triumvirate of American interests in the region: guaranteed access to oil, the survival and protection of Israel, and the exclusion of Russian/Soviet influence. All three remain, although the Russian problem has decreased since the disassembly of the Soviet Union.

Military problems and solutions have varied from area to area. The Russian problem is basically unique in three senses. First, it is currently a threat from a single state against Ukraine and, by extension, the Western democratic system rather than the NATO–Warsaw Pact configuration of the Cold War. Second, it is basically the flailing of a declining power against the changing demographics of Europe, a competition in which the Russians are disadvantaged greatly in the long haul. Putin's last stand is arguably Russia's last act as a military superpower opponent of the West. Third, it has proceeded and been grounded in the context of nuclear weapons, the possible use of which Putin has raised in the Ukrainian context, despite the obvious apocalyptical consequence of "going nuclear" for his country. Nuclear weapons probably provided a useful guard rail around the parameters of the war; the dangers of accidentally breaching that inhibition added sizable uncertainty and anxiety to the war. Adjustment of the nuclear relationship should be a major postwar imperative for the principals in the war once order is restored.

The Middle Eastern component is compartmentalized and diverse. The internal regional dynamic remains largely the same as before from an American viewpoint, if with somewhat different emphases. Israel remains the linchpin. As the only indigenous regional nuclear weapons state and with large and capable military and paramilitary assets, Israel is no longer the weak orphan in need of protection that it was in the 1940s when American policy was originally designed. Rather, Israel is *the* major military force in the region, a country to be courted, not threatened, as recent regional politics (e.g., the Abraham Accord) demonstrates. If there is a "highlight" conflict, it is now Israel vs. Iran, something of an irony since under the Shah, Iran was as close to an Islamic friend as the Israelis had in the region. Today, the possibility that Iran will convert its nuclear power program to nuclear weapons construction is the single most dangerous regional problem, with escalatory and proliferation possibilities seldom discussed in detail. The Israelis have bluntly said that they will counteract the Iranian commencement of an active weapons program, which in the past (e.g., Iraq) has meant attacking and destroying the location of that program. In the past, such threats and actions have occurred in a nonnuclear environment; now nuclear possibilities exist.

The United States has found itself involved in situations where the basis of actions in countries like Iraq and Afghanistan involved unconventional opponents, and American actions have not been spectacularly successful. These have been tied to radicalism in the places the United States has gone, and the actions have had some ties to terrorism, notably in Afghanistan. Whether terrorism will reemerge as a reason for the United States to insert itself in regional violent politics is problematical, but the lessons of the past have been instructive. When an opponent like Iraq confronted the American military on American fighting terms as the United States and its allies blocked an Iraqi advance into Saudi Arabia, the Iraqis were soundly and easily defeated. They retreated to their homeland, and when the Americans returned in 2003 to occupy Iraq, the Iraqis did not resist but instead absorbed the occupation as best they could. The Afghan Taliban were similarly pushed out of their country in the American pursuit of Al Qaeda in 2001, and only reemerged shortly before the fall of the American-backed Afghan government. They are now firmly in control of the country.

The American military experience in Afghanistan and Iraq are emblematic of the kinds of problems and solutions the United States faces in the developing world. Iraq tried to emulate the West in the structure and orientation of its forces, and its military efforts were easily brushed aside by an American military for whom that kind of fighting was the epitome emblematic of the "American way of war." The rest of the world watched the scenario unfold, and the clear lesson they learned was that it was suicidal folly to confront the Americans on their terms. In Afghanistan, the Taliban learned their lesson when they returned to their country from Pakistani exile, and they went back to fighting unconventionally, which worked. The Americans left in 2021 unbroken but unsuccessful.

The Past as the Model of the Future?

Ukraine and Afghanistan are models of the warfare the United States has confronted in the recent past and of the kinds of situations that they may encounter in the future. They have been distinctly different experiences both in why and how they were engaged and fought, and in the outcomes they produced. They both represent situations that differ both in their vitality to the United States and in the means and consequences of pursuing them: they have very different IF profiles to the point that generalizations that apply within each category do not necessarily provide for answers that apply in the other. A brief look at each reveals the differences between and importance of each.

The Ukrainian War

The Ukrainian case is the first instance since the Cuban missile crisis in 1962 of determining how to apply force in a situation where major nuclear-armed rivals face one another. It is the first occasion where American and major-power antagonistic forces have faced one another since American and Chinese armies confronted one another in Korea in the early 1950s and the United States and the Soviet Union confronted one another but avoided a "hot" shooting conflict. The lesson of Cuba was that the possibility of nuclear engagement meant that direct confrontation between nuclear-armed rivals must be avoided in the future, and it is a lesson that was adhered to carefully by both sides for over sixty years before Russian troops invaded Ukraine. How the Ukrainian crisis is ultimately concluded is an important harbinger for nuclear futures.

In IF terms, the American reaction and response to the Russian invasion has been one where outcome of the conflict is highly interesting to the United States but where the United States and its European allies are reluctant to commit their own armed forces because doing so would clearly raise the question of how doing so would affect acceptable and unacceptable outcomes and how these might be achieved short of war between Russia and NATO. Clearly, the governing exogenous variable in the situation is the impact of nuclear weapons. Without their existence and possession by both sides, there would be a very different set of potential options for trying to achieve the objectives for the United States. The Americans, like their European counterparts, have an interest in a free and independent Ukraine, and were the totality of military means held by either side to secure that objective limited to conventional weaponry, there would be a broader set of possible means to achieve those goals available. The potential devolution of the situation to nuclear exchange (a possibility that Putin has annoyingly raised occasionally through the conflict) greatly reduces the range of potential actions available that might cause a downward spiral to nuclear escalation. This possibility clearly and openly limited American responses to Russian actions; Putin tantalized those making decisions with his reminders of the Russian arsenal.

Without nuclear weapons, the obvious objective of the American action would have been to force Russia to leave Ukraine, possibly including the use of American military force. Since those weapons do exist, the objective constricts to forcing a Russian retreat without the realistic threat that the failure of the Russians to comply could lead to physical American escalation. The potential for nuclear escalation is a major qualification that makes attaining the broader goal more difficult; the poor performance of the Russian military makes the success of the Ukrainian countereffort more plausible.

The United States and its partners chose to use the economic instrument of power as the major means to compel Russian acquiescence to its demands. At one level, the response could be weak, even ineffective, to counter Putin. A believable military threat might have brought about more rapid Russian compliance, but it also might not have. Although Putin hinted at the possible uses of nuclear weapons in some unspecified way at various points, is there any reason to believe that a threat of possible nuclearization would have caused Putin to end the Russian invasion and savage campaign and retreat behind Russian boundaries accepted by the rest of the world?

The IF principles applied to the Russian invasion help clarify the situation. There were clearly important American and other NATO interests in denying Russia their goal of conquering and recolonizing Ukraine. At the most general level, the Russian act upset a three-quarter-century peace in what had historically been the most fractious part of the world, as two world wars in the last century provide clear testimony. The West could neither accept nor condone that forceful change in the global and regional balances of power and maintain the peaceful status quo that Europe has enjoyed. As Fazal put it in *Foreign Affairs*, "With Russia's invasion, the norm against territorial conquest has been tested in the most threatening and vivid way since the end of World War II." At the same time, the United States has never had a particularly distinct or close relationship with Ukraine, whereas bordering Russia does. Had the invasion not been the bloody, destructive spectacle that Russia made it, some Russian activity to bring Ukraine closer to Russia might have created a different set of emotions and responses. Given Ukrainian animosity toward Russia arising from their history and effective colonization from the Soviet era, it is not clear what kind of accord with Ukraine that Russia could have negotiated that would have satisfied both countries. Russia, of course, consistently rejected that interpretation of the situation, since it maintains that Ukraine is not an independent state but a part of Russia.

What exactly was the level of American interest in Ukraine and in opposing the aggressive conquest of that spinoff country of the old Soviet Union? These are two distinct questions that had to impact the decision process in contrary ways. Historically, there has not been a strong relationship between the United States and Ukraine, except indirectly. The Ukraine is the granary of Europe, producing large crops of various grains that feed both the Russians and West Europeans. American interest at this level is thus indirect, since American partners in NATO and the EU both get major amounts of their grains from Ukraine. That, however, is not a sufficient reason for conflict over the Ukraine.

Ukraine's geographic location is the source of its importance, certainly to Russia and to a lesser extent to Western Europe. Ukraine is a critical part of the invasion route back and forth between Russia and the rest of Europe, and the guarantee that this approach to Russia will be unavailable to those who might threaten Russia is a core element of Russian national security policy. This geopolitical element is clearly important to those on the European continent and is a derivative interest of the United States since it is a potential invasion route in either direction. Self-determination for the former Soviet republics has been an American policy goal since the breakup of the Soviet Union, although not one of the highest priority, as American verbal but not physical disapproval to the Russian effective takeover of Georgia is testimony.

Given this context, a free and independent Ukraine is a policy goal of the United States, but it is not one that probably rises to the level of vitality that would justify military action by the United States to enforce with its own armed forces. Russia maintains that the Ukraine is a rightful part of Russia based in historic Russian preference and the Soviet precedent. Ukrainians other than Russian transplants from the Soviet period (part of Soviet policy for control and legitimacy revolved around there being Russian populations in the various republics) reject this kindred attachment. Except in instances where Russian immigrants are discriminated against, however, this division is not great enough to create a sufficient American interest to justify the dangers (notably nuclear) that intervention would create.

The egregiousness and brutality of the Russian invasion made some form of American and other allied response inevitable in a way that actions in other parts of the former Soviet Union have not. Animosity between Russians and Ukrainians is long-standing, much of it based in the Russian belief that the Ukraine is a generic part of Russia and Ukrainian denial of that claim, and that animosity is multiplied by the geopolitical importance of Ukraine both as an invasion route and as a major source of grain that feeds the Russian people. They have a long and turbulent past that was reprised in the invasion and subsequent surprising acquittal of the war by a vastly outnumbered but clearly more dedicated Ukrainian force.

In the circumstance, the United States could not ignore the Russian invasion and the subsequent calls to come to the aid of the Ukrainians globally, but especially from members of NATO and the EU. The NATO connection was particularly irksome to the Russians, since Ukrainian advocacies to join the Western alliance had been a major source of Russian concern that apparently helped motivate the invasion. Whether any affiliation between NATO and Ukraine would have occurred if the Russians had limited their response to discouraging that expressed desire is not clear (it was certainly not a desire widely known or discussed in the United States), but the invasion itself greatly increased the likelihood of some affiliation between Ukraine and the West after the war ended—the exact opposite of Russian motivation and the ultimate irony of the situation.

In this situation, what was the United States to do? It could not ignore or downplay Russia's actions without undercutting the viability of the alliance, but it also could not stage a counterinvasion without running the risk of a direct military confrontation with Russia that could, under circumstances impossible to predict, turn into general war with the prospect of escalation to a nuclear World War III. This was a contingency that would clearly run the risk of obviating any sense of belief in the feasibility of attaining the objective. With the extremes of doing nothing or intervening with American forces having catastrophic consequences, the Nixon Doctrine solution of coming to the physical aid of Ukraine with massive amounts of assistance but short of physically inserting its forces seemed the only responsible, prudent, but also potentially effective response, and it was the option chosen.

The response arguably was also the best and probably the only alternative available to the United States, and at least in public, it was accepted by the Ukrainian government as the best deal it was likely to get. It arguably fulfilled the IF principles of defending American interests in promoting (in this case helping to restore) a peaceful Europe and in frustrating Putin's geopolitical power grab. Putin clearly miscalculated two aspects of what would happen if he invaded. First, he clearly overestimated the prospect of a quick and easy conquest of Ukraine and thus the likelihood that substantial global opposition would emerge in support of the Ukrainians. The invasion was supposed to be a Russian walk in the park; instead, Russian forces performed poorly, and the military "story" was the valor and success of Ukrainian forces that were no match on paper for the Russian armed forces. Just as the outcome of the Russian occupation of Afghanistan in the 1980s, the result was to diminish, not enhance, Russia's geopolitical place in the world and hence to accelerate rather than to impede the demographic time bomb under which Russia labors. Afghanistan was partly responsible for the demise of the Soviet Union; will Ukraine have the same effect on Putin's Russia?

Second, because Putin mistook the global response to the invasion, the result was to tarnish, not enhance, Putin's prestige and the way he will be remembered in Russian history. Ignoring the possibility of a reprise of the Afghan debacle, he plunged ahead with the invasion, and it was militarily a failure. Since the outcomes of wars are not calculated like the scores of athletic contests, the Russians will likely be able to claim success that may (or may not) be accepted in Russia itself, but not much of anywhere else. The reputation of Russia as the "frozen banana republic with nuclear weapons" was reinforced by their incursion. Afghanistan was instrumental in the collapse of the Soviet Union; will Ukraine be the experience that causes "Putinism" to collapse as well? It may be instructive that by May 2022 (three months into a war expected to last three days), there were rumors of coup attempts leaking out of Russia, and they have continued.

If the interests of the United States and its allies were to restore Ukrainian sovereignty and to avoid becoming embroiled personally in a shooting war with nuclear weapons use possibilities, it has apparently succeeded, for which we all should be grateful. How well (or if) Russia accepts the failure of its actions depends on the terms of the peace. The most notable issue is how to facilitate the Ukrainian recovery from the disastrous physical consequences of the Russian assault, an undertaking that will require the infusion of massive amounts of international financial and physical assistance to rebuild the devastated country, and a major question is the extent to which Russian petroleum resources will be included in the process and the terms on which such recovery is calculated. The Ukrainian people are unlikely to be in a forgiving or reconciliatory mood toward Russia, and the precedent established will have a good deal to do with whether the settlement quiets the region or contributes to the future stability of the fringes of the old Soviet Union. It has already brought Sweden and Finland to NATO's doorstep, a clear strategic defeat for Russia.

The second case is the profile of committing forces in developing world contests. Conflict and violence are more prevalent in this part of the world than in Europe, but these potential engagements tend to fall shorter in both interest and feasibility terms. In some cases, they may be important enough to tempt American intervention, as in the invasion of Afghanistan to pursue Al Qaeda in 2001, but they lack the geopolitical salience a Russian annexation of Crimea potentially makes for European and global purposes.

Asymmetrical War in the Developing World

The other forum for American forces usage has been in developing world conflicts. Most of these have been of a smaller order of magnitude or consequence to the United States and the overall international system than was the bloodletting in Ukraine, but these kinds of conflicts cumulatively have otherwise defined American military action since the late twentieth century.

The early involvements in places like Vietnam were motivated by the Cold War and the contest between communism and noncommunism. After the 9/11 catastrophe ushered in the new century, concerns with the war on terror became more prominent motivators.

Developing world involvements have distinctly different profiles than European conflicts in places like the war in Ukraine. Once again, these differences can usefully be described in terms of the IF criteria. Generally speaking, developing world internal conflicts occupy a lower level of interest for the United States for a variety of reasons that include geographic factors, cultural proximity, and political connections, and are thus likely not to be viewed as being as important to the United States as European-based conflicts. They were more prominent during the Cold War because of the American concern with the global communist-noncommunist competition for global ideological sway. When that competition ended with the implosion of communism, the justification became much less compelling. With a few exceptions like parts of the Middle East, it is difficult to argue that American vital interests are engaged in most developing world instability. The exceptions, of course, are areas that have connections to international terrorism directed at the United States, the suppression of which is clearly an American vital interest.

The toughest IF problem in dealing militarily with wars in the developing world is that those whom the United States ends up opposing in these conflicts tend to fight asymmetrically. Most developing world conflicts occur in countries that are geographically challenging for the application of the kinds of heavy, mechanized forces in which the United States specializes. As already noted, this problem is a combination of physical attributes of the area involved such as primitive infrastructure (on which to transport highly mechanized forces like those of the United States rapidly to the battlefield) and geographic features like highly vegetated—often with thick jungle—terrains that may inhibit the movement of weaponry based in advanced technology but that are well suited to the kinds of low technology warfare like booby trapping trails and roads and providing cover for ambushes. The environment, and the ways in which it is exploited militarily, are largely foreign to highly technological forces like those of the United States, which is, of course, one of the reasons it is employed against us.

Historically, the United States has misunderstood and underestimated the problems into which it was intervening and the difficulty of confronting those problems. During the Cold War, for instance, American interest in places like Southeast Asia was virtually nonexistent other than as an extension of the Cold War, and it is essentially inconceivable that the United

States would have involved itself in places like Vietnam had the argument not been convincing that the issue was a communist insurgency attempting to overthrow a noncommunist government in Saigon, to replace it with a Soviet-style dictatorship and thus lose a part of the world to communism. This consideration was present in Vietnam, but it was not the primary motivation of most of those who opposed the South Vietnamese regime. If stopping communist global expansion was the true nature of the conflict there, American intrusion might have been justifiable; if that nature was a struggle for land reform and the removal of excessive Chinese absentee land control, so that American military intrusion was, in Chua's estimate, "to keep the Chinese rich," it was a goal most Vietnamese opposed. At the same time, Americans (including the military) clearly underestimated the difficulty of defeating a determined adversary in a physically difficult setting where traditional European-style forces and ways of fighting did not necessarily apply or work. Phrasing the situation in IF terms makes it difficult to mount a spirited, credible case for American military intervention and would have added considerable fuel to anti-war sentiment in the United States.

The developing world intrusions of the United States into what are basically internal conflicts over who controls and governs which territories is apparently on the wane since the end of the Afghan intrusion. It is unclear where in the developing world the United States would be likely to wage a Vietnam- or Afghan-style conflict for reasons that derive from the influence of forces like those encapsulated in the IF principles.

Back to the Future: Where Should America Fight?

This book has had two basic purposes and themes that arise from the title. The first has been an examination of the kinds of situations into which the United States felt it necessary to use force to protect its interests. Since the United States emerged from World War II as one of the very few countries whose power and prestige were enhanced by the conflict and its outcome, this combination thrust the country into a position of power and influence that it had never experienced before in its history, and it was not entirely prepared for it physically or intellectually. The United States was the most powerful and influential state in the world, and this was a novel part of an American experience that is evolving.

Only the Soviet Union, its erstwhile ally during World War II, acted as a challenger to that status after the war, and it was the role it continued to occupy until the Soviet state dissolved. Each led a coalition of states with contrasting views of the world. Adding to the richness of the new system, the largest population concentration in the world, what became known as the developing or third world, was forming from the bankrupt ruins of European colonialism, and that struggle became a major geopolitical factor and source of contention as the postwar world evolved with the competition for dominion between Marxism and democracy as its major global military significance. The new states formed the most unstable and violence-prone part of the world, and thus the source of conflicts into which the Americans could be drawn. The major virtue of engaging in developing world indirect confrontations with the Soviets was that they posed a minimum danger of escalation to direct, including potential nuclear, conflict with the communists. The major drawback was that in many cases the United States did not fully understand the politics and physical dynamics of the places where we became involved. Nuclear war was avoided in this environment; engagements in conflicts that arguably violated the IF principles of adequate interests to engage and a clear way of how were not.

The other most striking aspect of the new geopolitical order was the advent of nuclear weapons, a novel form of massive mayhem that would set their possessors (the "superpowers") in a unique situation of geopolitical prominence and peril. The original research that led to these weapons occurred during World War II on both sides of the European theater, but since most of the prominent German scientists involved fled the country, the American Manhattan Project produced the first bombs, which were employed against Japan to end the war. The Soviets also pursued the weaponization of nuclear physics, and by the end of the 1940s, the dynamics that would produce the nuclear balance and the need to avoid the introduction of these weapons in war were in place (Clark, in a 1980 study, offers an interesting overview of this evolution).

Evolution in thinking about nuclear weapons has developed greatly over time. The consensus in the strategic community from the 1940s through the 1950s was very fatalistic: a civilization-destroying war between the two power blocs that would endanger the survival of humankind was viewed as virtually inevitable, and the notion of avoiding—deterring—such a catastrophe developed as a response during this period. The world looked over the brink into the abyss of the results of a nuclear conflict during the Cuban crisis of 1962, and the horror they saw made nuclear deterrence the prevailing goal and value for the remainder of the Cold War. The grim conviction that such a war was inevitable faded as, ironically, arsenals continued to grow, and by the time the Soviet Union dissolved, their influence had become part of the background constraints on conflict generally.

The end of the Cold War did not, of course, remove the physical possibility of a nuclear clash or its possible consequences. As the Soviet Union splintered, negotiations proceeded that transferred all the Soviet weapons to Russia, as noted. The dynamic that was not evident in the ensuing thirty years was the enhanced importance of their nuclear arsenal to Russia, as the de facto last pillar of Soviet world superpower status. As Russian performance in Ukraine has demonstrated, the Putin regime has reminded the world that they still exist and could become a factor in that conflict and in the future. Unless the outcome of the Ukraine war includes a radical change in the Russian leadership, they are likely to remain as a shadowy presence over the violent relations of those who possess them. They have not gone away, and at least the Putin regime feels they retain some significance that means they are a variable influencing conflicts to come. It is impossible to know with any confidence what that role might be—or become. It should be remembered that China also has a large arsenal of these weapons.

Nuclear weapons provide an important and ambivalent role in international relations, and especially on the dynamics of using force. Because of the probable societal impacts of a war in which they were used, there is an understandable unease about their existence in the military arsenals of the largest, most powerful, and antagonistic powers. Were relations between the possessors ever to devolve to war between them, human civilization could be the victim, and this realization creates a natural predilection to do away with them. Moreover, obtaining nuclear power can greatly enhance the power and prestige of new members and, in effect, make "players" of otherwise less consequential states; North Korea is the prime example. While leaders everywhere recognize the potentially catastrophic nature of a war that included nuclear weapons and possessors have acted to reinforce their use, it is still conceivable that they could fall into the hands of an unstable, irresponsible, or ignorant leader who would not be deterred by the potential consequences of their employment. A world without these weapons would not be prone to that possibility. But is that necessarily a good thing for the world and the continuation of world civilization?

Peering into the Future

There is no universally agreed-upon answer to that question, and it is fundamental to the core of when the United States should use force in the future, and how those weapons would influence the outcome. At the end of World War II, a consensus grew in some national security circles that it was just a matter of time until a possibly civilization-ending war erupted led by the two superpowers. These prophecies began to appear when the United States was the only nuclear possessor and continued after the Soviets gained the capability as well. It was further hypothesized that such a war would occur in Europe, would be gruesomely bloody and destructive, and that world civilization as it existed would likely be destroyed in the process. These gloomy predictions extended through the 1950s, and it spawned a fatalistic culture "highlighted" by motion pictures like *Dr. Strangelove* and *On the Beach*. It was a strange, even depressing, milieu in which to think about nuclear weapons, war, and the future of civilization.

The pessimism and gloom gradually receded as the major nuclear possessors came to realize that these weapons could not be used against one another in a way that could lead to any outcome that anyone would equate to "victory" or the accomplishment of geopolitical goals. The shock treatment crystalized around the 1962 Cuban Missile Crisis, when analysts agree the world came closer than at any previous time to a nuclear World War III, were appropriately appalled at the prospect, and lowered the temperature in the rivalry. It is not an exaggeration to say that the circumspection with which the United States and Russia have dealt with one another in the Ukrainian War is part of the legacy of Cuba. Put another way, realizations that emerged from the Cuban crisis have created the primary rule of superpower military relations ever since: any confrontation between nuclear weapons possessors must be regulated and kept well beneath the threshold where those weapons might be invoked. Since any conflict between nuclear possessors is a potential nuclear conflict, it means that the largest and most powerful states cannot fight one another directly. In the Ukrainian war, this dynamic created an arguable boundary over how far the two major powers could go in situations where their interests collide.

The consequences of this dynamic are, of course, ironic. They amount to saying that the reason there has not been war between the major players is not because of some improvement in the relations between them. Peace has not broken out! What it does say is that nuclear armed states do not fight because, at least to this point, they have not proven to be masochistic or self-destructive. The result has been that when they confront one another, it must be very carefully. The more real danger is that nuclear weapons might be used if it involved relatively minor states that did not have globally threatening arsenal sizes themselves but where these weapons are used to preclude a catastrophic outcome for them or for some other, possibly irrational reason. In the author's personal view, expressed in a 2021 book (*The Middle East and American National Security*), Israel may pose the greatest threat in this regard, since a number of Israeli commentators across time have suggested that "the bomb in the basement" might be used if Israeli was facing a state-threatening menace in a future conflict. It is exemplary that most of the discussions regarding nuclear weapons center on the consequences if a "crazy" state both acquires them and threatens to (or does) launch them, initiating nuclear war.

Developing world conflict remains a problem for the United States, but in a different way. The United States has prepared most extensively to fight over Europe (and more recently East Asia) for over three-quarters of a century, but it has physically fought in the developing world. For most of the period since 1945, its motivation was largely to blunt communist expansionism—which is no longer an operational imperative. Now most of the developing world conflict into which it potentially could be drawn has roots in international terrorism aimed directly or indirectly at the United States and its interests.

There are also two major problems posed by incidents of developing world violence. First, they occur in areas that are not of such high intrinsic interest to the United States that they pose the same depth of strategic, geopolitical interest that direct major power conflict does. Most of these places hold some geographic significance or resource of interest to the United States, but most problems and solutions are not of such high salience that they pose such a direct threat to important American interests that they demand a forceful response. The most dangerous and potentially consequential of these threats since the fall of the Shah in 1979 and the emergence of Iran as an opponent rather than an ally and stabilizing regional influence, have been in the Middle East, which is where the United States has projected force most consistently in this century. There is little obvious evidence that this is likely to change, although some analysts believe that relations with China could deteriorate in that direction. As the experience in places like Iraq and Afghanistan offer sober assessment, American military force has not been conspicuously effective in establishing the efficacy of force to achieve American interests in the developing world. The 2021 withdrawal from Afghanistan is the starkest testimony to this lack of spectacular outcomes and will dampen enthusiasm for such adventures for a time.

Second and relatedly, these are the places where the application of US force has produced the most ambivalent outcomes. Generically, these conflicts tend to be fought as asymmetrical wars, with the added difficulties that they involve physically hostile locations about which the United States has limited knowledge going in and where the setting is not convivial to the application of European-style forces fighting "conventionally." They are, in terms developed in these pages, asymmetrical wars, and they are not the kinds of conflict with which the United States is intimately familiar or in which they have enjoyed the most conspicuous successes. That is not so much a criticism of the US military as it is a statement about the consequences of using force in situations and for purposes for which it was not explicitly developed.

The mixed experience in developing world conflicts has created a bigger and better capability to deal with the experiences one encounters in developing world situations, although not yet one that is embraced universally within the services. There are at least two basic reasons for this. One is clearly that fighting in unfamiliar territory against foes with whom one is unfamiliar is difficult and for many military leaders and personnel not the kind of fighting for which they had signed up. The mindset for engagement against Afghan tribesmen, in other words, is different than the milieu one would encounter in a European conflict. This observation is part of the second problem: the level of American interests is lower in these kinds of contest.

By almost any criterion, for instance, the US effort in Afghanistan was a failure, but a year or more after the American withdrawal, it was not clear how the United States was physically or politically worse off as a result. By contrast, the outcome of Putin's war with Ukraine, in which the degree of American involvement in support has been substantial but did not include direct military participation, was ultimately more geopolitically significant than essentially any of its developing world involvements. The lesson seems clear enough for the time being: American reasons for fighting are still tied to the European balance in the world, but the instances of that participation are potentially less frequent than developing world conflicts, which are more frequent and thus available for American participation but where the outcomes are less vital to the country. Where should America fight?

Projecting Forward

It is sometimes said, slightly tongue-in-cheek, that it is easier to predict the past than the future, since the past has already occurred and the future has not. Certainly that is true of the present that forms the basis for guessing where the United States should and will employ force in the upcoming years. When the writing of this book began, there was no Russian invasion of Ukraine occurring, and hardly anyone predicted it would occur. But it did happen, and it has become a very expensive part of the current American military experience; the ramifications are likely to be a major part of policy negotiation and resolution for some time to come. The elements of that future will begin with how to deal with a basically humiliated Russia whose military performance was surprisingly incapable, how to rebuild Ukraine (notably how much of the burden will come in the form of Russian energy revenues), and how to reconcile Russia's sense of security with the new reality of a formidable NATO presence at its doorstep (ironically, of course, the very condition their invasion sought to avoid). It is difficult to see how a seventy-year-old Putin can politically survive this trauma; a major goal must be to soften the blow enough that Putin does not try to lash out with his nuclear arsenal but fades from the world geopolitical stage. This problem may be the real test of the outcome in terms of global, and especially European-based, peace and stability. The degeneration of the situation to nuclear exchange would be the ultimate failure of the system.

The situation in the Middle East has at least temporarily become less dangerous, although potential conflict between Israel and Iran over the dual and related issues of Israeli nuclear hegemony and the related issue of Iranian domain in the area continue. As American attention pivoted to the Ukrainian crisis, it moved temporarily away from the developing world, and one hopes that relative lack of emphasis can be maintained. So, where should America fight? A definitive substantive answer is impossible in a predictably unpredictable future environment and would be ultimately idle. What can be said is that one hopes that the tenets of the IF Principle will form some of the basis of those decisions.

Bibliography

Allison, Graham T. *The Essence of Decision: Explaining the Cuban Missile Crisis*. New York: HarperCollins, 1972.

Aslund, Anders. "Putin Is Going to Lose His War: And the World Should Prepare for Instability in Russia." *Foreign Affairs* (online), May 25, 2022.

Bacevich, Andrew J. *Washington Rules: America's Path to Permanent War*. New York: Henry Holt and Company, 2010.

Betts, Richard K. "Pick Your Battles: Ending America's Permanent State of War." *Foreign Affairs* 93, no. 6 (November/December 2014): 15–24.

Bildt, Carl. "NATO's Nordic Expansion: Adding Finland and Sweden Will Transform European Security." *Foreign Affairs* (online), April 29, 2022.

Chua, Amy. *Political Tribes: Group Instinct and the Fate of Nations*. New York: Penguin, 2018.

Clark, Ronald W. *The Greatest Power on Earth: The International Race for Nuclear Supremacy, Earliest Theory to Three-Mile Island*. New York: Harper and Row, 1980.

Clausewitz, Carl von. *On War*: Translated and edited by Michael Howard and Peter Paret. Princeton, NJ: Princeton University Press, 1984.

Drew, Dennis M., and Donald M. Snow. *Making Strategy for the Twenty-first Century*. Montgomery, AL: Air University Press, 2006.

Farrow, Ronan. *War on Peace: The End of Diplomacy and the Decline of American Influence*. New York: W. W. Norton, 2018.

Fazal, Tanisha M. "The Return of Conquest: Why the Future of Global Order Hinges on Ukraine." *Foreign Affairs* 101, no. 3 (May/June 2022): 20–27.

George, Roger, Harvey Rishikoff, and Brent Scowcroft, eds. *The National Security Enterprise: Navigating the Labyrinth*. 2nd ed. Washington, DC: Georgetown University Press, 2017.

Jarmon, Jack. *The New Era in U.S. National Security: An Introduction to Emerging Threats and Challenges*. Lanham, MD: Rowman & Littlefield, 2014.

Kagan, Frederick W., and Mason Clark. "How Not to Invade a Nation: Russia's Attack on Ukraine." *Foreign Affairs* (online), April 29, 2022, 64–79.

Kennedy, Robert F., and Arthur Schlesinger Jr. *The Thirteen Days: A Memoir of the Cuban Missile Crisis*. New York: Norton, 1969.

Kotkin, Stephen. "Realist World: The Players Change, But the Game Remains." *Foreign Affairs* 97, no. 4 (July/August 2018): 10–15.

———. "Ukraine, the China Challenge, and the Revival of the West." *Foreign Affairs* 101, no. 3 (May/June 2022): 64–79.

Preble, Christopher A., and John Mueller. *A Dangerous World: Threat Perceptions and U.S. National Security*. Washington, DC: CATO Institute, 2014.

Reid, Anna. "Putin's War on History: The Thousand-Year Struggle over Ukraine." *Foreign Affairs* 101, no. 3 (May/June 2022): 40–53.

Reveron, Derek S., and Nikolas Gvosdev. *The Oxford Handbook of U.S. National Security*. Oxford, UK: Oxford University Press, 2018.

Snow, Donald M. *Cases in U.S. National Security: Concepts and Processes*. Lanham, MD: Rowman & Littlefield, 2019.

———. *The Middle East and American National Security: Forever Wars and Conflicts?* Lanham, MD: Rowman & Littlefield, 2021.

Stoessinger, John G. *Why Nations Go to War*. 11th ed. Belmont, CA: Wadsworth, 2010.

Index

The Absolute Weapon (Brodie, B.), 21
Afghanistan, 17, 110, 132, 170; in asymmetrical warfare in Europe, 166, 168; asymmetrical warfare with, 116–17, 199; defeating intervention dynamics in, 125–26; Ukrainian-Russian conflict compared to, 3–4; unconventional opponents in, 186–87. *See also* Vietnam, Afghanistan, and beyond; Vietnam, Afghanistan, and Ukraine legacy
Afghanistan war, 73–77, 191. *See also* 9/11 avenging
Afghanistan withdrawal, 7–10, 198; AQ related to, 1, 14, 79; IF contribution in, 12–14; IF Factor introduction, 4–6; new way of fighting in, 11–12; public opposition in, 12–13; Taliban in, 1, 2; Vietnam compared to, 2, 13, 14, 15
Afro-Asia, 58, 85, 106
All-Volunteer Force (AVF), 14, 33–34
ambushes, 119, 193
America, 158–60. *See also specific topics*

America in Iraq, 78–79; Gulf War and beyond in, 67–69; Hussein in, 66–67; IF criteria justification in, 71–73; invasion and conquest of, 69–71; Iran compared to Iraq related to, 66; Iran-Iraq War related to, 65–67; Israel related to, 66; Kuwait in, 67; Saudi Arabia in, 67; Sunni and Shiites related to, 66
American Civil War, 17–18, 31–32, 58, 111
American Manhattan Project, 21, 46, 195
American Revolution, 10
anti-communism, 35, 85, 117; communism compared to, 124, 125, 134; instabilities related to, 159; "revolution" of, 184
anti-war sentiment, 27, 33, 132, 167, 194
AQ. *See* Al Qaeda
Army of the Republic of Vietnam (ARVN), 27
The Art of War (Sun Tzu), 10, 108

ARVN. *See* Army of the Republic of Vietnam

asymmetrical and conventional forms: America related to, 159–60; asymmetrical pasts and futures in, 164–66; asymmetrical warfare in Europe in, 166–69; comparisons in, 157–60; Cuban missile crisis and, 158–59; economics in, 158; European-style warfare in, 157–58, 160; in future, 196–98; IF Factor and Ukrainian War in, 175–78; NATO and, 158, 159; nuclear weapons in, 158–59; Russian invasion of Ukraine, American response in, 172–75; "traditional" war in, 160–64; Ukraine War in perspective in, 169–72; Ukrainian precedent in, 179–80; when should America fight in, 194–96

asymmetrical pasts and futures: Israel-Iran in, 165; Middle East in, 164–65; post-World War II intervention in, 164; Russian invasion of Ukraine and, 165–66; terrorist attacks in America, 164

asymmetrical warfare, viii, 10, 79, 198; with Afghanistan, 116–17, 199; in contemporary warfare, 107–8; in developing world, IF Factor, 108, 110, 193; developing world and, 11–12, 31, 192–94; European-style warfare compared to, 30, 31, 123; in invasion and conquest, 69–70; in Korean War, 18; in Russian invasion of Ukraine, American response, 141; terrain of, 31; in Ukrainian crisis resolution, 102; in Vietnam, 11, 30. *See also* contemporary warfare

asymmetrical warfare 101: in Cold War, 117; definition of, 118; developing world in, 117; IF Factor and, 117; postcolonialism and, 117; in Vietnam, 118, 119

asymmetrical warfare challenges: definition of, 111; in Iraq, 112; in Vietnam, 110–11

asymmetrical warfare in Europe: Afghanistan in, 166, 168; conscription in, 167; errors in, 166–69; hybrid in, 168; international response to, 168; morale in, 167; predictions on, 169; Russian attack on Ukraine in, 166–69; Russian forces' quality in, 166; Ukrainian resistance in, 167–68; unconventional resistance in, 169; war crimes in, 167, 169

asymmetrical warfare not easy: "liberators" in, 123; terrain related to, 122–23

asymmetrical wars, 198–99

asymmetry and IF Factor: feasibility in, 120; firepower in, 121–22; in Iraq, 120–21; Kuwait in, 120–21; terrain in, 122; Vietnam and, 119–20; vital interests in, 121

AVF. *See* All-Volunteer Force

Balkans, 86, 95
Biden, Joe, 15, 99, 147; Kabul airport related to, 2–3; Trump and, 56–57
bin Laden, Osama, 67
briar patch of intervention: Afghanistan in, 132; Chernobyl in, 132; "constant" in, 131; developing world instability in, 131; IF principles in, 133; Iraq in, 131–32; modal threats in, 133–35; Nixon Doctrine in, 132; nuclear weapons in, 132, 133; Russia and Ukraine in, 132, 133; threats in, 131, 133; Vietnam War in, 132. *See also* Russian invasion of Ukraine
Brodie, Bernard, 19–20, 21, 150
Brodie, Fawn, M., 150

Budjeryn, Marianne, 173
Bush, George W., 62, 68, 69

Cases in International Relations (Snow), 78
Chernobyl, 86–87, 90, 132, 164
China, 7, 61, 78, 128, 129; aspiration of, 116; energy-deficiency of, 113; in nuclear age and traditional war, 54, 56–57; in nuclear weapons age, 50, 83, 85; Russian invasion of Ukraine related to, 147; in twentieth-century legacy, 40–41
coconspirators, 74
Cold War, vii, viii, 35, 45, 102, 116; communism in, 117, 124; defeating intervention dynamics in, 124, 125; developing world, IF Factor and, 108–9; developing world and, 193–94; in Middle East quagmire, 112; nuclear age and traditional war related to, 53, 56; in post-WWII transition, 18–19; protection in, 140; Putin related to, 94, 140; in recent past as prologue, 185, 186; Russia and Ukraine related to, 86, 87, 128, 160, 163; in Ukraine 2022 crisis, 90, 180; in Ukrainian case, 88, 89; Vietnam, Afghanistan, and beyond related to, 9, 11; Vietnam related to, 5, 24, 28–29, 35, 146
communism, 5, 48, 184, 198; anti-, 35, 85, 117, 124, 125, 134, 159; in Cold War, 117, 124; terrorism compared to, 30–31, 112–13; Vietnam and, 7–8, 193–94
communist "empire," 61–62
competition, 85
conscription, viii–ix, 31–34, 167. *See also* Vietnam draft end and Americans' connection
contemporary warfare: Afro-Asia in, 106; asymmetrical warfare in, 107–8;
decolonization in, 106–7; Korean War in, 105; Middle East in, 105, 107; Ukraine in, 105–6; weaponry in, 107. *See also* asymmetrical warfare 101; asymmetrical warfare challenges; asymmetry and IF Factor; defeating intervention dynamics; Middle East quagmire; Russian invasion of Ukraine
conventional military plans, 41–42
conventional war, 54–55, 84, 107. *See also* asymmetrical and conventional forms; contemporary warfare
Costa, Robert, 40
counterinvasion, 191
Crimean annexation, 94, 127, 137
Cuba, 62
Cuban Missile Crisis, 49, 160, 183, 188, 195; asymmetrical and conventional forms and, 158–59; nuclear weapons in, 22–23; Ukraine 2022 war worthiness related to, 95–96

deaths, 2, 45, 64; in Vietnam impact, 26, 27, 126
decolonization, 85; in contemporary warfare, 106–7
defeating intervention dynamics: in Afghanistan, 125–26; AQ and, 125; asymmetry in, 124; in Cold War, 124, 125; interests and feasibility in, 127; NATO and, 126; in Vietnam, 124–25, 126–27
Democratic People's Republic of Korea (DPRK), 61
deployments beyond traditional Middle East conflict, 116–17
developing world, 131; in asymmetrical warfare 101, 117; asymmetrical warfare and, 11–12, 31, 192–94; asymmetrical wars in, 198–99; Cold War and, 193–94; in nuclear age and traditional war, 56; potential

deployments with, 116–17; in recent past as prologue, 184–85
developing world, IF Factor: asymmetrical warfare in, 108, 110, 193; Cold War and, 108–9; frustration in, 110; interest and feasibility in, 109–10; in Middle East, 109; military "mass" in, 110; Soviet Union collapse in, 108
"domino effect," 25–26, 32–33
DPRK. *See* Democratic People's Republic of Korea
draft, viii–ix, 31–34, 167

Eastern and Western warfare styles, 10–11
economics, 99, 158, 174–75; in Russian invasion of Ukraine, 143, 148, 149–50, 153–54, 163, 189
Eisenhower, Dwight D., 22
EU. *See* European Union
European-style forces, 42–43
European-style Russian forces, 157–58
European-style warfare: in American Civil War, 17–18, 58; in asymmetrical and conventional forms, 157–58, 160; asymmetrical warfare compared to, 30, 31, 123; in Cold War, 45; evolution of, 43; in France, 44; industrialization and, 44; nationalism related to, 43–44; nuclear age and traditional war compared to, 52, 56, 57–58; nuclear weapons related to, 45–46; standards of, 44; technology in, 44–45; terrain in, 44–45; total war in, 45–46; in Vietnam, 118–19; in world wars, 21; in WWII, 45
European Union (EU), 177

Fazal, Tanisha M., 189
feasibility, 179; in asymmetry and IF Factor, 120; in defeating intervention dynamics, 127; in developing world, IF Factor, 109–10; in Russian invasion of Ukraine, 148, 150; in Vietnam impact, 26–27
Finland, 178, 192
firepower, 121–22
France, 44

geopolitics, 89, 117–18; in 9/11 avenging, 75, 77; in nuclear weapons age, 50–51; in nuclear weapons impact evolution, 47–52; in Ukraine 2022 crisis, 90
Georgia, 147, 180
German Jews, 46
Germany, 174–75
global military power, 34–35
Groves, Lesley, 21
guerrilla mobile warfare, 10–11
Gulf War, 34
Gulf War and beyond: in America in Iraq, 67–69; bin Laden in, 67; Kurds in, 68–69; Kuwait in, 67–68; Persian Gulf War in, 67–68; Saudi oil in, 67

Harris, Kamala, 127
"heavy" warfare, 107
heroin, 76
Hiroshima, 19, 39, 55
Ho Chi Minh, 25, 28
Holocaust, 46
Humphrey, Hubert H., 33
Hussein, Saddam, 68–69, 70–71; in America in Iraq, 66–67; in IF criteria justification, 72–73

IF contribution, 12–14
IF criteria justification: accusation truth in, 71–72; Hussein in, 72–73; Israel related to, 73; of occupation, 72; Operation Northern Watch and, 73; plausibility of success in, 72; speculation on, 73; of WMDs, 72–73

Index · 207

IF Factor, 78, 119–22; asymmetrical warfare 101 and, 117; cautions of, 5; communism in, 5; interests in, 6, 179; intersubjectivity in, 6; *LTV* in, 6; "No More Vietnams" in, 5; Vietnam in, 4–5, 25, 26; vital interests in, 6

IF Factor and Ukraine: aberration in, 148; engagement rules change in, 148; NATO in, 148; nineteenth-century power politics in, 147–48; Putin in, 147–48

IF Factor and Ukrainian War: economic sanctions for, 176; geopolitics in, 175–76; NATO/EU in, 177; NATO in, 175, 177; nuclear weapons in, 175–76, 178; option for, 176; U.S. formal relations in, 176–77

IF principles, 191; in briar patch of intervention, 133; in recent past as prologue, 185

India, 96, 159, 173

interests: in IF Factor, 6, 179; in IF Factor and Ukraine, 149–50; in Russian invasion of Ukraine, 148, 149; in Vietnam, Afghanistan, and beyond, 7–8; in Vietnam impact, 26–27; in Vietnam longer-term effects, 28–29

interests and feasibility, 109–10, 127

intersubjectivity, 6

invasion and conquest: asymmetrical warfare in, 69–70; IF formula of, 70; misguidance of, 69–71; 9/11 related to, 71; without evidence, 70–71; WMD in, 69, 70–71

Iran, 186; Israel and, 113–15, 159, 165, 200

Iranian Revolution of 1979, 65–66, 114

Iran-Iraq War, 65–67

Iraq, 12, 65–69, 186–87; asymmetrical warfare challenges in, 112; asymmetry and IF Factor in, 120–21; in briar patch of intervention, 131–32. *See also* America in Iraq

Iraq War, 73–74

Islam and Judaism, vii–viii, 46

Isoroku Yamamoto, 63

Israel, 105; America in Iraq related to, 66; IF criteria justification related to, 73; initiatives of, 7; Iran and, 113–15, 159, 165, 186, 200; as linchpin, 186; after 9/11, 64, 65; nuclear weapons of, ix, 48, 186; threat of, 197–98

Jews, German, 46

Johnson, Lyndon B., 28, 33, 119, 126, 146

Judaism and Islam, vii–viii, 46

Kabul airport, 2–3, 13

Karzai, Hamid, 76, 77, 126

Kashmir, 96

Kennedy, John F., 22–23

Khrushchev, Nikita, 22–23, 89

Korea, 35, 61. *See also* North Korea

Korean War, 19, 35, 188; asymmetrical warfare in, 18; in contemporary warfare, 105; nuclear weapons and, 20; Vietnam draft end and Americans' connection and, 32

Kosovo, 57–58

Kurds, 68–69

Kuwait, 34, 67–68, 120–21

Latin America, 78

less than vital (LTV), 6

"liberators," 123

linchpin, 186

LTV. *See* less than vital

"manly" assistance, 179

Mao Dzedung, 11, 30

McGovern, George, 33

Middle East, 78–79, 116–17, 198, 200; in asymmetrical pasts and futures, 164–65; in contemporary warfare, 105, 107; developing world, IF Factor in, 109; international politics in, 65; Iran in, 65; 9/11 related to, 64; oil in, vii, 64; power competition in, ix; in recent past as prologue, 184, 185–86; Shah in, 65

The Middle East and American National Security (Snow), 15, 114

Middle East quagmire: Arab-Israeli conflicts in, 113–14; China in, 113; Cold War in, 112; Israel and Iran in, 113–15; North Korea in, 115; nuclear weapons in, 114–15; populations in, 114; religious terrorism in, 112–13; Saudi Arabia in, 114; Trump in, 115

Milley, Mark, 40, 41, 56–57

modal threats, 133–35

Nagasaki, 19, 39, 55

Nasser, Gamal Abdul, 66, 68

nationalism, 43–44; of Putin, 138, 143–44, 152–53

National Liberation Force (NLF), 2

National Security (Snow), 4–5

NATO. *See* North Atlantic Treaty Organization

Nazi Germany, 46

9/11, 34; China in, 61; civilian targets in, 64; communist "empire" in, 61–62; Cuba before, 62; declaration of war after, 63; introspection before, 61; invasion and conquest related to, 71; Israel after, 64, 65; Middle East related to, 64; NATO related to, 62; Pearl Harbor compared to, 62–63; Soviet Union collapse in, 61; Vietnam in, 61–62; vulnerability related to, 64; "war on terror" related to, 62, 63. *See also* America in Iraq; Gulf War and beyond; IF criteria justification; invasion and conquest

9/11 avenging: Afghanistan war related to, 73–74; AQ in, 74–75, 76, 77; future from, 77–79; geopolitics in, 75, 77; heroin in, 76; Northern Alliance in, 75–77; occupation as, 76–77; Pashtuns in, 75

Nixon, Richard M., 14, 28, 33

Nixon Doctrine, 132, 150, 153, 168, 180, 191

NLF. *See* National Liberation Force

"No More Vietnams," 2, 5, 14, 34

North Atlantic Treaty Organization (NATO), 95; asymmetrical and conventional forms and, 158, 159; defeating intervention dynamics and, 126; in IF Factor and Ukraine, 148; in IF Factor and Ukrainian War, 175, 177; 9/11 related to, 62; Russia and Ukraine related to, 87, 127, 161, 163; in Russian invasion of Ukraine, American response, 172–73, 174; Russian invasion of Ukraine and, 138–39, 140, 147, 148; in Ukraine 2022 crisis, 90–92; Ukraine 2022 war worthiness related to, 96–97; in Ukraine Russian's Vietnam, 147, 151; in Ukrainian case, 89; in Ukrainian crisis resolution, 97, 98, 100, 101, 102; Ukrainian War and, 190–91

Northern Alliance, 75–76

North Korea, 35, 50, 115, 174, 196

nuclear age and traditional war: assured destruction in, 53; China in, 54, 56–57; Cold War related to, 53, 56; developing world in, 56; European-style warfare compared to, 52, 56, 57–58; force in, 52; Kosovo related to, 57–58; legacy of, 53; nuclear deterrence in, 53, 57, 85; "petrolist" strategy in, 53–54; potential in,

52–53; proximity in, 53; Special Forces in, 54; Ukraine in, 53–54, 57; U.S. conventional force structure in, 54–55
nuclear deterrence, 151, 195; in nuclear age and traditional war, 53, 57, 85; in Russia and Ukraine, 86, 129, 133; in twentieth-century legacy, 39–42, 43
nuclear prophylactic, 102–3
nuclear science, 46
nuclear weapons, 3, 4, 13; analysts on, 21–22; in asymmetrical and conventional forms, 158–59; in briar patch of intervention, 132, 133; in Cuban Missile Crisis, 22–23; European-style warfare related to, 45–46; future of war and, 30–31; in IF Factor and Ukrainian War, 175–76, 178; of Israel, ix, 48, 186; Korean War and, 20; "manly" assistance related to, 179; in Middle East quagmire, 114–15; in post-WWII transition, 19–21; in recent past as prologue, 185; Russia and Ukraine related to, 84–85, 128–29, 161–62, 164, 196; in Russian invasion of Ukraine, American response, 141–43, 173–74, 178; Russian invasion of Ukraine and, 135, 148–49, 153–54; of Soviet Union, 19, 20–21, 22, 83; traditional warfare related to, 23–24; Ukraine related to, 23; in Ukraine Russian's Vietnam, 147; in Ukrainian case, 87–88; in Ukrainian crisis resolution, 99–100; in WWII, 21
nuclear weapons age: China in, 50, 83, 85; distance in, 50; economy in, 50–51; fear in, 49–50, 58; geopolitics in, 50–51; global warming in, 50–51; human extinction in, 49–50; peace in, 49; Taiwan in, 51; WWIII in, 51–52

nuclear weapons impact, 46
nuclear weapons impact evolution: all war in, 52; communism in, 48; Cuban Missile Crisis related to, 49; delivery in, 47; distribution in, 48; geopolitics in, 47–52; limitations in, 47; new nuclear powers in, 48; Soviet Union in, 48, 51; unpredictability in, 47; U.S. in, 48, 51

Operation Northern Watch, 68, 73

Pakistan, 96, 125, 126, 159, 173
Pashtuns, 75
past as model of future, 187–92
Pearl Harbor, 62–63
People's Republic of China (PRC), 61
Persian Gulf oil, 64
Persian Gulf War, 12, 67–68, 77–78
petrostate, 93
popular culture, 20, 197
post-Cold War, 140
post-WWII: Soviet Union, 18; warfare evolution in, 18–21, 83
post-WWII transition: Cold War in, 18–19; nuclear weapons in, 19–21; popular culture in, 20
Powell, Colin, 69
PRC. See People's Republic of China
projecting forward, 199–200
Putin, Vladimir, ix, 3, 84, 127, 158; aggressiveness related to, 139–40; as champion, 136–37; Cold War related to, 94, 140; in IF Factor and Ukraine, 147–48; IF Factor and Ukrainian War and, 175, 176, 177; longevity of, 93–94; motivations of, 95, 129, 143–44, 151–52, 191–92; nationalism of, 138, 143–44, 152–53; primary status from, 94; in recent past as prologue, 184; reminders from, 93–94; retribution from, 137;

210 ~ Index

in Russia and Ukraine, 87, 92–95;
in Russian invasion of Ukraine,
American response, 135–40,
143–44, 177–78; in Ukrainian crisis
resolution, 97; vulnerability and, 93,
152–53, 200; Yeltsin compared to,
137
"Putin Solution," 140

Al Qaeda (AQ), 7, 8, 62–63, 125;
Afghanistan withdrawal related to,
1, 14, 79; in 9/11 avenging, 74–75;
Taliban and, 74

recent past as prologue: Cold War
in, 185, 186; Cuban Missile Crisis
in, 183; decommunization in,
184; developing world in, 184–85;
IF Principle in, 185; Iraq and
Afghanistan in, 186–87; Israel and
Iran in, 186; Middle East in, 184,
185–86; nuclear weapons in, 185,
186; preparation in, 184; Putin in,
184
Rumsfeld, Donald, 69
Russia: China and, 128; economics of,
99; Europe related to, 127–28; as
petrostate, 93; size of, 98–99, 128.
See also "traditional" war
Russia and Ukraine: Balkan situation
related to, 86; buildup related to,
161; Cold War related to, 86, 87,
128, 160, 163; conventional
war and, 84; escalation in, 84;
geography of, 163; geopolitics from,
162–63; NATO related to, 87, 127,
161, 163; nuclear deterrence in, 86,
129, 133; nuclear weapons related to,
84–85, 128–29, 161–62, 164, 196;
population related to, 161; postwar
relations of, 164–65; Putin and,
87, 92–95, 163; rivalry of, 86–87;
Russian aggression and, 161;
Soviet Union dissolution in,
86, 87; superpowers related to,
83–84; Syria and, 161; territory
related to, 162; trigger for, 163;
Ukrainian reconstruction after,
162

Russian invasion of Ukraine: as
aberration, 148; buffer zones related
to, 138, 152; China related to,
147; colonization related to, 137;
Crimean annexation related to, 137;
demands in, 151–52; economics
in, 143, 148, 149–50, 153–54,
163, 189; feasibility in, 148, 150;
Georgia related to, 147; "high road"
motive for, 138; interests in, 148,
149; legacy of, 150–54; NATO and,
138–39, 140, 147, 148; neutrality
related to, 139; nuclear weapons
and, 135, 148–49, 153–54; outcomes
from, 146–47, 153; pariah state in,
136; power status from, 152–53;
Putin in, 135–40, 143–44; puzzle of,
135–36; reconstruction from, 138;
rules of engagement in, 149; Soviet
Union collapse in, 136; speculation
regarding, 136–37; Ukraine and IF
Factor in, 147–50; unity against,
135; U.S. related to, 139; Western
responses and, 138–39

Russian invasion of Ukraine, American
response: asymmetrical warfare in,
141; decisions in, 142, 143–44, 175–
76; economic sanctions in, 143, 174–
75; failure related to, 140–41; fear in,
142; formal relations and, 176–77;
interests in, 176; NATO in, 172–73,
174; nuclear weapons related to,
141–43, 173–74, 178; optimism of,
141; options in, 142; post-Cold War
related to, 140; Putin in, 135–40,
143–44, 177–78; reorientation in,
143; Russian petroleum in, 174–75;

sovereignty guarantee related to, 173–74
Russia's size, 171

Saudi Arabia, 67, 71, 114
Shah, 65, 113, 186
Southeast Asia, 122–23
South Korea, 35
Soviet Union: in nuclear weapons impact evolution, 48; nuclear weapons of, 19, 20–21, 22, 83; pinnacle of, 93; post-WWII, 18; U.S. versus, 35. *See also* Russia
Soviet Union collapse, 61, 86, 87, 108, 136
Special Forces, 29, 54
Sun Tzu, 10, 18, 30, 108
Sweden, 178, 192

Taiwan, 51, 153
Taliban, 3, 8; in Afghanistan withdrawal, 1, 2; AQ and, 74; U.S. and, 125–26
terrain, 31, 44–45, 122–23
terrorism, 62, 63, 164, 187, 198; communism compared to, 30–31, 112–13; Iraq War and, 73–74
Tet offensive, 27–28, 33
total war, 45
"traditional" war. *See* Russia and Ukraine
traditional warfare, 23. *See also* nuclear age and traditional war
Trump, Donald, 40, 41, 115; Biden and, 56–57
twentieth-century legacy, 13–15, 150–54; adaptability in, 42; anomaly in, 42–43; China in, 40–41; conventional military plans in, 41–42; dynamics of violence in, 40; European-style forces in, 42–43; India and Pakistan in, 42; nuclear deterrence in, 39–42, 43; nuclear

weapons in, 39–40; tradition in, 42; triggers in, 40–41. *See also* European style warfare; nuclear age and traditional war; nuclear weapons impact

Ukraine, 78; in contemporary warfare, 105–6; geography of, 86–87, 190; in nuclear age and traditional war, 53–54, 57; Vietnam compared to, 146; Vietnam effects on warfare thought related, 23. *See also* Russia and Ukraine; "traditional" war
Ukraine 2022 crisis: agreement in, 105–6; anti-Russian construct in, 91–92; Cold War in, 90, 180; European facing in, 89–90; geopolitics in, 90; NATO in, 90–92; partisan virtue in, 92; protection in, 92; settlement in, 91. *See also* Putin, Vladimir
Ukraine 2022 war worthiness: Cuban Missile Crisis related to, 95–96; NATO related to, 96–97; Soviet empire and, 96; world wars related to, 95
Ukraine and IF Factor, 147–50
Ukraine Russian's Vietnam: consequences in, 145; deterrence durability in, 151; excuse in, 145; Georgia compared to, 147; hybrid in, 146; without invitation, 146; NATO in, 147, 151; nuclear weapons in, 147; organization in, 146; outcomes in, 146–47; resistance in, 145; test case of, 151; Vietnam compared to, 146
Ukraine War, American response. *See* Russian invasion of Ukraine, American response
Ukraine War in perspective: Afghanistan in, 170; America's fight in, 170–71; asymmetrical model in, 169; as developing world conflict,

169; geopolitics of, 170; power in, 172; Russian failures in, 170; Russia's size in, 171; traditional sphere of influence in, 172; Ukraine's reintegration in, 171; Ukrainian disadvantages in, 170; war crimes in, 170

Ukrainian case: autonomy in, 88; buffer role in, 89; Cold War in, 88, 89; geopolitics in, 89; intimidation in, 88; Khrushchev in, 89; NATO in, 89; nuclear weapons in, 87–88

Ukrainian crisis nuclear prophylactic, 102–3

Ukrainian crisis resolution: accommodation in, 98, 100–101; aggressors in, 101; asymmetrical warfare in, 102; Cold War related to, 102; credibility in, 101; demographics in, 98; escalation in, 97–98; face-saving in, 101, 102; as "model," 102; NATO in, 97, 98, 100, 101, 102; nuclear prophylactic in, 102–3; nuclear weapons in, 99–101; Putin in, 97; Russia population in, 98–99; superpower in, 98–99; trust in, 97; United Nations in, 99–100. *See also* nuclear prophylactic

Ukrainian precedent, 179–80

Ukrainian-Russian conflict, vii–viii, ix; Afghanistan compared to, 3–4; European balance and, 7; media coverage of, 14; U.S. restraint in, 4; in Vietnam, Afghanistan, and beyond, 9–10; Vietnam compared to, 13–15. *See also* Vietnam, Afghanistan, and Ukraine legacy

Ukrainian War, 187–92; geography and, 190; grains and, 189–90; NATO and, 190–91; nuclear weapons and, 188–91

Ukrainian War and IF Factor, 175–78

unconventional warfare, 10–12, 107–8
United Nations, 35, 99–100
United States (U.S.), ix; in nuclear weapons impact evolution, 48; restraint of, 4; to Russian invasion of Ukraine related, 139; Soviet Union versus, 35; Taliban and, 125–26
U.S. conventional force structure, 54–55

Vietnam, viii, 4, 61–62, 164; Afghanistan withdrawal compared to, 2, 13, 14, 15; asymmetrical warfare 101 in, 118, 119; asymmetrical warfare challenges in, 110–11; asymmetrical warfare in, 11, 30–31; asymmetry and IF Factor and, 119–20; in briar patch of intervention, 132; Cold War related to, 5, 24, 28–29, 35, 146; communism and, 7–8, 193–94; context for, 17–18; defeating intervention dynamics in, 124–25, 126–27; draft end and Americans' connection related to, 31–34; European-style warfare in, 118–19; future of war related to, 30–31; IF Factor of, 25, 26–27, 29; impact of, 24–28; post-WWII evolution related to, 18–21; precedent of, 25; as prototype, 24; student knowledge about, 17–18; Ukraine compared to, 146; Ukraine-Russian conflict compared to, 13–15; world wars related to, 18. *See also* nuclear weapons; World War II

Vietnam, Afghanistan, and beyond: American Revolution in, 10; China related to, 7; Cold War related to, 9, 11; Eastern and Western warfare styles in, 10–12; force in, 8–9; interest in, 7–8; "myth of

invincibility" in, 9; peace-war-peace model in, 12; Ukraine-Russian conflict in, 9–10
Vietnam, Afghanistan, and Ukraine legacy, 13–15
Vietnam draft end and Americans' connection: Civil War and world wars related to, 31–32; deployment limitations and, 34; "domino effect" in, 32–33; Korean War and, 32; 9/11 related to, 34; opposition in, 32; party politics of, 33
"Vietnam hangover," 34
Vietnam impact: assumptions in, 26; deaths in, 26, 27, 126; "domino effect" in, 25–26; draft in, 27; feasibility in, 26–27; interests in, 26–27; Tet offensive in, 27–28, 33; war outcomes political definition of, 24–25
Vietnam longer-term effects: citizen connection in, 29–30; congeniality in, 29; future opponents in, 29–30; IF Factor in, 28; interests in, 28–29; Special Forces in, 29
Vietnam or Afghanistan and Iraq, 144–47
Vietnam Wall, 29, 120, 126–27

war crimes, 167, 169, 170, 175
weapons of mass destruction (WMD), 69, 70–71

When America Fights (Snow), vii, 4
when should America fight, 194–96
where and should America fight: asymmetrical war in developing world in, 192–94; back to future in, 194–96; past as model of future in, 187; peering into future in, 196–99; projecting forward in, 199–200; recent past as prologue in, 183–87; Ukrainian War in, 188–92
Wilson, Woodrow, 55
WMD. *See* weapons of mass destruction
Woodward, Bob, 40
worldview, 48, 136
World War I, 55
World War II (WWII), 4, 13, 17, 195; deaths in, 45; entry into, 55; European-style warfare in, 45; nuclear weapons in, 21, 39; Pearl Harbor in, 62–63; U.S. emergence from, 18. *See also* post-WWII
World War III (WWIII), 21, 22, 48, 106, 191, 197
world wars, 18, 34–35, 55–56; conscription in, 31–32; European-style warfare in, 21; Ukraine 2022 war worthiness related to, 95
WWII. *See* World War II
WWIII. *See* World War III

Yeltsin, Boris, 137, 173

www.ingramcontent.com/pod-product-compliance
Lightning Source LLC
Chambersburg PA
CBHW032043300426
44117CB00009B/1166